The 21st Century at Work

Forces Shaping the Future Workforce and Workplace in the United States

LYNN A. KAROLY, CONSTANTIJN W. A. PANIS

Prepared for the U.S. Department of Labor

RAND LABOR AND POPULATION

The research described in this report was conducted by RAND Labor and Population. The views expressed herein are those of the authors and do not necessarily reflect the official position of the U.S. Department of Labor.

0-8330-3492-8

The RAND Corporation is a nonprofit research organization providing objective analysis and effective solutions that address the challenges facing the public and private sectors around the world. RAND's publications do not necessarily reflect the opinions of its research clients and sponsors.

RAND® is a registered trademark.

Cover design by Stephen Bloodsworth

Published 2004 by the RAND Corporation
1700 Main Street, P.O. Box 2138, Santa Monica, CA 90407-2138
1200 South Hayes Street, Arlington, VA 22202-5050
201 North Craig Street, Suite 202, Pittsburgh, PA 15213-1516
RAND URL: http://www.rand.org/
To order RAND documents or to obtain additional information, contact
Distribution Services: Telephone: (310) 451-7002;
Fax: (310) 451-6915; Email: order@rand.org

In labor as in other policy domains, government action plays out in a context of powerful trends, some strongly affected by other government activities and some not. Understanding this context is a prerequisite to sound policy formation. To aid understanding of the forces impinging on the workforce and workplace of the twenty-first century, the U.S. Department of Labor (DOL) asked RAND to conduct a study of the future of work. Specifically, we seek to answer two sets of questions about work in the twenty-first century:

- What are the major factors that will shape the future of work in the current century and how are those factors likely to evolve over the next 10 to 15 years?

- What are the implications of these future trends for key aspects of the future workforce and workplace, including the size, composition, and skills of the workforce; the nature of work and workplace arrangements; and worker compensation?

To address these questions, we take a closer look at three major factors that are expected to shape the world of work in the coming decades: shifting demographic patterns, the pace of technological change, and the path of economic globalization. In doing so, our objective is not so much to predict the future but rather to understand key structural forces under way in the economy today, the factors associated with those trends, and whether we can expect such trends to continue or to deviate from their present course. We also aim to identify the implications of those trends and the challenges they pose for decisionmakers in the public and private sectors.

CONTENTS

FIGURES

TABLES

BOXES

SUMMARY

In the next 10 to 15 years, work in the United States will be shaped by demographic trends, technological advances, and economic globalization. Formulation of sound labor policy will require an understanding of how those trends will evolve and affect the size and composition of the labor force, the features of the workplace, and the compensation structures provided by employers. It is our purpose here to contribute to that understanding. In the following pages, we summarize current trends in each of the three principal forces acting on the world of work. In the final section, we draw out some implications that the combination of those forces will have for the future of work. Our key findings are as follows:

- The U.S. workforce will continue to increase in size, but at a considerably slower rate, while the composition will shift toward a more balanced distribution by age, sex, and race/ethnicity. Slower workforce growth may make it more difficult for firms to recruit workers during periods of strong economic growth, although greater participation in the workforce by the elderly, women with children, persons with disabilities, and other groups with relatively low labor force participation could cause the workforce to grow faster. Immigration policy offers another lever for changing the growth and composition of the workforce. Many of the trading partners of the United States are undergoing slower workforce growth and population aging on a more dramatic scale, thus offering a new comparative advantage to the United States.

- The pace of technological change—whether through advances in information technology (IT), biotechnology, or such emerging fields as nanotechnology—will almost certainly accelerate in the next 10 to 15 years. Synergies across technologies and disciplines will generate advances in research and development (R&D), production processes, and the nature of products and services. Further technological advances are expected to continue to increase demand for a highly skilled workforce, to support higher productivity growth, and to change the organization of business and the nature of employment relationships.

- The future reach of economic globalization will be even more expansive than before, affecting industries and segments of the workforce relatively insulated from trade-related competition in the past. The new era of globalization—marked by growing trade in intermediate and final goods and services, expanding capital flows, more rapid transfer of knowledge and technologies, and mobile populations—is partly the result of inexpensive, rapid communications and information transmission enabled by the IT revolution. Globalization will continue its record to date of contributing economic benefits in the aggregate. Although market share and jobs will be lost in some economic sectors with short-term and longer-term consequences for affected workers, the job losses will be counterbalanced by employment gains in other sectors.

- Rapid technological change and increased international competition place the spotlight on the skills and preparation of the workforce, particularly the ability to adapt to changing technologies and shifting product demand. Shifts in the nature of business organizations and the growing importance of knowledge-based work also favor strong nonroutine cognitive skills, such as abstract reasoning, problem-solving, communication, and collaboration. Within this context, education and training become a continuous process throughout the life course involving training and retraining that continues well past initial entry into the labor market. Technology mediated learning offers the potential to support lifelong learning both on the job and through traditional public and private education and training institutions.

- A number of forces are facilitating the move toward more decentralized forms of business organization, including the transition away from vertically integrated firms toward more specialized firms that outsource noncore functions and more decentralized forms of organization within firms. Some sectors may be comprised of "e-lancers," businesses of one or a few workers linked by electronic networks in a global marketplace for products and services. More generally, we can expect a shift away from more permanent, lifetime jobs toward less permanent, even nonstandard employment relationships (e.g., self-employment) and work arrangements (e.g., distance work). These arrangements may be particularly attractive to future workers who seek to balance work and family obligations or such workers as the disabled and older persons who would benefit from alternative arrangements. These changes call attention to the importance of fringe benefits that are portable across jobs, or even independent of jobs (in the case of freelancers, for example).

SHIFTING DEMOGRAPHIC PATTERNS AND THE FUTURE LABOR FORCE

In the next 10 to 15 years, important demographic shifts will continue to influence the size and composition of the workforce. The size and composition of the population, as well as labor force participation rates, determine the number and makeup of people who want to work. Demographic parameters also influence the consumption patterns of the population and thus the mix of goods and services produced and of the labor required to produce them. These factors continue to evolve, in some ways that perpetuate recent trends, and in other ways that suggest changes from the recent past.

Slower Labor Force Growth Ahead

The labor force has been growing more slowly over the past 20 years than it had previously been. During the 1990s, the workforce grew at an annual rate of just 1.1 percent, in contrast to the 1970s when it grew at an annual rate of 2.6 percent. This is partly because, in the years following the end of the baby boom in 1964, the fertility rate (the number of live births per capita) fell by about a quarter, and these smaller cohorts reached working age during the 1980s. It is also partly because of a trend toward earlier retirement by male workers. That the labor force has been growing at all has been the result of progressively higher labor force participation by women (see Figure S.1) and a continuing large inflow of immigrants. Immigration tends to increase the workforce disproportionately to their numbers, because immigrants include many young adults of working age.

Most notably, workforce growth will slow even more dramatically over the next several decades. Between 2000 and 2010, the annual growth rate is projected to equal the rate in the 1990s of 1.1 percent. In the decade that follows, the rate of growth is projected to slow to just 0.4 percent, followed by an even lower 0.3 percent annual growth rate between 2020 and 2030. The slowdown of the workforce growth rate may make it more difficult for firms to recruit workers in the future, especially in periods of more rapid economic growth.

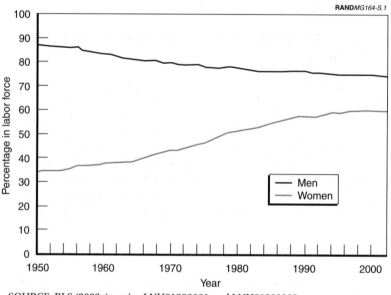

RAND*MG164-S.1*

SOURCE: BLS (2003a), series LNU01300001 and LNU01300002.
NOTE: Population is those age 16 and above.

Figure S.1—Labor Force Participation Rate, by Sex, 1950–2002

Shifting Workforce Composition

The composition of the workforce will also continue to shift, largely reflecting demographic changes that have been under way for some time. Because the U.S. population as a whole has been growing older as the baby boom generation ages, the workforce has also been aging or, looking at it another way, has come into greater balance across age groups. Older people bring strengths to the workforce different from those younger people bring. However, to the extent that they are not part of the labor force and are supported by such largely pay-as-you-go programs as Social Security and Medicare, an older population imposes greater support costs per working person. These greater costs, which impinge on the quality of life for the labor force, are still less than those faced by most other developed countries. By 2050, there will be three working-age adults per elderly person in the United States compared to two in the United Kingdom, France, and Germany, and 1.4 in Japan, Spain, and Italy.

The inflow of immigrants has been largely responsible for a continuing increase in the racial and ethnic diversity of the workforce. Hispanics and Asians are the fastest-growing racial and ethnic groups in the population and workforce. In the case of Hispanics, a high birth rate is partly responsible for that, but immigration is the main driver. In addition, the steadily increasing female labor force participation rates, combined with decreasing male rates, have brought the labor force close to gender balance. The rise in female rates holds for married women and single women alike. It holds as well for women with and without minor children, and, for the latter, it holds whether they are married or not and no matter how old their children are. As a result of population aging and the increased labor force participation of women, another dimension of change is that more workers have responsibilities outside of work. This may involve caring for children, elderly parents, or both.

The Growing Importance of Worker Skill

While these attributes provide one way of characterizing the future workforce, an even more important dimension as we look to the future is the skill that potential workers bring to the workplace. The rapid pace of technological change is expected to continue to propel

demand for highly skilled workers who can develop the new technologies and bring them to market and who can exploit the new
technologies in the production of goods and services. Moreover, the
transition to a knowledge-based economy continues to fuel demand
for well-educated workers. Maintaining a high-skilled workforce is
also a key component of U.S. comparative advantage in the world
economy. Shifts in organizational forms and the nature of employment relationships, brought about by new technologies and global
competition, also favor such high-level cognitive skills as abstract
reasoning, problem-solving, communication, and collaboration, attributes associated with so-called "knowledge work."

On the whole, educational attainment (i.e., years of schooling completed) in the United States has been rising and will probably continue to do so. Achievement scores of U.S. students, however, have
been only about average when compared to those in other developed
nations, despite greater public and private expenditures on education in the United States. Likewise, adults in the U.S. rank near the
middle of other developed countries on tests of skill measures
important for workplace literacy. Notably, the United States also
tends to have a wider spread in the distribution of such skills, with
more very low-skilled and very high-skilled individuals based on
these assessments. Education reforms, such as those that address the
funding and institutional organization of schools, and the degree of
competition among schools promise to raise the productivity of education. In addition, technological developments, such as technology-
mediated instruction, have the potential to improve educational outcomes and support lifelong learning through on-the-job training or
training through other public and private institutions.

Options for Raising Workforce Growth in the Future

The slowdown in the growth of the workforce may have far-reaching
consequences for the U.S. economy. In general, further growth of
economic activity depends on a growing labor force or increases in
worker productivity. Thus, the growth rate of the future labor force
limits the growth rate of the economy for any given rate of productivity growth. Slower economic growth is a concern, given the rising
costs of such entitlement programs for the elderly as Medicare and
Social Security, which will be largely paid for by taxes on a workforce

that is growing more slowly. To the extent that it is desirable to raise the rate of labor force growth, in the short to medium term the two primary options are to increase the labor force participation rate for the current population or to increase the overall size of the population through immigration.

Given the right environment, more older workers may be motivated to retire later and continue to contribute to the nation's prosperity. Indeed, the rates of labor force participation for men age 55 and older, previously on the decline, have begin to level off and even increase at older ages. A variety of factors, including changes in incentives associated with pension plans and reforms to Social Security, mean that the reversal in the trend toward earlier retirement will likely continue. The rise in female labor force participation rates holds for women with and without minor children, regardless of marital status and the age of their children. Clearly, women with responsibilities at home are willing to work outside the home. Data from the United States and from other countries suggest that labor force participation by women with children could rise further if work could be more easily balanced with family responsibilities, such as through less-expensive child care, greater availability of public preschool programs, or more-flexible scheduling. While the overall effect on female labor force participation may be modest, the effect would likely be larger for women with lower earnings prospects. It may also be possible to raise labor force participation by groups underrepresented in the workforce. For example, fewer than one in three working-age individuals with disabilities are currently in the workforce, leaving around 12 million persons with disabilities out of the workforce. Finally, immigration offers opportunities for workforce growth. In particular, immigration policy may be applied to target highly skilled aliens, thus raising the overall skill levels of the U.S. workforce.

Demographics Will Shift the Demand for Goods and Services

So far, we have emphasized the effect of demographic trends on the characteristics of labor supply. However, those trends will also alter the mix of goods and services demanded and thus the characteristics of labor demanded by firms. Older households tend to spend their money differently from younger ones: an aging population is likely to employ more health care workers and increase the demand for other health care–related products and services. Furthermore, such household activities as child care, cooking, cleaning, and gardening that used to be performed by household members may be "outsourced" to the paid workforce as women (in particular) take paid work in greater numbers.

THE EXPANDING REACH OF TECHNOLOGY

By the end of the twentieth century, the U.S. economy was shifting from one based on production to one based on information. New technologies had spawned new products and industries and had transformed the way firms in established industries were organized and labor was employed. In the coming decades, technological advances promise to further shape what is produced; how capital, material, and labor inputs are combined to produce it; how work is organized and where it is conducted; and even who is available to work.

Rapid Advance in Information Technologies

To anticipate the future consequences of technology for the work-force and workplace, consider the remarkable pace of change in the incorporation of information technologies into the U.S. economy. Computing power and storage capacity, data transmission speed, and network connectivity have increased dramatically while costs have fallen rapidly. For example, between 1970 and 1999, as the capacity of a fingernail-size silicon chip grew from a few thousand transistors to 44 million, the cost of 1 megahertz of processing power fell 45,000-fold from $7,600 to 17 cents. At the same time, greater user-friendliness of new software has led to rapid adoption of computer systems: levels of business investment in computer hardware during the mid- to late 1990s were several times those of previous years (see Figure S.2).

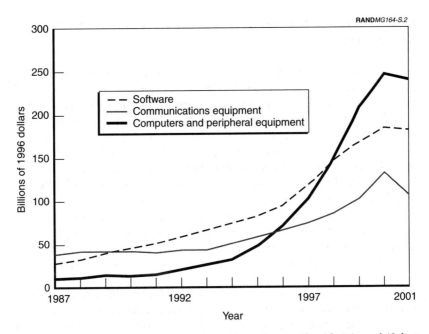

RAND*MG164-S.2*

SOURCE: BEA NIPA Tables, Table 5.9 (http://www.bea.gov/bea/dn/nipaweb/Select Table.asp).

Figure S.2—Real Private Fixed Investment in Information Technology, 1987–2001

While the technological advances experienced in the last several decades in IT have been remarkable, the pace of change will almost certainly continue for the next decade or more. The practical implications of further technical advances will include greater processing speed, higher storage capacity, and a wider array of applications. For example, advances in microprocessors will support real-time speech recognition and translation, and the fields of artificial intelligence and robotics are likely to advance further. The use of more intelligent robotics in manufacturing will support agile manufacturing—the ability to quickly reconfigure machines for the production of prototypes and new production runs—with implications for manufacturing logistics and inventories.

Other Evolutionary and Revolutionary Technologies Are on the Horizon

Technological progress, however, is not limited to communications and information technologies. A wide array of such technological advances as biotechnology and nanotechnology are expected to have equally profound consequences for the U.S. economy in the next several decades. In the health care sector, for example, recent progress against a variety of diseases will be married to molecular-genetic advances spawned by the Human Genome Project to yield "personalized medicine" in which drugs might be individually tailored to increase their effectiveness and reduce side effects. In the near future, progress in biotechnology is expected to generate medical advances that will further extend life expectancy and improve the quality of life for those with a chronic illness or disability, often in ways that will enhance their productive capacity in the workplace.

Nanotechnology—the manipulation of matter at the atomic scale—could afford even more-drastic revolutions in products, services, and quality of life over the next half-century. In addition to applications in electronics and IT, nanotechnology is expected to lead to breakthroughs in pharmaceuticals and other aspects of biotechnology, energy technology, and aerospace and materials technology, among others. As a cross-cutting technology, nanotechnology will facilitate technological change that extends and enhances existing technologies—further computing power for semiconductors, for example—as well as more revolutionary applications—computers no bigger than a bacterium and new materials displaying paradoxical properties of strength and flexibility and performance in heat and cold. The earliest applications in the next 10 to 15 years are likely to be in the first category, while those in the second category may be further in the future.

Many of the advances in biotechnology and nanotechnology raise social, legal, and ethical implications, among other concerns, that need to be addressed as the technologies evolve. If public acceptance of the new technologies is slow to materialize, their adoption and diffusion may not match the pace of discovery.

New Technologies Demand a Highly Skilled Workforce

Job skill requirements have been shifting across all sectors as a result of new technologies. Machines with microprocessors can now be programmed to do the sort of routine activities that less-skilled workers used to do. At the same time, business computer systems generate demand for highly skilled labor in the form of technical staff who operate and repair the equipment, develop and install the software, and build and monitor the networks. In addition, computer systems often generate more data that may be profitably analyzed, thereby increasing the demand for the analytical, problem-solving, and communication skills of workers, managers, and other professionals. Increasingly, the term "knowledge workers" is applied to workers who go beyond just providing information to now being responsible for generating and conveying knowledge needed for decisionmaking.

While the recent technological advances may favor either skilled or unskilled workers, depending on the application, the overwhelming evidence is that on balance, recent technological advances favor more-skilled workers and the same can be expected for future advances. Not surprisingly, those demand differentials have been driving up the salary premium paid to workers with higher education levels (see Figure S.3). For example, between 1973 and 2001, the wage premium for a college degree compared with a high school diploma increased 30 percentage points, from 46 percent to 76 percent. Researchers consistently find that technological progress that increased the demand for more-skilled workers explains a sizable portion of the rise in the wage differential by education level since the 1980s, although other factors played a role as well.

The Organization of Firms and the Workplace Respond to Technological Change

The new information technologies adopted in recent decades have had implications for other aspects of the production process, from the capital equipment used in the goods-producing sectors to the ways firms across all sectors are organized and conduct their business. Such changes have taken place in "old economy" goods-

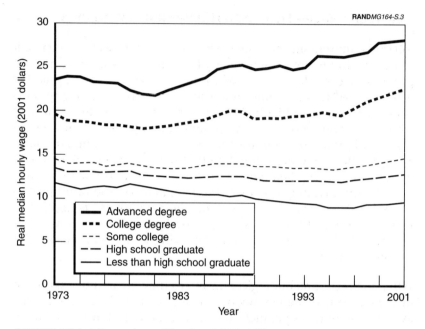

SOURCE: Mishel, Bernstein, and Boushey (2003), Table 2.17.

Figure S.3—Real Median Hourly Wage by Education Level, 1973–2001

producing sectors, such as the steel and machine tool industries, as well as services-producing sectors, such as retailing, trucking, and banking.

The vertically integrated corporation was the dominant organizational model for much of the twentieth century. This model provided the means to control and coordinate the various stages of production, especially in an era when markets were underdeveloped and supply networks were more uncertain. While this model has by no means disappeared and revenues and production volumes may be as large as before, some sectors of the economy are moving toward more specialized, vertically disintegrated firms. With vertical disintegration, firms divide up the production pipeline and specialize broadly in products and services that define core competencies while outsourcing noncore activities. Such activities might include steps on the production chain, such as industrial design or the manufacturing of intermediate goods, or support activities, such as computing services or human resources. This trend is facilitated by the power of information technologies and their associated networks to coordinate and control across organizations and within organizations in a more decentralized manner.

Technology also shapes firms' decisions about how to organize production within the firm and how to structure the compensation system to motivate workers at various levels of the organization. With increased investment in IT, companies have been moving toward more participatory, "high-performance" work systems. Such practices invest greater authority and problem-solving responsibilities in front-line employees rather than managers. Jobs become more flexible and broadly defined, employees work in collaborative teams requiring a high degree of information-sharing and communication, and outcomes focus on timeliness, quality, and customer service. A related development is the increased reliance on performance-based pay to improve employee motivation. Production-based pay, profit-sharing, and stock-option plans allow employees to share directly in the profitability of their employers.

Technology also facilitates telecommuting and other forms of distance work. As of 2001, nearly 20 million workers, or 15 percent of the workforce, usually did some work at home (at least one day a week) as part of their primary job. Using a broader definition of off-site work, about four out of five workers either work off-site themselves or work with others who work at a distance.

Technology Supports the Process of Lifelong Learning

As technology operates to increase the demand for more skilled labor, workers often need to undergo retraining in order to take advantage of how new technologies are utilized in the workplace or to operate within new organizational structures. At the same time, technology has great potential to support the education and training of the workforce prior to labor market entry and as a part of lifelong learning. Technology-mediated learning—the use of computers and other information technologies as an integral part of the learning process—is gaining ground through such applications as computer-based instruction, Internet-based instruction, and other methods for customized learning. Information technologies potentially allow access to instructional materials any time, any place.

New technologies in the next 10 to 20 years offer tremendous potential to revolutionize the way education and training is delivered in order to improve efficiency and effectiveness in learning. For example, one application that goes beyond traditional distance learning is the use of electronic performance support systems, typically wearable computer devices that provide real-time access to information needed on the job to perform increasingly complex, dynamic tasks. Just as individualized medicine is envisioned as an outgrowth of biotechnology, individualized learning programs that are optimized for a given person's knowledge base and learning style are expected for the future. Such learning programs will become increasingly sophisticated over time with advances in hardware and software, including artificial intelligence, voice recognition and natural language comprehension. They will also benefit from improvements in intelligent tutoring systems that allow self-paced, interactive, self-improving learning.

Productivity Benefits from New Technologies

After a long period in which it seemed that the information revolution was having no impact on worker productivity, an acceleration of the annual rate of productivity increase began in 1995 and has not been slowed by the post-2000 economic downturn. The productivity gains were not limited to a few industries but applied to a range, including durable-goods manufacturing and such services as wholesale and retail trade and finance. Analyses by economists indicate that the rise in economywide productivity can be attributed to growing productivity within the IT sector itself, as well as increased productivity in other sectors of the economy. Given that these new technologies have yet to reach saturation in the economy, most analysts expect the boost to productivity from the IT revolution to continue for the near term.

GLOBAL ECONOMIC INTEGRATION

With the growth of economic globalization in recent decades—whether measured by flows of goods and services, direct investment and other capital flows, the transfer of knowledge or technology, or the movement of people—the economies of the world are tied together even more so than in the past. In the decades ahead, the era

of economic globalization will affect the size of the markets we produce for, the mix of products we consume, and the nature of the
competition in the global marketplace. It also has implications for
the labor market that U.S. workers compete in and the sources of
domestic and international labor available to U.S. firms.

The Dimensions of Economic Globalization

Recent decades have been marked by dramatic increases in trade.
Total trade activity (exports plus imports) has increased from about
one-tenth of U.S. gross domestic product (GDP) in 1960 to about a
quarter at the turn of the century (see Figure S.4). Meanwhile, the
sectoral distribution of trade has changed. Trade in services has
grown from 18 to 30 percent of the total over the last 20 years.
Another important new aspect of trade patterns, called "vertical

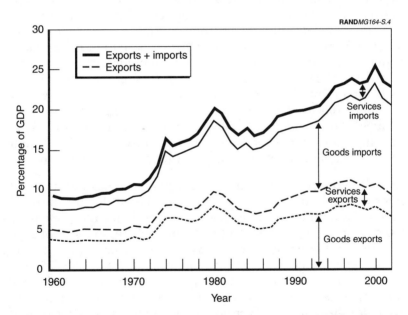

SOURCES: BEA U.S. International Transactions Accounts Data, Table 1 (http://
www.bea.gov/bea/international/bp_web), and BEA NIPA Tables, Table 1.1
(http://www.bea.gov/bea/dn/nipaweb/SelectTable.asp).

Figure S.4—U.S. Exports and Imports as a Share of GDP, 1960–2002

trade," is that finished products may be composed of inputs produced and assembled in stages in different countries. Multinational firms no longer limit production to a single country but carve up the production process into stages implemented in multiple countries through subsidiaries or contractors. This allows more labor-intensive stages of the production process to be located in lower-wage settings, as opposed to stages that are more capital-, knowledge-, or technology-intensive, which are located in higher-wage settings. This pattern of specialization extends on a global scale the vertical disintegration of the firm discussed above in the context of technological change.

Not only manufacturing jobs have been outsourced overseas but also higher-skilled white-collar jobs in the services sector, such as IT and business-processing services. Advances in communication technologies and falling prices associated with voice and data transmission facilitate the shift of IT-enabled services from the United States to overseas locations in such countries as China, Costa Rica, Hungary, India, Ireland, and the Philippines. Since the work products in many information-based and knowledge-based industries can be readily transmitted over high-speed computer networks, the physical location of the workforce is increasingly less relevant. Data to estimate the extent of international outsourcing in the services sector are not readily available, but some estimates suggest that the movement is relatively modest to date but growing. In the future, companies may choose to blend onshore and offshore models to offer greater flexibility as well as the capacity to work around the clock.

As trade flows have increased and production has become more internationalized, the United States has altered the mix of trading partners toward countries with lower wages. While Canada remains the largest trading partner with the United States in terms of goods exported and imported, Mexico assumed the second-place ranking as of 1999, displacing Japan from that position. Trade with China has also grown dramatically, from less than 1 percent of U.S. goods imports in 1980 to 11 percent in 2002, exceeding goods imports from Japan for the first time. Even so, more than half of U.S. goods trade takes place with other industrialized countries where wages are more comparable.

Globalization has extended to capital flows and labor skills. U.S. acquisition of foreign assets increased sixfold between 1980 and 2000, and foreign acquisition of U.S. assets grew even more. Capital flows increasingly take the form of direct investment in companies overseas as a means to control production and expand into new markets. Worldwide migration has doubled in the last quarter-century, resulting in greater circulation of workers, not only the less-skilled but also the highly skilled. At the same time, IT advances have enabled highly skilled workers on different continents to collaborate without physically relocating. The internationalization of labor is also tied to the greater ease with which new knowledge and technologies are transferred across international boundaries.

Forces Propelling Globalization Will Continue

What is driving the current wave of economic globalization? First, over the past 50 years, communication and information transmission costs have declined precipitously, along with transportation costs. For instance, a call from New York to London that would have cost $1 in 1950 cost just 6 cents as of 1990, and the call is essentially free today using the Internet (although the quality might not be as good). Through voice, video, and electronic communications, firms can work with subsidiaries or suppliers in other countries and ensure the quality and timeliness of product delivery necessary to meet their own production processes. The revolution in information technologies also provides a mechanism for rapid transmission across electronic networks of inputs and outputs in the IT-enabled services sector, as well as the means for supervising work products and monitoring quality. Second, since the end of World War II, a series of trade agreements have reduced barriers to trade, while the move to flexible exchange rates in the early 1970s, combined with other financial reforms and new financial instruments, increased capital mobility.

On balance, we believe the trend toward a globally integrated economy is likely to continue, driven by further IT advances and reductions in trade and capital market barriers. However, there may be efforts to link further trade and capital market liberalization with particular countries or regions to concerns over labor standards, the environment, human rights, the existence of democratic institutions, or the protection of property rights. There are also signs that other countries, especially low-income nations, are more reluctant to seek further liberalization without the major industrialized countries relaxing some of their remaining barriers (e.g., subsidies for agricultural products, patent protections on pharmaceuticals). If so, this may limit the pace of expansion of trade between the United States and developing countries.

Economic Globalization Generates Aggregate Benefits to the Economy

The consensus among economists is that globalization has had and can be expected to continue to have, at the aggregate level, a favorable effect on income, prices, consumer choice, competition, and innovation in the United States. In terms of long-run growth, at the same time that trade's share of the U.S. economy more than doubled in the last four decades of the twentieth century, real GDP per capita—a measure of U.S. standard of living—did so also.

From the perspective of U.S. consumers, trade typically expands the range of choices available and results in the reduction of prices for some goods when foreign suppliers can produce them at less cost. For U.S. firms, a more open world economy expands the size of the market they can sell to, elevating sales and possibly reducing costs and raising productivity through economies of scale. At the same time, the increased openness of U.S. markets, both through export competition and import competition, pressures U.S. firms to remain competitive in the global marketplace. Such forces spur innovation and adoption of technologies and production processes that can reduce cost. Trade also provides access to foreign technology and ideas (e.g., business organization practices), which further allow productivity gains for U.S. firms.

Globalization Also Has Distributional Consequences

While greater integration in world trade and capital markets can enhance welfare at the national level and over the long term, there can be short-term and longer-term consequences for particular segments of the U.S. economy and workforce as labor, capital, and other inputs are reallocated to their most efficient uses. Some industries facing greater import competition will lose jobs. At the same time, trade generates new jobs for U.S. workers in domestic exporting industries. As of 1999, for example, an estimated 11.6 million jobs in the United States were supported directly or indirectly by goods and services exports, representing about 9 percent of employment. With continued growth in exports relative to GDP, that share is likely to expand. In two industries—computers and electronic products and primary metals—more than one-third of jobs were tied to exports as of 1997. On balance, research suggests that the effect of trade on overall employment levels is, at most, small, with job losses caused by import competition counterbalanced by job gains that stem from expanding exports.

Economywide, most workers displaced due to a plant move or closing, elimination of a position or other factors that lead to involuntary job loss find new jobs although they may experience spells of unemployment and face permanent wage losses. For example, the typical, or median, worker displaced in the late 1990s experienced a little more than five weeks of unemployment before finding a new job. Earlier in the 1990s, when the labor market was weaker, the typical unemployment spell was about three weeks longer. Studies of the longer-term consequences of job displacement suggest permanent earnings losses in the range of 5 to 15 percent. More-educated workers tend to be reemployed more rapidly than their less-educated counterparts and their relative earnings losses tend to be smaller, presumably because their skills transfer more easily from one job to the next. This suggests that, while painful, future job loss associated with higher-skilled services-sector employment might not be as costly in terms of unemployment and permanent wage loss as were earlier waves of blue-collar trade-related job displacement.

Globalization has also been linked to the relative decline in earnings among less-skilled workers over the last few decades. Research suggests that, while trade made a modest contribution to the trend, other factors, such as technology and immigration, were more important. It must also be kept in mind that many less-skilled workers are employed in nontradable services and thus will not be directly affected by globalization. In the future, if trade in services that involve more highly skilled jobs continues to grow, trade will affect a larger share of the workforce, so the effect on the wage structure could become larger over time.

THE IMPLICATIONS FOR THE FUTURE OF WORK

The three forces we have examined do not move independently of one another but can be expected to have important interactive effects. Given these interactions, we seek to anticipate the implications of these interrelated and interacting forces for the future of work. These issues are relevant from the perspective of current and future workers who wish to anticipate future trends and how they might respond in terms of investments in their human capital and other decisions throughout their working lives. Other issues pertain to choices that employers make about how to organize their workplaces, invest in their employees, and structure employee compensation. Policymakers at the federal, state, and local levels also make decisions that shape the laws and regulations governing the workplace and other policies that may provide incentives or disincentives for behavior on the part of workers or employers. Other interested parties include public- and private-sector education and training institutions that help shape the quality of the future workforce.

The Organization of Production

Technological advances and globalization are changing the way production is structured, pushing firms toward vertical disintegration and specialization, decentralized decisionmaking, and attaching a premium to acquiring and sustaining knowledge as a means of achieving competitive advantage. Such specialization allows firms, which may remain as large as ever, to exploit their comparative advantage in the provision of particular goods and services, while outsourcing those functions peripheral to the core business. With more decentralized decisionmaking, striking the right balance between empowerment and control will be an important management element in the future workplace.

In some sectors, these trends could result in the disintegration of firms to the individual level in the form of numerous IT-enabled, networked, self-employed individuals or "e-lancers." In this new business model, individuals may compete in a global market for project opportunities and may work on multiple projects at any given time. Project teams continually dissolve as old projects are completed and form as new projects begin. Issues associated with a more decentralized e-lance model of production include access to the full range of tangible and intangible benefits that come with traditional employment relationships: economic security through employment continuity and subsidized employee welfare benefits, professional development through training and other opportunities, social connections to workplace colleagues, and a sense of professional identity. In the future, some or all of these functions may be provided by worker associations, organizations independent of particular employment relationships. Existing organizations (e.g., professional or community groups) may take on these functions or new organizations may be established defined by occupational groups or geographic areas to take on this role.

The evolution of organizational forms in the next 10 to 15 years is not expected to rapidly converge on any one particular model. Instead, organizations are expected to adapt in the future in response to the nature of innovation, markets, networks, and information costs. Thus, we can expect large corporations to continue to exist, albeit with greater specialization of function than in the past, at the same time that the prevalence of decentralized networks of small organizations grows. Within these new paradigms of specialized firms, decentralized decisionmaking, and knowledge-based organizations, employers in the coming decades will require a workforce with well-developed analytical skills and communication and collaboration skills.

The Nature of Employer-Employee Relationships and Work Location

The conventional model of employment is that of full-time jobs of indefinite duration at a facility owned or rented by the employer. The forces driving the reorganization of production are expected to decrease the fraction of workers in such traditional arrangements and increase the fraction in such nonstandard arrangements as self-employment, contract work, and temporary help. Already, about one in every four U.S. workers is in some nontraditional employment relationship. These alternative work arrangements may become more prevalent in the face of rapid technological change and competitive market pressures. A further increase could result from increases in labor force participation among subgroups of the population, such as the disabled or older workers who have a preference for more flexible work arrangements. To the extent that the ranks of workers in nonstandard work arrangements grow in the future, one issue will be access to traditional workplace benefits. It may be worthwhile to implement policies promoting health and pension coverage among workers in nonstandard arrangements, whether through the tax code or access through business or professional associations. The latter may be modeled on the worker associations as discussed above.

As advances in IT continue to weaken the bonds between work and workplace, a greater proportion of the labor force will be working at home or in other locations removed from their employer's headquarters (or client's office). Part-time or full-time telecommuting can allow employers to accommodate the needs of workers who care for children at home or a sick family member. Older workers and the disabled may also benefit from nontraditional workplace arrangements. This geographical separation, where it crosses state boundaries, will increasingly raise questions about which jurisdiction's work-related policies apply.

Changes in business organization, management structures, and employment relationships have other implications for the relationship between employers and their employees in more-traditional employment relationships. On the one hand, shifts in organizational form and the use of nonstandard work arrangements weaken the bonds between employers and their employees. On the other hand, many employers increasingly recognize the human capital and knowledge base of their employees as a critical asset. Within this context, the use of high-performance workplace practices that give greater decisionmaking authority to front-line employees is blurring the traditional distinction between "labor" and "management." Changing employer-employee relationships will also alter the opportunities and challenges faced by labor unions.

Workplace Safety, Security, and Privacy

While workplace safety and security concerns focused in the past on high-risk industries in the goods-producing sector, these issues now resonate with virtually all employers and the entire workforce. In the coming decades, the aging of the workforce may raise new safety concerns in traditional or emerging industries. For example, workers age 65 and older have been shown to experience higher rates of permanent disabilities and workplace fatalities compared with their younger counterparts in the same industries and occupations. Emerging technologies may present new health and safety concerns (e.g., those associated with nanotechnology or biotechnology). At the same time, technological advances may provide new solutions for improving worker safety. Workplace security, in the face of terrorist or other security threats to workers in the United States or overseas, raises issues regarding the balance between public-sector investments in workplace security and private-sector security investments. Privacy concerns will become more prominent as a result of various technological advances that facilitate employee monitoring and access to sensitive information.

The Nature of Work and Job Skill Requirements

Future technological developments will increase the demand for highly skilled workers who can develop and market the new technologies, while other workers will be involved in production processes or in the production of goods and services based on these technological advances. A growing emphasis on knowledge workers and knowledge-based organizations can further define a source of competitive advantage for U.S. workers and employers. The shift in organizational forms and the nature of employment relationships also favor strong cognitive and entrepreneurial skills. Workers who increasingly interact in a global marketplace and participate in global work teams will require the skills needed to collaborate and interact in diverse cultural and linguistic settings. At the same time, demographic and other factors will drive demand for traditionally lower-skilled jobs in retail trade, health services, and other personal services. None of these jobs typically require postsecondary education, although training often is an important component of job preparation. In addition, more of these jobs in the future are likely to incor-

porate new technologies but typically with intuitive interfaces accessible to individuals who are not technologically sophisticated.

A variety of forces appear to be shifting the workforce away from
more permanent or lifetime jobs toward less permanent, even nonstandard employment relationships. Thus, the labor market will
require a workforce adaptable throughout the life course to changing
technology and product demand. As less-competitive sectors of the
economy lose jobs, workers who can retrain will be better able to
adjust and find productive reemployment. The prospects of continued or even accelerating job displacement as a result of technological change and trade also invite consideration of current and future
policies to help workers adjust to these shocks.

In this context, consideration must be given to how the U.S. education and training system can evolve to better meet the needs of the
twenty-first-century workforce. Workforce education and training in
the future will involve continuous learning throughout the working
life, involving training and retraining that continues well past initial
entry into the labor market. Challenges for the private and public
sectors include improving educational outcomes at the primary and
secondary levels of education, developing opportunities for career-
long learning through formal and informal training opportunities,
and meeting the growing need for scientists and engineers who can
advance new technologies in the laboratory, develop the applications, and bring them to market.

Technology-mediated learning, which offers the advantage of individualized learning programs that can be accessed "any time any
place," may help meet training challenges and support life-long
learning. In addition, as e-learning materials become more common
in routine work processes (e.g., the use of wearable devices with procedural information to supplement prior training and reduce errors),
continuous training and lifelong learning can become a reality.

The Size and Composition of the Workforce

Current demographic forecasts estimate no change in the growth
rate of the labor force over the coming decade and even a likely
slowdown after that. Such projections depend critically on assumptions regarding underlying population growth rates (immigration

being one important factor) and rates of labor force participation among demographic subgroups. Labor force growth rates can exceed current projections to the extent that labor force participation can rise for groups not fully employed.

Thus, an important issue is whether tapping underutilized labor force capacity can contribute substantially to a larger workforce. Some older workers are lengthening their careers, and more might do so if employers show more flexibility in job responsibilities, hours worked, and pay (and if government permits such flexibility). There is room for progress in this regard: 63 percent of workers age 59 or over say that their employer would not let them move to a less demanding job with less pay if they wanted to. Greater attention to work-family balance issues may increase the labor force participation of women, particularly women with children. Technological advances may aid the labor force participation of people with disabilities by alleviating the disabilities themselves or their impact on ability to work. Other demographic groups that may be targets for greater inclusion are low-income women with children, former military personnel, and immigrants.

From the perspective of employers, strategies to make work more attractive than remaining out of the labor force are not cost-free. In tight labor markets, employers may offer higher wages. They may also offer more attractive work conditions (such as flexible scheduling or telecommuting) or more generous fringe benefits (such as time off for family emergencies, on-site child care, or assistance with elder care). In their negotiations about compensation, prospective workers and firms may trade off among cash wages, working conditions, and benefits. The key challenge will be to identify the compensation mix that attracts the most new workers for any given total cost increase. Government policies may constrain employers' abilities to increase participation among some groups. For example, government policies currently limit employers' ability to adjust benefits for older workers to account for changes in preferences for health insurance, pension benefits, and other employee benefits as workers age.

Compensation in the Form of Wages and Benefits

Future trends in technology, globalization, and demographics are also likely to affect the level and distribution of wages, just as they have in the past several decades. Continued technological progress has the potential to lead to further productivity gains that would support growth in real wages (or total compensation to the extent that compensation patterns shift from wages to benefits). At the same time, mechanisms driving greater wage disparities in the recent past, namely technological change and globalization among others, can be expected to exert the same pressures in the near term. In the absence of a strong increase in the supply of skilled workers in response to the higher returns to education, wage dispersion—particularly as measured by the gap between more- and less-educated workers—will likely remain at current levels or continue to widen.

Meanwhile, a variety of factors may weaken the tie between employment and access to fringe benefits. Greater turnover within traditional employment relationships and shifts to nonstandard employment relationships also spotlight the importance of fringe benefits that are portable across jobs or even independent of jobs (in the case of freelancers, for example). Employers that do offer benefits may move toward more personalized structures, tailored to meet the circumstances of each employee. Younger and older workers, for example, might be allowed to select those benefits that fit their circumstances with corresponding adjustments in cash wages to retain current compensation levels. Information technologies and outsourcing may support this trend by reducing the costs associated with managing a more complex system of employee benefits.

We have identified a number of ways in which the workforce and workplace are likely to differ in the early decades of the twenty-first century compared with the experience of the twentieth century. At the same time, many of the institutional features of the U.S. labor market—such as the laws and regulations that govern employment, hours, wages, fringe benefits, occupational health and safety, and so on—evolved in the context of an earlier era. In some cases, these policies need to be reexamined in light of the evolution of the labor market in the coming decades. Are there distortions or unintended consequences associated with current policies that preclude desirable market adjustments? Are policies put in place to address market failures in the past less relevant, given parameters that exist today and their likely future evolution? Are there new market failures that policy can address? Are there distributional consequences that could make a case for government intervention? These questions merit a

more detailed examiniation in the context of the future of the workforce, workplace, and compensation in the twenty-first century.

ACKNOWLEDGMENTS

We wish to acknowledge the U.S. Department of Labor, including Christopher T. Spear, Assistant Secretary for Policy, for its funding under contract number J-9-9-2-0033. In addition, during the course of preparing the book, we had valuable discussions and received a wealth of insightful comments from many other DOL staff.

We benefited from comments on the study provided by a group of academic experts consisting of Amar Bhide (Columbia University), Gary Burtless (The Brookings Institution), Eric Hanushek (Stanford University), Marvin Kosters (American Enterprise Institute), Olivia Mitchell (University of Pennsylvania), June O'Neill (City University of New York), Robert Smith (Cornell University), and Finis Welch (Texas A&M University).

We are indebted to Jeannette Rogowski for the extensive management support she gave the project in her role as Director of the RAND Center for Employer-Sponsored Health and Pension Benefits which housed this project. We are also grateful for discussions and feedback provided by our RAND colleagues Philip Antón, Beth Asch, Phil Devin, Carole Roan Gresenz, James Hosek, Michael Hurd, Arie Kapteyn, M. Rebecca Kilburn, M. Susan Marquis, Robert Reville, and Cathleen Stasz. David Loughran and Jacob Klerman at RAND provided constructive and comprehensive technical reviews of the book.

Giacomo Bergamo and Maria Dahlin served as research assistants to the project, contributing extensive support in assembling the data and literature that we draw on. James Chiesa provided superb editorial assistance with the entire book and especially with the summary. We also thank Dan Sheehan for editing the manuscript, Stephen

Bloodsworth for the cover design and graphics, Denise Constantine for coordinating the document production, and Diana Malouf and Mechelle Wilkins for project administrative support.

ABBREVIATIONS

ADL   Advanced Distributed Learning (Initiative)

AFDC   Aid to Families with Dependent Children

ASTD   American Society for Training and Development

BCIS   Bureau of Citizenship and Immigration Services

BEA   Bureau of Economic Analysis

BLS   Bureau of Labor Statistics

CEA   Council of Economic Advisors

CBO   Congressional Budget Office

CPS   Current Population Survey

DB   defined benefit

DC   defined contribution

DHHS   Department of Health and Human Services

DHS   Department of Homeland Security

DI   (Social Security) Disability Insurance

DOC   Department of Commerce

DoD   Department of Defense

DOL   Department of Labor

EBSA   Employee Benefits Security Administration

EITC   Earned Income Tax Credit

FDI   foreign direct investment

GATT	General Agreement on Tariffs and Trade
GDP	gross domestic product
HI	Hospital Insurance (Medicare Part A)
HTML	hypertext markup language
IALS	International Adult Literacy Survey
IMF	International Monetary Fund
INS	Immigration and Naturalization Service (now the Bureau of Citizenship and Immigration Services)
IRS	Internal Revenue Service
IT	information technology
ITAA	Information Technology Association of America
ITAC	International Telework Association and Council
ITU	International Telecommunications Union
MEMS	microelectromechanical systems
MSTs	microstructure technologies
NAFTA	North American Free Trade Agreement
NAS	National Academy of Sciences
NCHS	National Center for Health Statistics
NHIS	National Health Interview Survey
NIC	National Intelligence Council
NIH	National Institutes of Health
NIPA	National Income and Product Accounts
NNI	National Nanotechnology Initiative
NSF	National Science Foundation
NTIA	National Telecommunications and Information Administration
OASDI	(Social Security) Old-Age, Survivors and Disability Insurance

OECD	Organisation for Economic Co-operation and Development
OMB	Office of Management and Budget
PC	personal computer
PDA	personal digital assistant
PISA	Programme for International Student Achievement
PRWORA	Personal Responsibility and Work Opportunity Reconciliation Act
R&D	research and development
SAG	Screen Actors Guild
SARS	Severe Acute Respiratory System
SMI	Supplemental Medical Insurance (Medicare Part B)
SSA	Social Security Administration
TAA	Trade Adjustment Assistance
TANF	Temporary Assistance for Needy Families
TCU	transportation, communications, and utilities
TFR	Total Fertility Rate
TPA	trade promotion authority
TRIPS	Trade-Related Aspects of Intellectual Property Rights (agreement)
UNCTAD	United Nations Commission on Trade and Development
UNDP	United Nations Development Programme
UPS	United Parcel Service
USDA	U.S. Department of Agriculture
WDM	wavelength division multiplexing
WTO	World Trade Organization

Chapter One

INTRODUCTION

In the next 10 to 15 years, work in the United States will be shaped by a number of forces, including demographic trends, advances in technology, and the process of economic globalization. In many respects, these key factors have already played a role in shaping the world of work in today's economy. They have influenced the size and composition of the labor force, the features of the workplace, and the compensation structures provided by employers. How these factors continue to evolve will further influence the workforce and the workplace, often in ways that can be predicted. In some cases, however, conditions will change in ways that are, as yet, more uncertain. The evolution of these trends and their eventual consequences will clearly depend, to a great extent, on the decisions made by workers, employers, educators, and policymakers. To make informed decisions, these individuals need to understand their evolving context, and that is what we hope to bring about in the study that has resulted in this book. In particular, we attempt to answer two sets of questions about work in the twenty-first century:

- What are the major factors that will shape the future of work in the current century and how are those factors likely to evolve over the next 10 to 15 years?

- What are the implications of these future trends for key aspects of the future workforce and the future workplace, including the size, composition, and skills of the workforce; the nature of work and workplace arrangements; and worker compensation?

To address these questions, this book focuses on three major factors expected to shape the world of work in the coming decades: shifting demographic patterns, the pace of technological change, and the path of economic globalization.

When we have finished, we hope that current and prospective workers will benefit from an understanding of how the future world of work is likely to evolve and how they might respond in terms of investments they make in their education and training and other labor market choices. Employers can use the information in their decisionmaking regarding their business approach, investments in their employees, the nature of the employer-employee relationship, and the structure of compensation, including fringe benefits. The perspective we provide will inform policymaking at the federal, state, and local level with regard to laws and regulations that govern the workplace, the workforce, and compensation. Other interested parties include decisionmakers at public and private education and training institutions that contribute to the skills and knowledge development of current and future workers.

We seek to provide an assessment based on relevant data and research. Our focus is on a medium-term horizon—10 to 15 years— and a broad-brush perspective on the trends that are likely to shape the future. We are less concerned about the inevitable ups and downs of the business cycle as that future unfolds. Even aside from such fluctuations, the future is difficult to predict. Some developments can be foreseen with more confidence than others. In demographics, for example, the composition of the future population, outside of immigration patterns, is well defined for our time horizon because future cohorts of adults are today's children and youth. However, more uncertainty will be associated with the path of other forces.

In the remainder of this chapter we set the stage for our analysis of the forces shaping the future world of work in the United States. We begin by identifying some of the challenges associated with anticipating the future direction and implications of such complex systems as the U.S. labor market. We then outline a conceptual framework that guides our analysis, particularly our focus on the three key forces: demographics, technology, and globalization.

THE CHALLENGES OF LOOKING TO THE FUTURE

Efforts to anticipate the course of future events range from simple extrapolation of existing trends to wishful thinking. One of the earliest systematic efforts to anticipate the future that lay ahead was the Commission on the Year 2000 established in the late 1960s under the auspices of the American Academy of Arts and Sciences. The seminal volume published by the Commission in 1967, *Toward the Year 2000: Work in Progress*, has been viewed as the forerunner of what would become the field of futurism (Bell and Graubard, 1967). Rather than setting out to *predict* the future, the contributors to the Commission aimed to identify the *structural changes* under way and the issues they raised and challenges they posed for society (Bell and Graubard, 1997). Actual predictions were viewed as less relevant, given the complexity of the interrelated systems of interest and the potential for behavioral responses to forces that might not be anticipated. History is also often marked by important unforeseen turning points—the assassination of Archduke Franz Ferdinand in 1914, for example—that in turn set in motion other events that could not have been predicted. Thus, *Toward the Year 2000* did not feature findings but conjectures on possible future courses.

Among the conjectures, many were prescient. Although the commission did not focus explicitly on the world of work, their deliberations anticipated the continued emergence of a postindustrial society and the associated changes in the structure of industry and occupations. They also anticipated the communications revolution and the associated growth of a national information infrastructure. The changing age distribution of the population was highlighted, as well as the growing importance of education. The rise of biology, including genetic engineering, within the sciences was also anticipated. Looking back with 30 years of hindsight, the original editors of the commission report note with regret their most serious omission: the failure to anticipate the changing role of women in the economy and society (Bell and Graubard, 1997). Another omission was the lack of focus on the role of minorities and the persistence of economic disparities across groups. The editors note the latter oversight may have been due to optimism that minorities would be integrated into society in much the same way as past waves of immigrants. Finally, the growing interconnectedness of economies and societies around the world was underappreciated.

Two other studies speak more directly to the subject matter of this book. In 1987, the Hudson Institute published *Workforce 2000*, a study commissioned by then Secretary of Labor William E. Brock to provide "basic intelligence on the job market" in order to evaluate then existing policies and for undertaking new initiatives (Johnston and Packer, 1987). Based on analysis of trends and forecasts using an econometric model, the study reached four central conclusions:

- Economic growth would be strong, propelled by exports, a strong world economy, and rising productivity.

- Manufacturing's share of employment would continue to decline, with most new job creation in the services sector.

- The workforce would become steadily older, more female, and include more minorities.

- New jobs in the services sector would require a more highly skilled workforce.

By and large, these predictions held up, along with some of the other findings of the study. Perhaps the greatest oversight was the lack of attention to the information technology (IT) revolution, although in 1987, personal computers (PCs) were just starting to penetrate the workplace.

A decade later, the Hudson Institute published a follow-up volume to the original study titled *Workforce 2020* (Judy and D'Amico, 1997). Like the first study, this follow-up analysis continues to emphasize the aging of the workforce, along with the increased share of the future workforce that will be made up of females and minorities. The study projects that automation, as a result of accelerating technological change, will continue to displace unskilled and lower-skilled workers, although technology is expected to create more jobs than it destroys. The greater integration of the U.S. economy with the rest of the world is highlighted as well, with implications that include a high reliance of the manufacturing sector on exports and a shrinking, but higher-skilled, employment base in manufacturing. The combination of globalization and technological change is expected to increase volatility in product and services markets, as well as their associated labor markets, implying, for example, more frequent job changes. While it is too soon to grade these forecasts with respect to eventual outcomes, many of the same themes emerge from our analysis based on more recent data.

Like the Commission on the Year 2000, we seek in this book to identify the underlying structural forces likely to shape the future world of work. The next section provides our underlying conceptual framework that links the roles of demographics, technology, and globalization to the key labor market outcomes of interest:

- Who will be working and what skills they will they bring to the labor market.

- The types of jobs the future workforce will fill and the type of work arrangements future workers will make.

- How much workers will earn and how their compensation will be structured in terms of wages and such employment benefits as health insurance, pensions, and other benefits.

In general, our objective is neither to provide future estimates of the number of workers in a given industry or occupation nor to pinpoint the expected growth rate in real wages or the future level of wage dispersion. Rather, we seek to understand key structural trends under way in the economy today, the factors associated with those trends, and whether we can expect such trends to continue or to deviate from their present course. We also aim to identify the implications of the trends and the challenges they pose for decision-makers in the public and private sectors. In some cases, our inferences will be more speculative because future outcomes are not predetermined. They depend not only on the future evolution of key forces but also on how behavior might change in response to those forces. Unanticipated events and the uncertain timing of business cycle upturns and downturns further complicate efforts to forecast even broad trends with certainty.

In some cases, we will draw on existing forecasts of future economic outcomes to illustrate the likely trend in the outcome, given the best available forecasts. However, all such forecasts are inherently limited in that they do not typically anticipate the ways in which economic actors—consumers, workers, firms—may respond to shifts in economic forces and other social, political, or cultural phenomena. For example, future projections of the wage premiums offered to highly skilled workers assume that technological change will continue its rapid pace and that workers' educational attainment will increase only modestly, as it has in the recent past. Instead, it is possible that young people will anticipate the increasingly large rewards to skills and respond by seeking more education. This would change the relative supply of highly skilled workers and reduce future wage disparities.

As another example, forecasts of the future labor force may assume that older workers will retire at the same rate at each age as they do today. Instead, it is possible that older workers may choose to extend their careers in the future in response to other external forces, such as improving health and longevity or changes in such social insurance programs as Social Security. Nevertheless, it can be useful to present relatively naive forecasts, so that policymakers, employers, and future workers can prepare and benefit from upcoming opportunities. At the same time, we exercise caution in placing too much weight on mechanical forecasts, especially when we can identify important changes under way that would induce behavioral responses.

A GUIDING FRAMEWORK

In undertaking our analysis of the forces that are likely to shape the future of work in the United States, we are guided by the conceptual framework illustrated in Figure 1.1. Our ultimate interest is in understanding the outcomes of the labor market (bulleted above and shown in the box at the bottom of the figure).

To address these labor market outcomes, we first require an understanding of the forces that will shape them—the subject of our first question on p. 1. In seeking to answer this question, we adopt an economic perspective that views the labor market outcomes in the bottom half of the figure as determined by labor supply and demand.

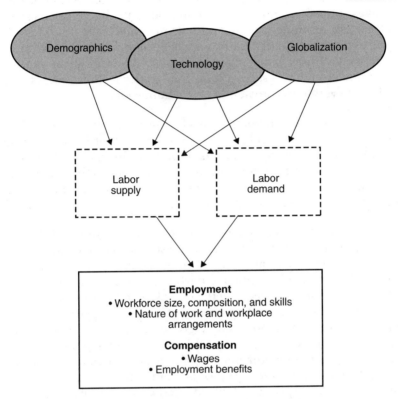

Figure 1.1—Conceptual Framework

By labor supply, we mean those willing and available to work, how much they can work, and what skills they bring to the labor market. By labor demand, we mean the number of jobs employers seek to fill, and the associated skill requirements, to produce the goods and services demanded. In such a market, following the neoclassical economic tradition, compensation is assumed to adjust to balance supply and demand. This will occur separately for each type of labor—both more- and less-skilled workers—to adjust both the demand for each type of labor and the relative demand for different types of labor. Finally, compensation should be viewed broadly. Firms compensate workers in the form of cash wages, noncash benefits (e.g., pensions, health insurance), and working conditions (e.g., flex time, attractive work sites). Workers and firms may negotiate a varying mix of wages, benefits, and working conditions in the compensation package. For example, working parents may prefer greater scheduling flexibility in exchange for lower cash wages. While this is a simplistic view of how labor markets actually operate, given various deviations from the assumptions that underlie the neoclassical model, it nevertheless provides a useful framework.

The key then is understanding which factors are likely to shift underlying supply and demand in the U.S. labor market in the coming years. We view three key forces as important drivers of future outcomes in the U.S. labor market through their effect on the supply and demand for labor (shown in the ellipses at the top of the figure): demographics, technology, and globalization.

The demographic force encompasses the manner in which births, deaths, and net migration determine the size and composition of the U.S. population. The total supply of labor is obtained by multiplying the population by the labor force participation rate, the percentage of the population working or actively looking for work. Labor force participation is determined by, among other factors, people's health, family structure, and nonlabor income (Blundell and Macurdy, 1999). The labor supply can be broken down demographically by considering the population and labor force participation rate specific to people of the same sex, age, race and ethnicity, marital status and family composition, country of birth, and education. In addition to affecting the available supply of workers, demographic factors also influence the demand side of the labor market. The mix of jobs employers seek to fill by industry and occupation is derived from the underlying demand for goods and services, either for consumption by U.S. residents or, through export, by populations in other countries. To the extent that consumption needs vary with different characteristics of the U.S. population or populations abroad, demographic factors can influence the types of jobs required. For example, older individuals consume more health care goods and services than younger individuals do. Thus, if the population composition becomes older, that will increase the demand for physicians, nurses, home health care workers, pharmaceuticals, medical devices, and so on.

The force of technology captures the ongoing, and by all evidence accelerating, process of technological innovation across a wide range of applications that can influence the world of work. Like the demographic force, technology affects both the demand and supply side of the labor market. New technologies may generate new products that give rise to new industries and occupations. The invention of the PC, for instance, generated an entire new industry dedicated to its production and the associated occupations required to create software and install, service, and repair the machines. New technologies may also change the process of producing goods and services in new and in established industries and thus alter the nature of work and worker productivity. Again, the incorporation of the PC and microprocessors more generally into machine tools and office processes has fundamentally altered a wide array of manufacturing processes and services-sector occupations, shaping how and where work is performed. The supply side of the labor market can also be affected by technological change. For instance, medical advances may improve the physical and mental functioning of individuals with disabilities or individuals as they age, thereby affecting who is available for work. Technology may also alter the process of workforce preparation in secondary and postsecondary education, as well as the ability of older workers to retrain, thereby altering the mix of skills in the workforce.

Finally, the force of globalization represents the economic integration of the U.S. economy with those of the rest of the world in terms of trade, capital flows, labor mobility, and knowledge transfers. As the U.S. economy becomes more integrated with others, the markets for goods and services and even the market for labor become global rather than domestic. Thus, the demand for labor is driven not only by domestic demand but by world demand for U.S. goods and services. Just as U.S. firms compete in a global marketplace, U.S. workers increasingly compete with workers in other countries as employers make decisions, on the basis of labor and other cost differentials, whether to locate production facilities in the United States or overseas.

As Figure 1.1 is drawn, the three ellipses representing the forces of demographics, technology, and globalization overlap to indicate that in many ways, these factors are not acting independently but are interacting with one another. As we detail in our analysis, for example, the process of economic integration across the world's economies is driven by technological innovations that are reducing the cost and raising the speed of communications and transmission of data and information. In turn, the competitive pressures brought about by a more open economy stimulate further technological innovation and more rapid adoption of new technologies. In many respects, these interactive effects across the forces we focus on make them even more powerful than if they were operating independently.

Our focus on demographics, technology, and globalization as major drivers of future labor market trends is consistent with the important role that these forces have played in shaping the world of work in the twentieth century as well. For example, one of the salient changes in the demographic composition of the labor force in the last century was the substantial rise in the rate of labor force participation among women. Figure 1.2 illustrates this trend from 1900 to 2002. At the turn of the last century, only about one in five U.S. women worked for pay in the labor market. By 2002, that fraction had tripled to three in five women. The rate of increase was markedly faster from about 1960 to the late 1980s, when the rate advanced almost 2 percent per year, more than three times the rate of increase for the early part of the century or of the 1990s. The transformation in women's paid work is even more dramatic among married women. For example, just 6 in 100 married women worked in paid employment as of 1900 in contrast to 61 in 100 a century later (Goldin, 1990; U.S. Bureau of Census, 2002c). In the Chapter Two, we consider not only the role of women in the labor market but a number of other aspects of population growth and change that will influence the labor market over the next several decades. We show that the U.S. workforce will continue to increase in size, but at a considerably slower rate, while the composition will shift toward a more balanced distribution by age, sex, and race/ethnicity. Slower workforce growth may make it more difficult for firms to recruit workers during periods of strong economic growth, although greater participation in the workforce by the elderly, women with children, persons with disabilities, and other groups with relatively low labor force participation could cause the workforce to grow faster.

The twentieth century was also marked by a revolution in technology that has transformed the economy from the industrial age to the

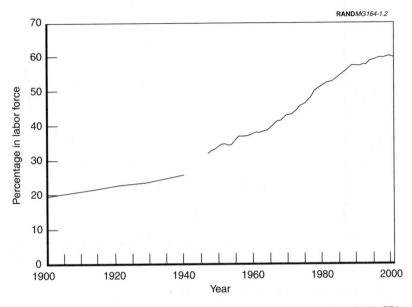

RAND*MG164-1.2*

SOURCE: 1900–1954: U.S. Bureau of Census (1975), Series D29-41; 1955–2002: CEA (2003), Table B-39.
NOTE: Participation rates for 1900–1940 are for women age 14 and above. Participation rates for 1947 onward are for women age 16 and above.

Figure 1.2—Female Labor Force Participation Rate, 1900–2002

information age. As an illustration of the remarkable pace of change in the past century, Figure 1.3 charts the rapid rise in the number of U.S. patents granted since the middle of the last century. While the number of patents granted has oscillated somewhat, there has been a rapid pace of growth in patent awards since the late 1940s and what appears to be an acceleration of the upward trend since the mid-1990s. These patents capture everything from advances in telecommunications to the introduction and evolution of computing hardware and software to the revolution in biotechnology. These past and future trends in technological change are the subject of Chapter Three. There, we describe how trends in IT, biotechnology, and nanotechnology have led experts to conclude that the pace of technological change will almost certainly accelerate in the next 10 to 15 years. Synergies across technologies and disciplines will generate

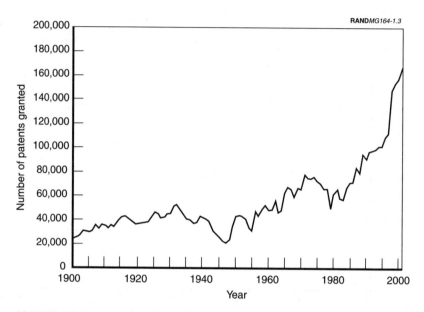

RAND*MG164-1.3*

SOURCE: U.S. Patent and Trademark Office (2002b).

Figure 1.3—Patents Granted, 1900–2001

advances in research and development (R&D), production processes, and the nature of products and services, with wide-ranging implications for the workforce and workplace.

Another marked change in the past half-century was the increased integration of the U.S. economy with the rest of the world. Although the U.S. economy experienced considerable trade and capital flows in the early part of the twentieth century, protectionist pressures and other factors substantially dampened the importance of those flows within the U.S. economy in the interwar period. However, the U.S. emerged from World War II on a path toward greater openness. Figure 1.4 illustrates this trend with respect to trade in goods and services. As a share of gross domestic product (GDP, a measure of economic activity), exports and imports combined have climbed from about 10 percent of GDP in the late 1940s to 26 percent at the peak in 2000. Expanded trade has come through growth in both exports and imports, although since 1976 the U.S. trade account has been in deficit as exports have been smaller than imports. While the bulk of

U.S. trading activities is in goods, trade in services, especially exports, has been growing in importance over time. We address the extent and nature of globalization and its implications for the labor market in Chapter Four. The central lesson we infer is that globalization will continue its record to date of contributing economic benefits in the aggregate. Although market share and jobs will be lost in some economic sectors with short-term and longer-term consequences for affected workers, the job losses will be balanced by employment gains in other sectors. The future reach of global competition will be even more expansive than before, affecting industries and segments of the workforce relatively insulated from trade-related competition in the past.

These patterns provide a preview of the forces that have shaped the world of work in recent decades and ones that we think will play an

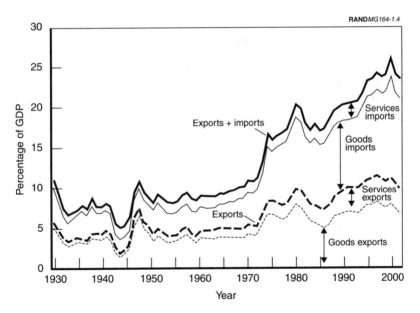

SOURCE: BEA NIPA Tables, Tables 1.1 and 4.1 (http://www.bea.gov/bea/dn/nipa web/SelectTable.asp).

Figure 1.4—Exports and Imports as a Share of GDP, 1929–2002

important role in the labor market in the next several decades as well. It is our intent that our assessment of these forces provide a framework for considering their implications for important dimensions of the workforce and the workplace. Thus, in the concluding chapter we discuss the implications for important dimensions of the workforce, workplace, and compensation that arise from the major forces shaping the world of work. Among those are the following:

- Employees will work in more decentralized, specialized firms.

- Employer-employee relationships will become less standardized and more individualized.

- Greater emphasis will be placed on retraining and lifelong learning as the U.S. workforce tries to stay competitive in the global marketplace and respond to technological changes.

- Slower labor force growth will encourage employers to accommodate women, the elderly, and persons with disabilities to increase their participation in the labor force.

- Future productivity growth will support rising wages and may affect the wage distribution. The tie between employment and access to fringe benefits will be weakened.

Chapter Two

SHIFTING DEMOGRAPHIC PARAMETERS SHAPING
THE FUTURE WORKFORCE

In the next 10 to 15 years, important demographic shifts will continue to influence the size and composition of the workforce. The size and composition of the population, as well as labor force participation rates, determine the number and makeup of people who want to work. Demographic parameters also influence the consumption patterns of the population and thus the mix of goods and services produced and the labor required to produce them. These factors continue to evolve, in some ways that perpetuate recent trends, and in other ways that suggest changes from the recent past.

In this chapter, we elaborate on the relationships among population size and composition, labor force participation, and labor demand and supply. We begin with the basics: slower workforce growth and shifting labor force composition. These developments have been under way for some time and will continue in the next couple of decades. The labor force has been growing more slowly because of smaller birth cohorts following the baby boom that ended in 1964 and a trend toward earlier retirement on the part of male workers. While workforce growth has been slowing for some time now, the upcoming slowdown is far more dramatic than at any time during the twentieth century. That the labor force has been growing at all has been the result of progressively higher labor force participation by women and the continued large inflows of immigrants. As the female labor force participation rate approaches that of men, the growth of female labor force participation is slowing, thus further slowing the expansion of the overall workforce.

The U.S. population as a whole has been growing older as the baby boom generation ages. Older people bring strengths to the workforce different from those of young people. However, the increase of nonworking elderly can be costly for society because of their reliance on social insurance programs. These costs in the United States, however, are less than those faced by other developed countries. A continuing large inflow of immigrants has shifted the composition of the workforce. Hispanics and Asians are the fastest growing racial and ethnic groups in the population. In the case of Hispanics, a high birth rate is partly responsible for that, but immigration is the main driver. The steadily increasing female labor force participation rates, combined with decreasing male rates, have brought the labor force close to gender balance. The rise in female rates holds for married women and single women alike. It holds as well for women with and without minor children, and, for the latter, it holds whether they are married or not and no matter how old their children are. As a result of population aging and the increased labor force participation of women, another dimension of change is that more workers have responsibilities outside of work. This may involve caring for children, elderly parents, or both.

An important theme of this chapter is the growing weight of education and skills in defining the future workforce. We outline the educational attainment, achievements, and skill levels in the United States, both compared to years past and to other countries. On the whole, the educational attainment (i.e., years of schooling completed) of the U.S. population has been rising and will probably continue to rise. Achievement scores, however, have been only about average compared to those in other developed nations despite greater public and private expenditures on education. In addition to education reforms, such as those that address the funding and institutional organization of schools and the degree of competition among schools, technological developments, such as technology-mediated instruction, might raise the productivity of education.

The slowdown of the workforce growth may make it more difficult for firms to recruit workers in the future. We therefore explore the potential for faster workforce growth. First, given the right environment, more older workers might choose to retire later and continue to contribute to the nation's prosperity. Second, data from the United States and from other countries suggest that labor force participation by women with children could rise further if work could be more easily balanced with family responsibilities. Third, there is the potential to raise labor force participation by such underrepresented groups as the disabled. Finally, immigration offers opportunities for workforce growth or changes in the skill composition of the workforce.

Most of this chapter is directed to the effect of demographic trends on the characteristics of labor supply. Those trends will also alter the mix of goods and services demanded and thus the characteristics of labor demanded by firms. Older households tend to spend their money differently than younger ones do, and household tasks formerly performed by household members may be "outsourced" to the paid workforce as women (in particular) take paid work in greater numbers. We take up such issues briefly toward the end of the chapter.

SLOWER WORKFORCE GROWTH AHEAD

The workforce grew from 83 million individuals in 1970 to 107 million in 1980, 126 million in 1990, and 141 million in 2000. These figures correspond to annual growth rates of 2.6 percent in the 1970s, 1.6 percent during the 1980s, and 1.1 percent in the 1990s (see Figure 2.1). The rate of increase has thus abated. Between 2000 and 2010, the Bureau of Labor Statistics (BLS) projects a continuing annual growth rate of 1.1 percent to 158 million individuals in 2010 (Fullerton and Toossi, 2001). After 2010, the workforce growth will slow further. Between 2010 and 2020, the annual growth rate is projected to be just 0.4 percent, followed by an even lower 0.3 percent annual growth rate between 2020 and 2030 (Toossi, 2002). (See Box 2.1 for a discussion of what factors determine the size of the labor force and methods for projecting the size of the future labor force.)

Why has the rate of growth decreased and why will it slow even more? The high labor force growth rates of the 1970s and 1980s were the results of strongly increased workforce participation among women combined with fairly robust population growth. The rapid increase in female labor force participation strongly dominated a gradual decrease in male participation. However, as female and male participation rates converge, the rate of female participation growth

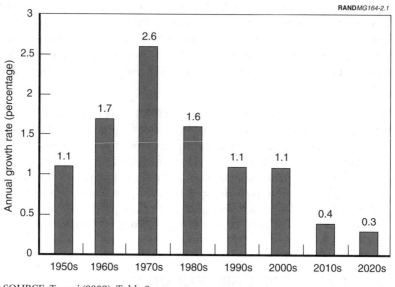

SOURCE: Toossi (2002), Table 2.

Figure 2.1—Annual Growth Rates of the Labor Force, 1950–2000, and Projected, 2000–2030

Box 2.1

What Determines the Size of the Future Workforce?

A study about the twenty-first century workforce and workplace inherently relies on many projections. How do we, or rather, how does the BLS, project the number of people in the future workforce?

First a definition: the workforce includes both people who are employed and people who are unemployed. It is also known as the labor force. Unemployed people are people without a job who are actively seeking one. Thus, the term "unemployed" does not count a student, disabled person, homemaker, or retiree who does not have a job and is not looking for one. Similarly, someone who would like a job but has given up on finding one is not unemployed and thus not in the workforce.

The size of the future workforce depends on the size of the future population and the future labor force participation rate—that is, the fraction of the

Box 2.1—continued

population that is employed or unemployed. The size of the future population, in turn, depends on the current population, fertility, mortality, and immigration (see Figure 2.2). Labor force participation rates vary greatly by age, sex, and race/ethnicity. The BLS therefore generates separate population projections for 136 age, sex, and race or Hispanic origin groups. It does this every two years with a 10-year horizon. It also projects labor force participation rates for each of the 136 subpopulations. It first calculates the rate of change over the past eight years and applies this to the most recent labor force participation rate to get an estimate for the next eight. It then reviews each projected rate and manually adjusts implausible ones, namely when they appear inconsistent with the results of cross-sectional and cohort analyses. This second step aims to ensure consistency in the projections across the various demographic groups. Finally, the size of the anticipated labor force is calculated by multiplying the labor force participation rates by the population projections (BLS 1997; Fullerton and Toossi, 2001).

Workforce measures do not take number of hours on the job into account. Someone who works full-time is counted the same as someone who works 20 or 30 hours a week. This can sometimes be misleading—for example, when labor force participation rates are compared across subpopulations or countries with different fractions of part-time workers.

Naturally, there is uncertainty in projecting the various elements contributing to the labor force estimate. If the horizon is only 10 to 20 years, uncertainty about fertility is not very important, because future children will be mostly too young to work. Barring a major shock such as a particularly lethal disease or a war on U.S. soil, the effects of mortality are accurately predictable. Legal and illegal immigration are more uncertain, but those uncertainties are on the order of hundreds of thousands per year against a population pool in the most immigration-affected age classes in the tens of millions. The main source of uncertainty is future labor force participation. This will depend on job opportunities, wage levels, ability to balance work and family, retirement incentives, health, nonlabor income, and many more factors.

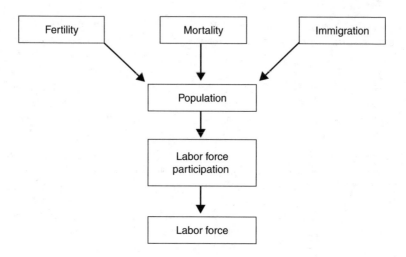

RANDMG164-2.2

Figure 2.2—Determinants of the Size of the Workforce

is slowing. BLS expects women to continue slowly increasing their *age-specific* workforce participation until 2015. But because the aging female workforce is gradually moving into age groups that traditionally have low participation rates, *overall* female labor force participation is expected to reach its highest level a few years earlier, in 2010. Men are also aging, resulting in a continuing slow decline in their overall participation rate. Since 1990, the total contribution of increased labor force participation rates to workforce growth has been very small; after 2010, the aging of the workforce is expected to reduce the overall labor force participation rate (Toossi, 2002). Workforce growth since 1990 has largely been fueled by immigration.

We now take a closer look at underlying childbearing trends, decreasing labor force participation rates among men, increasing labor force participation among women, and the large inflow of immigrants since the late 1970s.

Baby Boom, Baby Bust

The most notable development in fertility after World War II has been the baby boom of 1946–1964 (see Figure 2.3).[1] It was preceded by a baby dearth in the 1930s, so that the baby boom cohort is much larger than earlier birth cohorts. Fertility rates declined substantially after 1964 and have remained low through the present time (14.5 births per 1,000 residents in 2001).

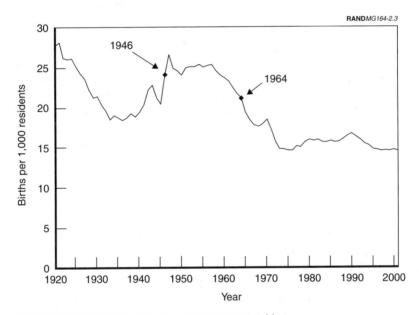

SOURCES: NCHS (2001), Table 1-1; NCHS (2002a), Table 1.

Figure 2.3—Fertility Rate, 1920–2001

---

[1]Because we are interested in explaining the growth of the population and its subgroups, we define fertility as the number of live births per x residents, conventionally, per 1,000. Fertility rate in this sense is affected by population age-gender structure, as well as by Total Fertility Rate (TFR), or the number of live births per woman of reproductive age over the course of her life. The TFR was 2.1 children per woman in 2001, precisely at the level to maintain a stable population in the long run.

In 2003, the oldest baby boomers will celebrate their 57th birthday. Over the next decade or two, many of them will be retiring. Since this cohort is so much larger than older cohorts, the number of people leaving the labor force will increase sharply.

At the young end of the workforce, the number of entrants will increase, but not in tandem with the large cohort that is retiring. The difference is not quite so dramatic as Figure 2.3 might suggest. The fertility rate since 1970 has been well below the rate in the baby boom years, but because the overall population has grown, the total number of babies born is not hugely lower than during the baby boom years. At the peak of the baby boom, in 1957, there were 4.3 million live births (or 25 per 1,000 residents) in the United States. The number declined to a low of 3.1 million in 1973, but has risen to around 4 million recently (National Center for Health Statistics (NCHS), 2002a). The number of young workforce entrants has been increasing correspondingly in recent years and may be expected to continue to slowly increase in the next couple of decades.

Men Start Working Later, Retire Earlier

The most striking workforce participation trends of the second half of the twentieth century are the declining labor force participation rates of men (especially older men) and increasing rates of women (see Figure 2.4 and the discussion regarding women below). In 1948, fully 90 percent of men age 55–64 were in the labor force. This rate declined to 87, 72, and 67 percent in 1960, 1980, and 2000, respectively (BLS, 2003a).

The effect of the trend toward earlier retirement is amplified by the population's aging. If the age structure of the workforce were stationary, earlier retirement would reduce the overall labor force participation rate. However, the population is also aging, thus gradually moving workers to age groups with traditionally low participation. The effect is clearly reflected in male labor force participation statistics. The overall male participation rate declined from 86 percent in 1950 to 74 percent in 2002 (BLS, 2003a). However, as we discuss in detail below, there are reasons to believe male labor force participation behavior at older ages will be different in the future.

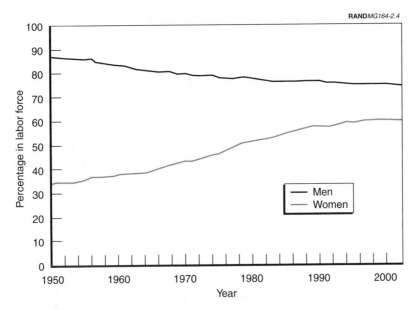

SOURCE: BLS (2003a), series LNU01300001 and LNU01300002.
NOTE: Population is those age 16 and above.

Figure 2.4—Labor Force Participation Rate, by Sex, 1950–2002

Male labor force participation has also decreased at younger ages. Between 1980 and 2000, labor force participation rates among men age 25–54 dropped by two to three percentage points. BLS projects further small declines (Toossi, 2002). Larger changes occurred at younger ages. Between 1980 and 2000, labor force participation among men age 16–24 fell by six percentage points to 69 percent in 2000, and it is expected to drop some more. Much of this reduced workforce participation is mirrored in sharply increased school enrollment rates. Between 1980 and 2000, school enrollment increased from 46 to 61 percent among 18–19-year-olds, from 31 to 44 percent among 20–21-year-olds, and from 16 to 25 percent among 22–24-year-olds (U.S. Bureau of the Census, 1981, 2001c). We elaborate on education issues below.

Women Greatly Increased Their Workforce Participation

While labor force participation among men, particularly older men, has gradually declined since 1950, among women it has increased at an extraordinarily rapid pace (see Figure 2.4). In 1950, 86 percent of men and 34 percent of women age 16 and older were in the labor force. By 2002, these rates had converged to 74 and 60 percent, respectively (BLS, 2003a). BLS expects the male and female labor force participation rates to continue to converge to 73 and 62 percent, respectively, in 2010 (Fullerton and Toossi, 2001; Toossi, 2002). The generally converging labor force participation among men and women implies that the fraction of workers that are women is increasing. It was 47 percent in 2000 and is expected to be 48 percent in 2010.

While male and female participation rates are converging in the population as a whole, the story is different in some subgroups. For example, at roughly the same age-specific participation rates, Hispanic men have higher overall labor force participation rates than non-Hispanic men because of their young age structure (61 percent of Hispanics are between age 20 and 44, compared to 46 percent of non-Hispanic whites [Fullerton and Toossi, 2001]). This does not hold for Hispanic women. Age-specific participation rates of Hispanic women are 12–14 percentage points lower than among non-Hispanic white women. However, because of the younger age structure among Hispanics, the overall labor force participation rate among Hispanic women age 16 and older is only 4 percentage points lower than among non-Hispanic white women (Fullerton, 1999). Overall in 1998, male and female labor force participation among Hispanics was 80 and 56 percent, respectively. The increasing prevalence of Hispanics in the population therefore counteracts the observed overall convergence of male and female workforce participation rates.

Figure 2.5 demonstrates that increased participation among women took place at all ages between 20 and 64 years. The figure also indicates that the changing age structure of the population has important implications for overall workforce participation. Among both men and women, labor force participation drops off strongly after age 55. While male labor force participation rates are projected to

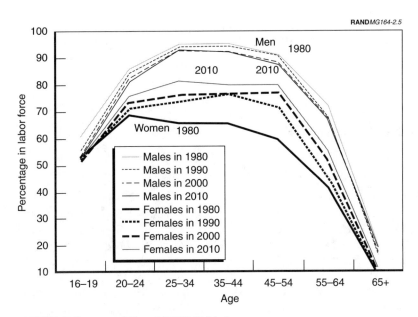

RAND*MG164-2.5*

SOURCE: Fullerton and Toossi (2001), Table 3.

Figure 2.5—Labor Force Participation Rate by Sex and Age, 1980–2010

change very little between 2000 and 2010, the aging of the workforce implies an overall reduction of male labor force participation. Among women, the continuing small increases in labor force participation between 2000 and 2010 and population aging counteract each other. BLS expects overall female labor force participation to continue to rise until 2010 and decline thereafter (Toossi, 2002).

Immigrants Fuel Workforce Growth

Immigration has dramatically influenced U.S. population and workforce trends in recent decades. Relative to population size, immigration was largest in the early part of the twentieth century. However, the absolute number of immigrants in the last two decades of the twentieth century exceeds that during the first two (INS, 2002, 2003a). To a small extent, immigration is offset by emigration. Since 1960, there has been approximately one emigrant for every four immigrants. (See Box 2.2 for a discussion of how immigrants are counted and comparisons between the United States and other countries in the relative size of their foreign-born populations.)

Box 2.2

Counting Immigrants

How does the United States differ from other developed countries in its absorption of immigrants? First, we must define what we mean by "immigrant."

Following the Bureau of Citizenship and Immigration Services (BCIS, formerly the Immigration and Naturalization Service, INS), we use the term "immigrants" to refer to foreign individuals (aliens) who become permanent residents of the United States. Their immigrant visa is commonly called a "Green Card" and their expressed intent is to live permanently in the United States. In addition to immigrants, the population contains nonimmigrants (aliens with a temporary visa) and illegal immigrants (aliens without a visa).

Some countries, including the United States, maintain statistics on the number of residents born abroad. Other countries keep track of the number of foreign nationals, which is not the same. Immigrants may later adopt citizenship of their host country, in which case they are no longer foreign nationals but still foreign born. The difference can be substantial, depending on naturalization policies. For example, the 1999 population of France consisted of 10.0 percent foreign-born, but only 5.6 percent of the entire population were not French citizens.

Table 2.1 indicates that large international differences exist in immigrant populations. Some countries have few immigrants because they are traditionally sending countries (Mexico, Spain, Italy, and Ireland). But low immigrant populations may also be the result of restrictive immigration policy. For example, Sweden apparently admitted many more immigrants than its neighboring countries (Denmark, Finland, and Norway), which are similar by many measures. The fraction foreign-born in the United States, at 10.4 percent in 2000 (up to 11.5 percent by 2002), is roughly in the middle of the international range.

Table 2.1

Percentage of the Population That Is Foreign-Born and Foreign National, Selected Countries, 2000

	Foreign-Born	Foreign National
Australia	23.6	
Austria	10.4	9.3
Canada (1996)	17.4	
Denmark	5.8	4.8
Finland	2.6	1.8
France (1999)	10.0	5.6
Germany		8.9
Hungary	2.9	
Italy		2.4
Luxembourg		37.3
Ireland		3.3
Mexico	0.5	
Netherlands	10.1	4.2
New Zealand	19.5	
Norway	6.8	4.1
Spain		2.2
Sweden	11.3	5.4
Switzerland		19.3
United Kingdom		4.0
United States	10.4	

SOURCE: OECD (2003c).

In 2002, the civilian noninstitutionalized population in the United States included 32.5 million foreign-born, representing 11.5 percent of the U.S. population (U.S. Bureau of the Census, 2003b). These individuals may be (permanent, legal) immigrants, temporary foreign residents, or illegal immigrants. Figure 2.6 shows the number of permanent, legal immigrants entering the country each year between 1950 and 2001, including individuals who already resided in the United States and converted from nonimmigrant to immigrant status (INS, 2003a). The annual inflow increased slowly to about 640,000 in 1988, jumped to over 1 million in the next year, reached a peak of 1.8 million in 1991, and settled in around 900,000 per year in the late 1990s. The jump in 2001, when the INS issued 1.1 million immigrant visas, is largely the result of an effort to reduce administrative backlog (INS, 2003a).

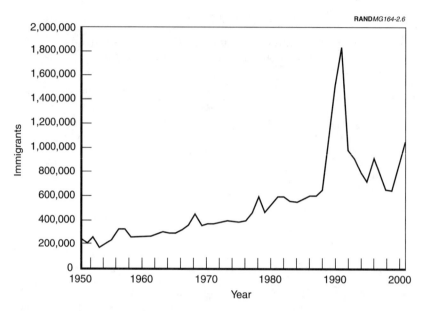

SOURCE: INS (2003a), Table 1.

Figure 2.6—Immigration to the United States, 1950–2001

Many aliens legally reside in the United States on a temporary basis. These include students, professionals, their family members, and others. Most temporary foreign professionals hold an H-1B or L-1 visa. H-1B visas are for well-educated or skilled so-called Specialty Occupation Workers; L-1 visas are for intracompany transferees—i.e., for aliens transferring from a foreign to a U.S. location of their employer. H-1B petitions are approved for up to three years with a possible extension of up to another three years; L-1 petitions are for a maximum of seven years. In fiscal year 2002, BCIS approved 198,000 H-1B petitions, down from 331,000 in the previous year (DHS, forthcoming). The number of L-1 visas issued was 58,000, slightly below that in the previous year (U.S. Department of State, forthcoming).[2] A

_____

[2]BCIS considers and approves petitions, thereby granting the right to work; the U.S. Department of State issues visas, thereby granting the right to enter the United States. Someone who converts from student (F-1) status to H-1B status without leaving the United States does therefore not need a visa, unless they leave and reenter. (In fiscal year 2002, 198,000 H-1B petitions were approved and 118,000 H-1B visas were issued.)

rough estimate, assuming an average stay of two years per H-1B approval and four years per L-1 visa issuance, is that the stock of H-1B and L-1 beneficiaries is about 800,000. Their labor force participation is, by the terms of their visa, 100 percent. Approximately 7 million illegal immigrants were thought to reside in the United States in 2000. A little more than half of them originated from Mexico. The population of illegal immigrants is estimated to grow at about 350,000 per year (INS, 2003b).

Migration flows can substantially alter the growth rate and the composition of the future workforce. Assuming no growth in the number of temporary (H-1B or L-1) workers, the number of people—other than business travelers and tourists—legally entering the United States each year is around 900,000. There is about one emigrant for every four immigrants and the illegal immigrant population increases by roughly 350,000 annually, so net migration is around 1.0 million. In 2001, the natural increase of the U.S. population—the difference between 4.0 million births and 2.4 million deaths—was about 1.6 million (NCHS, 2002c). Net migration thus boosted the U.S. population growth by about 60 percent. The effect on workforce growth is even larger, because immigrants are more likely to be of working age than the general population (71 percent of immigrants were age 20–64 in 2001 compared to 59 percent of the population).

Declining male labor force participation and slow population growth reduce labor force growth to a trickle. This has prompted some to become concerned about a future labor shortage (e.g., Lofgren, Nyce, and Schieber, 2003).[3] For economic activity to continue to grow, U.S. workers would need to become more productive or overall labor

---

For counting temporary alien workers, the number of H-1B and L-1 approvals is thus most relevant. BCIS does not publish L-1 approval statistics, but because L-1 beneficiaries are transferring from abroad, the number of approvals is close to the number of visas. (BCIS does publish admission statistics, but those double count individuals who entered the country twice in one year.)

[3]Some argue that the term "labor shortage" is a misnomer, because if labor supply is not sufficient to meet labor demand at current wage levels, the price of labor (i.e., total compensation) will increase. This will make work more attractive relative to leisure, thus inducing greater labor force participation to the point where firms can hire all the workers they desire. Strictly speaking, the concern is thus not about a labor shortage but about upward pressure on wages and benefit costs, which could erode corporate profits, reduce corporate investments, reduce productivity growth, or make U.S. goods and services less competitive on the world market.

force participation or immigration would need to increase. To the extent that the predictions of slower growth ahead are accurate and tight labor markets materialize, a central issue for the next couple of decades will thus be whether and how to increase the size of the labor force, perhaps through immigration or increasing labor force participation rates. We return to this issue later in the chapter.

THE WORKFORCE IS BECOMING EVER MORE DIVERSE

The Hudson Institute's *Workforce 2000* predicted that in the late twentieth century the workforce of the United States would become older, more female, and more "disadvantaged"—a term it used to capture black and Hispanic workers (Johnston and Packer, 1987). As we discuss in this section, as many of the underlying demographic forces remain the same, the workforce will continue to evolve along these same lines in terms of age, gender composition, and the racial and ethnic makeup. In addition, we will signal another dimension of diversity: more diverse in responsibilities outside work. The remainder of this section documents the forces leading to greater workforce diversity over the upcoming couple of decades.

The Workforce Is Becoming More Balanced in Age

As has been noted extensively elsewhere, the population of the United States is getting older. The median age is projected to increase from 35.5 years in 2000 to 40.7 years in 2050 (UN, 2001). During the same period, the number of elderly (age 65-plus) per 100 working-age adults (age 15–64) will nearly double from 18.6 to 34.9. In other words, the population of workers will support a relatively larger elderly population in the future, a population that participates in social insurance programs largely paid for by current workers. Most notably, under current law, expenses on Social Security and Medicare are projected to climb from 7.0 percent of GDP in 2002 to 13.1 percent in 2050 (Board of Trustees of the Federal Old-Age and Survivors Insurance and Disability Insurance (OASDI) Trust Funds, 2003; Boards of Trustees of the Hospital Insurance (HI) and Supplementary Medical Insurance (SMI) Trust Funds, 2003). The cost of these social insurance programs will thus fall on a relatively smaller base of workers. The population is aging mainly because of past fertility and mortality trends, which generate lower growth rates among the young and higher growth rates among the old. The result is a departure from the standard pyramid-shaped age-gender diagram of a growing population, in which relatively many young people outnumber smaller and smaller population sizes at older ages. The population diagram has instead become more pillar-shaped, with roughly equal population sizes at all ages except the old.

The top panel of Figure 2.7, for example, shows the pyramid-shaped distribution of 1960, with relatively many young children. These children are the baby boom generation, born between 1946 and 1964. Moving down the panels of Figure 2.7, the large baby boom cohort climbs the pyramid and shows up in the age 56–76 categories by 2020. Successive cohorts were generally smaller in size, so that the base of the population pyramid has not grown as rapidly as higher levels have. As a result, by 2020 the distribution of the population between birth and age 65 will be approximately rectangular or pillar-shaped rather than pyramid-shaped. The size of the population will be in the narrow 20–23 million range for every five-year age group from birth to age 64. Thus, none of these groups will differ by more than 6 percent from the average size. After age 65, mortality becomes increasingly strong and generates a pyramid-shaped pattern.[4]

Since the population "pyramid" will soon be pillar-shaped up to age 64, we speak of the population's "becoming increasingly balanced in age" in addition to just "aging." In the workforce, the trend toward greater age balance is even stronger than in the population, at least until 2010 because of projected increased labor force participation among mature and older workers (see below for details). In 2000, the median age of the population was 4.9 years higher than that of the workforce. By 2010, this difference is projected to shrink to 4.1 years (Fullerton and Toossi, 2001).

---

[4]In keeping with tradition, we have depicted the age distribution of the population separately for men and women in two-sided horizontal histograms. However, the differences between men and women do not change markedly over time. At birth, there are slightly more boys than girls. The sex ratio reverses at higher ages because women generally outlive men. In 2000, the sex ratio went from 105 boys per 100 girls at birth to 100 at about age 35 and only 50 at age 80 or above.

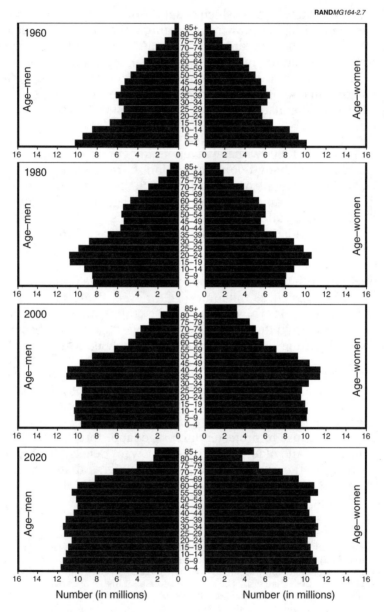

Number (in millions)

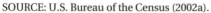

SOURCE: U.S. Bureau of the Census (2002a).

Figure 2.7—Age Structure of the Population in 1960, 1980, 2000, and 2020

Among Developed Countries, the United States Remains Relatively Young

At present, the U.S. population is somewhat younger than the populations of other developed nations. The outlook, however, shows much greater differences. All major countries will age, but the United States at a much slower pace than most other nations. Table 2.2 lists two indicators of population aging in the United States and other countries in 2000, 2025, and 2050. As mentioned above, the median age of the population and the old-age dependency ratio are both increasing in the United States. Most of this population aging process will have been realized by 2025.

Our neighbors to the north and south will also become older. The median age in Canada is already above that in the United States, and the gap will become wider. The number of elderly per working-age adult is currently about on par with the United States but will grow much faster. The Mexican population is currently much younger

Table 2.2

Indicators of Aging in Selected Countries (2000, 2025, and 2050)

	Median Age (Years)			Old-Age Dependency Ratio		
	2000	2025	2050	2000	2025	2050
United States	35.5	39.3	40.7	18.6	29.3	34.9
Canada	36.9	42.9	44.0	18.5	32.6	40.9
Mexico	23.3	32.5	39.5	7.6	13.8	30.0
Europe	37.7	45.4	49.5	21.7	33.2	51.4
France	37.6	43.3	45.2	24.5	36.2	46.7
Germany	40.1	48.5	50.9	24.1	39.0	54.7
Italy	40.2	50.7	54.1	26.7	40.6	68.1
Spain	37.7	49.2	55.2	24.8	36.1	73.8
United Kingdom	37.7	44.5	47.4	24.1	34.8	47.3
Russia	36.8	43.8	50.0	18.0	27.6	47.1
Japan	41.2	50.0	53.1	25.2	49.0	71.3
China	30.0	39.0	43.8	10.0	19.4	37.2
India	23.7	31.3	38.0	8.1	12.1	22.6

SOURCE: United Nations (2001).

NOTES: Old-age dependency ratio is defined as the number of elderly (age 65-plus) per 100 working-age adults (15–64 years). Europe includes all European countries, from Norway to Greece and Iceland to Russia.

than the U.S. population. The median age is fully 12 years lower and the old-age dependency ratio less than half. Until 2025, the gap will narrow, but the Mexican population will remain much younger than the U.S. population. After 2025, however, Mexico is projected to age at a much faster rate than the United States. By 2050, its age structure will be similar to ours.

The populations of most European countries are already older than the United States, and the difference is projected to grow substantially. The median ages in Germany and the United Kingdom, for example, are projected to rise by more than 10 years between 2000 and 2050, compared with an increase of five years in the United States. The median age of the Italian population will have risen by nearly 10 years by 2025 and 14 years by 2050; Spain will age even faster. In Europe as a whole, the median age is projected to rise by 12 years between 2000 and 2050. Similar patterns are reflected in the old-age dependency ratios. The large western European countries currently have ratios of about 25 elderly per 100 working-age adults—i.e., there are about four working-age adults per elderly person. By 2050, there will be as few as two working-age adults per elderly person in Germany, France, and the United Kingdom, and only 1.4 in Italy and Spain.

Japan's population is currently among the oldest in the world. Its median age, at 41 years, is slightly above the median ages of Germany and Italy. It is projected to rise by 12 years between 2000 and 2050. Similar to the oldest European countries, its number of working-age adults per elderly is projected to fall from four in 2000 to 1.4 in 2050.

The populations of such fast-developing countries as India and China are much younger than the U.S. population. China's median age is 30 and India's only 24, with correspondingly low old-age dependency ratios. However, both countries will age rapidly. By 2025, China's median age will be the same as that of the United States, and even higher by 2050. India will also age rapidly, but remain comparatively young.

As the age gap between the United States and other developed nations grows, so will the differences between their workforces. While older workers tend to have more experience, younger workers are generally more productive and more likely to acquire new skills through their own investments or investments by their employers (Lofgren, Nyce, and Schieber, 2003). The productivity of the U.S. workforce is thus likely to evolve more favorably than in other developed nations. The same holds with respect to India and China, whose populations are aging much faster than the U.S. population.

These demographic patterns may have implications for the relative competitiveness of the United States vis-à-vis other nations, particularly other developed countries where population aging is even more dramatic. Absent major changes in immigration levels in Japan and other European countries or unanticipated increases in birth rates, the U.S. population will remain relatively younger. A major issue facing all developed countries is the costs associated with old-age social insurance programs. Most developed nations largely fund their retirement benefit and health care programs on a pay-as-you-go basis—that is, current workers pay for the benefits of current retirees. Current tax and benefit structures cannot be sustained in light of the increasing size of the elderly population supported per worker. For all practical purposes, benefits must become less generous or tax contributions higher. Almost all developed nations are therefore currently reforming their retirement benefit and old-age health care programs, typically opting for a combination of reduced benefits and higher taxes.

Who will bear the burden of those higher taxes? Basic economic theory states that workers are compensated according to their marginal productivity, so that in the long run the higher burden will be borne entirely by workers and reduce their standard of living. In the short to medium term, it is possible that employers will shoulder some of the costs. As a result, the cost of production may go up which could reduce competitiveness in world markets.

The impending societal costs associated with an aging population are expected to weigh heavily on the United States. As mentioned above, under current law, expenses on Medicare and Social Security are projected to almost double as a fraction of GDP. However, other developed nations are facing even greater burdens. In part, this stems from the slower pace of aging in the United States. In addition, while Social Security and several government pension programs are largely funded on a pay-as-you-go basis, these programs account for only a portion of retirement benefits in the United States. Employer-provided pensions, which account for roughly the same share of retirement income as Social Security, are mostly prefunded. Few European countries have sizable funded pensions. (The Netherlands is a clear exception, as is the United Kingdom, to a lesser extent. Sweden recently carved out a funded portion of its retirement benefit program.)[5] Nevertheless, as the number of retirees increases relative to the number of workers in the United States, there will be rising fiscal pressure to pay for the elderly's entitlements and the government services that they use.

The Workforce Is Becoming More Diverse in Race and Ethnicity

Another major U.S. population development is the increasing diversity of its racial and ethnic composition. (See Box 2.3 for a discussion of racial and ethnic categories.) Figure 2.8 shows the population's composition for 1980 through 2020 (U.S. Bureau of the Census 2001a, 2001b, 2002b). Hispanics may be of any race; the other categories exclude Hispanics.[6] The most notable feature is the declining share of whites in contrast to the growth of all minority populations, particularly Hispanics and Asians and Pacific Islanders. The Hispanic population has grown the most, almost doubling its share from 6.4 percent in 1980 to a projected 12 percent in 2002. Hispanics are projected to keep increasing their share of the population, albeit at a slower pace, to 17 percent in 2020. Asians and Pacific Islanders increased from 1.6 percent in 1980 to 4.1 percent in 2002. They, too, are projected to continue increasing their share of the population, to 5.7 percent in 2020. The black population share increased slightly and is projected to continue to do so only slightly, from 12 percent in 1980 to 13 percent in 2020. Native Americans remain the smallest segment, with a projected growth from 0.6 percent in 1980 to 0.8 percent in 2020.

---

[5]A system of personal retirement accounts, much like Sweden's, is under consideration in the United States, but this will affect U.S. government cash flow negatively because of immediately lower tax revenues and much-delayed lower benefit payments.

[6]Unless explicitly stated otherwise, this study uses the racial identifiers "white," "black," etc., for non-Hispanic white, non-Hispanic black, etc.

Box 2.3

The Difference Between Race and Ethnicity

What is the distinction between race and ethnicity in the context of the demographic data we rely on for this study? The Oxford English Dictionary defines the two terms as follows: Race is "A group of persons ... connected by common descent or origin" or alternatively, "One of the great divisions of mankind, having certain physical peculiarities in common." Ethnic is "pertaining to or having common racial, cultural, religious, or linguistic characteristics." In other words, race categories tend to be associated with biology and ethnic categories with culture. However, the two concepts are not clearly distinct from each other. For example, 26 different racial terms have been used to identify populations in the 1900–1990 U.S. censuses. In the early twentieth century, Italian, Irish, and Jewish were listed as racial categories and seen as inherently and irredeemably distinct from the major-ity white population. Today, these are considered ethnicities. Genetically, no matter how racial groups are defined, two people from the same racial group are about as different from each other as two people from any two different racial groups (American Anthropological Association, 1997).

The U.S. government uses a distinction, which we follow here, based on the Office of Management and Budget (OMB) Directive 15 of 1977. OMB Directive 15 specified that all federal agencies use a four-race classification system (white, black, American Indian and Alaska Native, and Asian and Pacific Islander) and an ethnicity classification system that permits classifi-cation of all individuals as either Hispanic or non-Hispanic. Finer categories are allowed, provided that they can be unambiguously assigned to one of the primary categories. Thus, Hispanics can be of any race. For example, someone who is descended from slaves brought from Africa to Cuba is Hispanic and black; someone of Mayan descent who immigrated from southern Mexico is Hispanic and American Indian. Often, race and ethnicity are blended into five mutually exclusive categories: Hispanic, non-Hispanic white, non-Hispanic black, non-Hispanic American Indian and Alaska Native, and non-Hispanic Asian and Pacific Islander. While simpler, this classification does not permit analyses of racial differences within Hispan-ics or of ethnic differences within races.

Box 2.3—continued

The 1990 census asked respondents to identify themselves with one and only one racial category and one ethnicity. However, the U.S. population had become increasingly diverse since 1977 and opposition against the mutually exclusive racial categorization was building. More and more people were born with ancestors of different races. About half a million people ignored the instruction and selected more than one race (Wallman, Evinger, and Schecter, 2000). Large numbers of immigrants (especially from Latin American and Arab countries) complained that none of the four main racial categories applied to them, and many people (especially people of Hispanic origin) chose "other race" on the 1990 census form. Among those, many reported ancestries (on the ancestry question) indicating multiple racial backgrounds (Lee, 2001). OMB Directive 15 was therefore amended in 1997. There are now five basic race categories: American Indian or Alaska Native, Asian, black or African American, native Hawaiian or other Pacific Islander, and white. An important change is that federal survey respondents may now identify themselves with multiple racial categories. The two ethnic categories are now labeled "Hispanic or Latino" and "not Hispanic or Latino." Unlike mixed-race people, individuals with mixed ethnicity must select one and only one ethnic category.

Figure 2.9 reproduces the questions on ethnicity and race, as asked in the 2000 census. The questionnaire distinguishes several subdivisions of the primary ethnicity and race categories laid out in OMB's 1997 Directive 15. Nationwide, 2.4 percent of the respondents identified with more than one racial category. Among children under age 18, 4.0 percent were multiracial (Lee, 2001).

The growing diversity of the labor force in terms of the race and ethnic composition stems mainly from trends in fertility, immigration, and labor force participation. In short, minorities have more children, immigrants largely add to the minority population, and minority Hispanics participate more in the workforce because of their relatively young age.

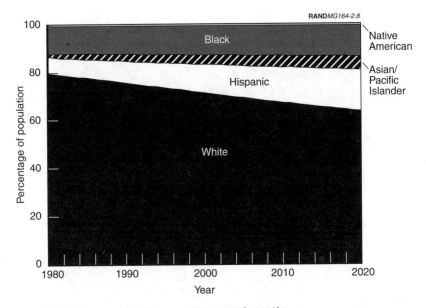

SOURCE: U.S. Bureau of the Census (2001a, 2001b, 2002b).
NOTE: Hispanics are excluded from the other categories. Hispanics can be of any race.

Figure 2.8—Racial and Ethnic Composition of the Population, 1980–2020

Fertility series by race show that whites have had lower fertility than other racial groups (see Figure 2.10). The differences, however, have not been sufficient to have a very large influence on the evolution of racial and ethnic diversity. More important are differences by Hispanic origin (available since 1989). Figure 2.11 breaks Hispanics out of the racial groups. It shows that birth rates among Hispanics have been substantially and consistently higher than among non-Hispanics. In 2001, the number of births per 1,000 Hispanic residents was 85 percent higher than the corresponding figure among non-Hispanic whites (26 versus 14). Part of the reason for Hispanics' higher birth rate is their younger age structure, in which more women are in their prime child-bearing years. The dominant reason, though, is their much higher age-specific birth rates.[7] However, large differences

---

[7]A commonly used summary measure of age-specific birth rates is the TFR, equal to the sum of age-specific birth rates. It measures the rate of childbearing absent the

RAND*MG164-2.9*

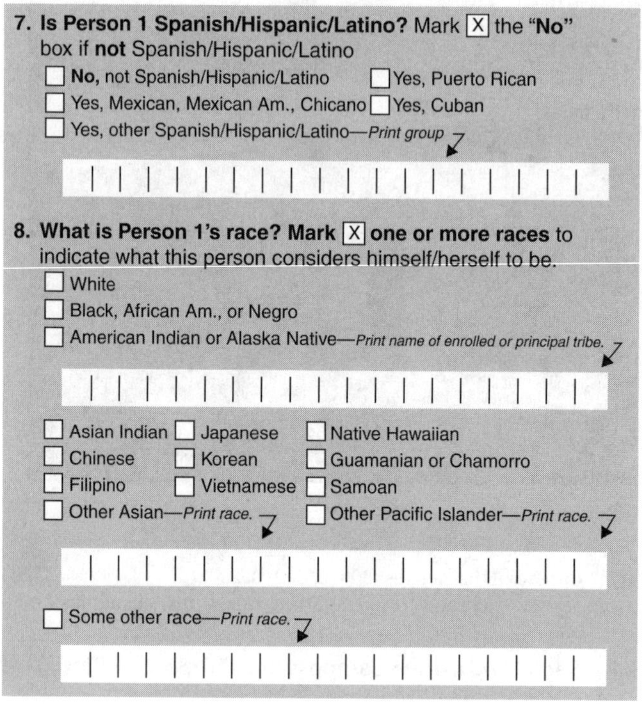

7. Is Person 1 Spanish/Hispanic/Latino? Mark ⊠ the **"No"** box if **not** Spanish/Hispanic/Latino

☐ **No,** not Spanish/Hispanic/Latino   ☐ Yes, Puerto Rican
☐ Yes, Mexican, Mexican Am., Chicano ☐ Yes, Cuban
☐ Yes, other Spanish/Hispanic/Latino—*Print group*

8. What is Person 1's race? Mark ⊠ **one or more races** to indicate what this person considers himself/herself to be.

☐ White
☐ Black, African Am., or Negro
☐ American Indian or Alaska Native—*Print name of enrolled or principal tribe.*

☐ Asian Indian ☐ Japanese   ☐ Native Hawaiian
☐ Chinese   ☐ Korean   ☐ Guamanian or Chamorro
☐ Filipino   ☐ Vietnamese   ☐ Samoan
☐ Other Asian—*Print race.*   ☐ Other Pacific Islander—*Print race.*

☐ Some other race—*Print race.*

Figure 2.9—Ethnicity and Race Questions on the 2000 Census

arise within the Hispanic population. Hispanics of Mexican descent account for much of the high birth rate. Their birth rate was 27.1 per 1,000 residents in 2000, much higher than among Puerto Ricans (20.2) and Cubans (10.4).

Immigration has strongly added to workforce diversity in recent decades because only a small fraction of immigrants are non-

influences of population age-gender structure. The TFR is the average number of life-time births women may be expected to have if they bore children at the rates that women of all ages did in the year or other period for which the TFR is taken. The TFR among Hispanics was 2.9 versus 1.8 children per woman among non-Hispanics in 1999.

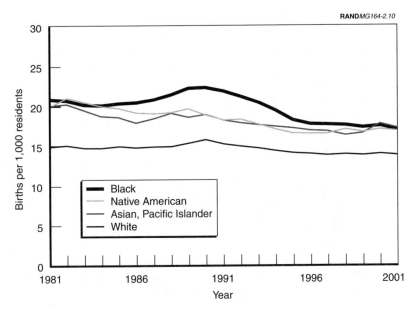

SOURCE: National Center for Health Statistics (2002a), Table 1.
NOTE: Hispanics can be of any race.

Figure 2.10—Fertility Rate by Race, 1981–2001

Hispanic white. Over the 1990s, only one in six legal immigrants came from Europe or Canada (see Figure 2.12). One in three came from Asia and almost one-half from Mexico, Central America, or South America. Among (temporary) H-1B workers, almost half are from India, 8 percent from China, and another 8 percent from Europe or Canada. As of 1996, about three in four illegal immigrants originated from Mexico, Central America, or South America (INS, 2002).

Along with minority status, nativity status—whether born in the United States or abroad—is often considered an important workforce characteristic. As calculated above, net migration adds about 1.0 million people per year to the U.S. population. The number of births is around 4 million per year, so that immigrants account for around 20 percent of new U.S. residents. The stock percentage of the

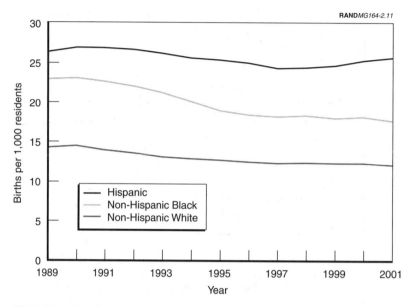

SOURCE: National Center for Health Statistics (2002a), Table 6.

Figure 2.11—Fertility Rate by Hispanic Ethnicity, 1989–2001

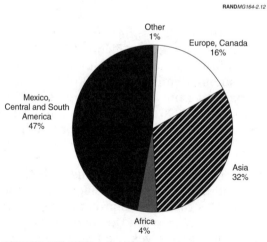

SOURCE: INS (2003a), Table 3.

Figure 2.12—Immigrants by Origin, 1991–2001

population that is foreign-born is 11.5 percent (U.S. Bureau of the Census 2003b). The foreign-born population is therefore increasing, with implications for the distribution of educational attainment and skills of the future workforce as we discuss below.

Finally, labor force participation among Hispanics is higher than among non-Hispanics, thus further contributing to ethnic diversity of the workforce. The main reason for Hispanics' greater participation in the workforce is their relatively young age structure. The Hispanic population is kept relatively young by its high fertility and by the large inflow of Hispanic immigrants. While the U.S. population as a whole is becoming more balanced in age (see Figure 2.7), the Hispanic population retains a younger age distribution. Hispanics have about the same age-specific workforce participation rates as the overall population, but 61 percent of Hispanics are between age 20 and 44, compared to 46 percent of non-Hispanic whites (Fullerton and Toossi, 2001).

Future Workers Will Have More Responsibilities Outside Work

While increased diversity of the workforce by sex, age, and race/ ethnicity has been widely signaled before, one more dimension of worker diversity deserves attention. Women with children at home have increased their labor force participation faster over the past 30 years than those without. While women with children are still less likely to work than similarly aged women without children, participation by women age 25–54 with children at home increased from 49 percent in 1975 to 74 percent in 2002, while that by their childless counterparts increased from 67 percent to 80 percent.[8] A working mother who is unmarried clearly has substantial responsibilities outside work; a working mother with a partner or spouse presumably shares some or all of the household responsibilities, particularly when the partner or spouse is also employed. Thus, increased workforce participation by mothers implies that more workers have substantial responsibilities outside work.

---

[8]Based on authors' calculations from unpublished BLS tabulations of the March 1975 and 2002 Current Population Surveys.

Family responsibilities frequently pertain to the workers' children, but they may also relate to the workers' parents. Increasing life expectancy and delayed childbearing imply that increasingly many workers find themselves in between both needy children and needy parents. Family members between needy children and needy parents are sometimes referred to as the sandwich generation (Raphael and Schlesinger, 1994). Based on the 1994 National Long-Term Care Survey, Spillman and Pezzin (2000) found that approximately 3.5 million individuals, primarily women, were dually responsible for an aging parent and a dependent child. Familial or other responsibilities outside work have implications for workplace arrangements and preferences regarding employee benefits. Sandwiched workers, in particular, are likely to attach a high value to scheduling flexibility, working from home, leave days for family emergencies, and employer-provided child care, among other aspects of their employment situation.[9] With these preferences, they may be willing to trade off various forms of working conditions or employment benefits for lower wages. Other workers may also prefer these types of flexible benefits and the associated trade-off with cash wages.

THE KEY CHARACTERISTIC OF THE FUTURE WORKFORCE IS SKILL

The workforce has become older, with greater numbers of women and more diversity in race and ethnicity, and all signs point to a continuation of that trend over the next couple of decades. Non-Hispanic whites will continue to form a majority, but the other racial and ethnic groups will constitute sizable minorities, represented in all sectors and at all levels of the economy. Women already make up almost one-half of the workforce. Many mature workers will remain in the workforce, given the aging population. While these attributes provide one way of characterizing the future workforce, an even more important dimension as we look to the future is the skill that potential workers bring to the workplace. As we discuss further in Chapter Three, the rapid pace of technological change is expected to continue to propel demand for highly skilled workers who can

---

[9]See Neal et al. (2001) for a discussion of ways in which employers can support employees with child and elder care needs.

develop the new technologies and bring them to market and who can exploit the new technologies in the production of goods and services. Chapter Four emphasizes the importance of high-skilled work to the U.S. comparative advantage in the world economy. As we discuss further in Chapter Five, shifts in organizational forms and the nature of employment relationships, brought about by new technologies and global competition, also favor such high-level cognitive skills as abstract reasoning, problem-solving, communication, and collaboration, attributes associated with "knowledge work" (Earl and Scott, 1999; Zack, 2003).

Skill acquisition is, of course, tightly linked to education as well as training, both on-the-job training and training that occurs outside the workplace. In the remainder of this section, we focus on the makeup of the future U.S. workforce in terms of educational attainment but also more broadly in terms of measurable skills. We consider how the United States ranks compared with other countries in terms of skills measures, and the prospects for technology to improve skill acquisition in the future.

Educational Attainment Will Continue to Rise

Educational attainment among the U.S. population increased rapidly throughout the twentieth century. About 80 percent of people born around 1950 graduated from high school, up from 40 percent among those born around 1900 (Day and Bauman, 2000). Similarly, the share of college graduates rose from 10 to 25 percent. These large cohort differences implied that there was a steep age gradient in educational attainment. By the end of the twentieth century, however, that age gradient had flattened considerably. The difference in educational attainment between cohorts entering and retiring from the labor force is becoming smaller.

Has educational attainment really stagnated? Day and Bauman (2000) took a very close look at the issue. Earlier findings of a stagnation were typically based on cross-sectional data and the assumption that educational attainment stops after a certain age. For example, according to the 1998 Current Population Survey (CPS), the fraction of white men that completed college was stagnant at 30 percent for the 1953–1957, 1958–1962, 1963–1967, and 1968–1972 birth cohorts (see Table 2.3). However, this understates college graduation rates for the younger cohorts because they have had fewer years to complete their degree. When measured during the same age range for every cohort (i.e., ages 26 to 30), college graduation rates rose from 26.3 percent among white men born in 1953–1957 (determined in 1983) to 30.4 percent among white men born in 1968–1972 (determined in 1998). College graduation rates among young white women, as of ages 26 to 30, now surpass those among their male counterparts. White female college graduation rates rose very strongly, from 22.7 percent in 1983 among women born in 1953–1957 to 34.2 percent in 1998 among women born in 1968–1973, again when measured as of ages 26 to 30 for each cohort. Here, even cross-sectional data show an upward trend, but they again understate actual attainment growth. It is therefore important to measure successive cohorts' educational attainment at the same age—i.e., one must use multiple years of data. Day and Bauman (2000) concluded that educational attainment has not stagnated but continued to increase.

Day and Bauman (2000) also investigated the effects of immigration. A sizable fraction of the immigrant population is very well educated, but most come to the United States with relatively little formal schooling. This has made educational progress among Hispanics, in particular, look low. The fraction of Hispanics that completed high school increased only 15 percentage points over the last 20 years,

Table 2.3

Percentage of College Graduates, by Sex and Birth Cohort, in 1998 and at Age 26–30

	White Men		White Women	
Birth cohort	In 1998	At Age 26–30	In 1998	At Age 26–30
1953–1957	30.4	26.3	28.8	22.7
1958–1962	29.5	25.7	28.3	24.5
1963–1967	30.4	27.2	32.6	27.1
1968–1972	30.4	30.4	34.2	34.2

SOURCE: Day and Bauman (2000), Table 1.
NOTE: White includes both Hispanic and non-Hispanic white.

compared with a gain of 30 percentage points among blacks. However, many more less-educated Hispanic immigrants are here today than were here 20 years ago. A cohort analysis excluding immigrants showed that educational progress among Hispanics has been nearly identical to that among blacks (Bean and Tienda, 1987). Smith (2003) applied an analogous analysis to the schooling and wages of three generations of Hispanic immigrants. He concluded that the apparent slow progress among Hispanics stemmed from immigration. Indeed, schooling and wages of the children and grandchildren of immigrants grew faster than that of native non-Hispanic whites, so that their economic statuses converged (also see Smith, 2001).

Based on characteristics of the youngest cohorts, Day and Bauman (2000) projected that educational attainment would continue to increase among the very youngest birth cohorts. Overall, over the next 25 years, they project the probability that a 25-year-old will have completed high school to rise four to seven percentage points above the current 84 percent. The probability of having completed college at that age will rise four to five percentage points above the current 24 percent. The largest gains will be booked by women, particularly non-Hispanic white and Asian women. Non-Hispanic white men are also projected to reach higher levels of educational attainment. Minority men should robustly increase high school graduation rates, but gains in college graduation rates are subject to more uncertainty.

However, educational attainment (or years of schooling) does not necessarily equate with the skills that workers need. It is clear that quality differences exist among schools, and the skills taught in school may differ from those needed in the workplace. As we discuss further in the next chapters, workers will increasingly be exposed to new technologies, new management practices, and development and production distributed over multiple countries and carried out by people from multiple cultures. Such new work circumstances call for skills not traditionally taught in school: communications, working in teams, problem-solving, and so on. These skills are already essential for the higher echelons of the workplace and will become increasingly important for workers at all levels. Unfortunately, as with on-the-job training, there is a paucity of data on such "soft skills."

Comparing Across Nations, Our Average Is in the Middle

How do the educational attainment, achievement, and skill levels of the U.S. population or workforce compare to those in other countries? There have been several large-scale international studies to consistently measure achievement. The National Center for Education Statistics (2003), for example, found that educational attainment (as measured by upper secondary and university completion) in the United States was the highest among all G-8 nations (Canada, France, Germany, Italy, Japan, the Russian Federation, the United Kingdom, and the United States). However, attainment is not achievement. Based on internationally comparable standardized test scores administered to students in primary or secondary schools, the United States typically falls somewhere near the middle of the G-8 countries (National Center for Education Statistics, 2003). Perhaps the most extensive international achievement comparison is the Programme for International Student Assessment (PISA) of the Organisation for Economic Co-operation and Development (OECD). It covers 43 countries and tests 15-year-olds on reading, mathematical, and scientific literacy. The results are consistent with those above: U.S. students score approximately in the middle of other developed countries (OECD, 2003b).

The explanation for the achievement gap between U.S. students and those of other developed countries remains unresolved. One possibility is that schools in the other G-8 nations are of higher quality than those in the United States. Yet, U.S. public and private expenses on schooling are far greater than among other G-8 countries. In 1998, schooling expenditures amounted to 2.3 percent of GDP. By contrast, Canada spent 1.9 percent, whereas the other six countries spent between 0.8 and 1.1 percent (OECD 2001, Table B2.1b). Other possible explanations center around differences in pedagogical methods, academic emphasis, the organization of schools, and other institutional differences between the U.S. schooling system and those of other countries.

Beyond the achievement test comparisons for school-age children, other internationally comparative data provide insights into differences in skill measures across adults. The 1994–1998 International Adult Literacy Survey (IALS), also coordinated by the OECD, tested adults aged 16 to 65 in three areas that mimic broad requirements of white-collar jobs: prose literacy (the ability to process narrative text), document literacy (the ability to process forms, charts, tables, schedules, and maps), and quantitative literacy (the ability to perform practical arithmetic operations). Similar to their student counterparts, U.S. adults ranked near the middle of the 21 participating countries on all three assessments (OECD, 2003a). (Sweden scored highest, on average, on all three tests.)

Notably, the United States had the largest spread (i.e., the difference between scores at the 95th and 5th percentiles) of all countries on two of the three tests, and was close to the largest spread on the third. In other words, many very low-skilled and very high-skilled individuals work in the United States. The relatively large fraction of very low-skill individuals may be stem, in part, from immigration. As noted above, about one-half of legal and three in four illegal immigrants are Hispanics (INS, 2002). The average educational attainment of foreign-born Hispanics is almost four years lower than that of white men (Smith, 2001). On the other end of the spectrum, the high quality of many colleges and universities in the United States may be responsible for the relatively large fraction very high-skilled individuals. By most evaluations, U.S. colleges and universities rank among the best in the world (Hanushek, 2002).

Since the IALS was administered to working-age adults, it offers the opportunity to correlate test scores to labor market outcomes. The OECD (2003a) study found that greater literacy skills, including mathematical literacy, are correlated in the expected direction with most labor market outcomes: labor force participation, unemployment, and earnings. These relationships held up even after controlling for educational attainment.

The international comparisons suggest that the educational delivery by U.S. schools is, at best, about average among developed nations. This is consistent with Hanushek and Kimko (2000), who found that the quality of U.S. schools could not take credit for causing the high growth rate of U.S. GDP over the twentieth century. Instead, the openness and fluidity of U.S. markets and the low level of intrusion by the government in economic operation—through relatively little regulation, low taxes, and few government-owned industries— stimulated more innovation and investment in the United States than in most other developed countries. Presumably, though, growth could have been even more impressive had U.S. schools been of higher quality.

Technology-Mediated Learning Offers the Potential for Improved Educational Outcomes

The U.S. performance on internationally comparative tests suggests there is room for improvement in educational outcomes. Indeed, considerable focus has been placed on various approaches to educational reform in the United States, including greater competition among schools (through charter schools, vouchers, and other reforms to school organization); setting educational standards; testing and other accountability reforms; reductions in class size and other changes in school resources; and such movements as home schooling (Grissmer et al., 2000; Gill et al., 2001).

In addition to these various reforms under way across the country, technology-mediated learning has been the source of one of the most exciting new developments. This term captures many types of learning, ranging from traditional classroom settings equipped with PCs or other technology tools to distance learning through videoconferencing or interactive software, possibly at remote locations, in the comfort of one's home, or at an hour of the day that best suits the student. Technology-mediated learning is also sometimes labeled e-learning: instructional content or learning experiences delivered or enabled by electronic technology. In the educational sector, distance learning has gained the most ground at the postsecondary level. In the 2000–2001 academic year, 56 percent of U.S. colleges offered distance education courses (U.S. Department of Education, 2003). Spending on e-learning by the federal government is expected to grow 34 percent a year, from $200 million in 2000 to $850 million in 2005 (Emery, 2001). As we discuss further in Chapter Three, technology-mediated learning has an even wider array of applications for learning opportunities throughout the life course, not only as part of kindergarten through twelfth-grade education or postsecondary education but also as part of a process of lifelong learning, in or out of the workplace.

Distance learning is an example of a production process that has become much more efficient through the application of IT. It can reduce costs by eliminating the need to bring in a live instructor or for geographically dispersed pupils to travel to a central location. The marginal cost of enrolling students is very low. Perhaps more important, technology mediated learning offers opportunities for faster and more effective learning. Distance learning, along with other forms of technology-mediated learning, is individually based rather than institutionally based (Commission on Technology and Adult Learning, 2001). Its delivery of content may be in the form of multimedia presentations or other effective methods. Technology-mediated learning may be complemented by other advances in the cognitive sciences with regard to how individuals learn and how best to tailor educational opportunities—whether using traditional pedagogical methods or technology-mediated methods—for optimal delivery given an individual's learning style (U.S. DOC, 2002).

One key issue in the diffusion of these advances in educational approaches is the extent to which these methods are available to children and adults of all backgrounds. At the same time, experts in the area have noted that realizing the benefits from technology-mediated learning requires more than just making computers available to all school-age children or placing computers in every library. It is important to pay attention not only to hardware and software but also to the support resources, infrastructure, and social context within which the individuals who will use the technology operate. Warschauer (2003) illustrates the issue in the case of an effort to make advanced placement courses available in underserved high schools in the Los Angeles area. The initial effort, an online course, allowed small, dispersed populations across several schools to participate, but the online instructional format lacked structure and sufficient teacher-student and peer-to-peer interaction given the learning styles of the students involved. A more successful revamped program brought students from several schools to a central location for an online course taught by an expert instructor but also included a local teacher to provide additional assistance in the classroom with the computer-based curriculum. Ultimately, researchers now argue that the issue is not so much unequal access to the technology but rather inequities in the way the technology is used.

ADDRESSING THE SLOWDOWN IN LABOR FORCE GROWTH

We began this chapter with the forecast that workforce growth will slow to a trickle in just a few years. This poses some challenging policy issues. In general, further growth of economic activity depends on a growing labor force or increases in worker productivity. Thus, the growth rate of the future labor force limits the growth rate of the economy for any given rate of productivity growth. While we discuss expectations for future productivity growth in the next chapter, here we focus on the size of the labor force.

Should we be concerned with aggregate output growth or should we be satisfied with greater output per worker (productivity)? Several arguments can be made in favor of a focus on aggregate growth. First, our standard of living is closely linked to GDP per capita, not per worker. As the population ages, overall labor force participation declines and GDP per capita shrinks for any given level of productivity. Second, expenses on such entitlement programs as Medicare and Social Security will rise sharply relative to GDP; a larger aggregate wage bill would reduce the tax rate that would be required to pay for those expenses. Third, the U.S. economy is currently the largest in the world, which in itself may bring advantages. For example, much of international trade is conducted in U.S. dollars, which generates seigniorage income for the United States. There may thus be benefits to maintaining a dominant role in the international marketplace.

To the extent that it is desirable to raise the rate of labor force growth, in the short term the two primary options are to increase the overall size of the population through immigration or to increase the labor force participation rate for the current population.[10] In the case of immigration, future immigrant flows and their composition are, to a large degree, under the control of policymakers. While it may be considered desirable to increase labor force participation from current levels, such increases may involve trade-offs. The current participation rates result from market forces and reflect a balance between desire for income on the one hand and health, family responsibilities, and other factors on the other. Thus, further increases may involve trade-offs between greater work effort and reductions in

---

[10]Over a longer horizon, higher birth rates would also be a source of increased labor force growth.

other uses of time. In some cases, greater work effort may follow from increasing the returns to work in the form of wage compensation or the structure of benefits. In other cases, some groups may desire to work more, but various barriers or disincentives preclude them from doing so now.

One perspective on the potential for increasing labor force participation rates comes from comparative data that show how the United States measures up against other developed countries in terms of labor utilization. By "labor utilization," we mean the extent to which potential labor is utilized—i.e., a combination of workforce participation, (lack of) unemployment, and annual hours worked per worker. Figure 2.13 displays labor utilization in selected countries, relative to the United States. The figures are standardized for age composition of the population, that is, a country with the same age-specific labor force participation, unemployment, and annual hours as the United States has a utilization of 100, even if its age structure is different.

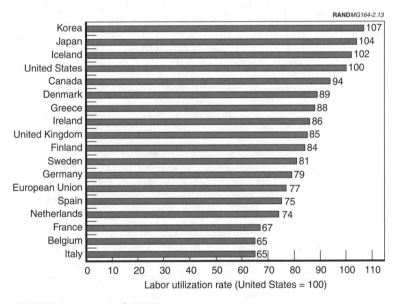

RAND*MG164-2.13*

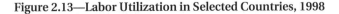

SOURCE: Scarpetta et al. (2000).

Figure 2.13—Labor Utilization in Selected Countries, 1998

Most European countries have labor utilizations well below that of the United States. The European Union as a whole uses only 77 percent of what the United States uses; France and Italy use as little as 65–67 percent. These low utilization rates reflect Europeans' earlier retirement, higher unemployment, higher enrollment in disability programs, shorter work weeks, and longer vacations. Some countries, such as Korea and Japan, have utilization rates above that of the United States, although only modestly so. The high utilization rate in Korea is driven by Koreans' long working hours. In 2001, Koreans worked an average of 2,447 hours per year, 34 percent above the U.S. and Japanese averages of 1,821 hours (DOL, 2003). Based on Figure 2.13's utilization rates, the scope for additional work effort among the U.S. population seems limited. However, several large subpopulations have a labor force participation that is relatively low or an unemployment rate that is relatively high. Given the right labor market structures, some members of these subpopulations may choose to work more.

In the remainder of this section, we investigate this issue in the context of labor force participation among older men, among women with children, and among the disabled. In addition, we explore immigration as a potential source for workforce growth.

Will Men Continue to Retire at Increasingly Younger Ages?

While we previously documented the trend toward earlier retirement among men, there are reasons to believe this trend will not continue. Figure 2.14 shows that workforce participation among men age 55 and older declined steadily during the second half of the twentieth century, but reversed its slide after 1995. A more detailed examination of this pattern for single-year ages, also shown in Figure 2.14, reveals that no recent reversal of the retirement rate occurred among 59-year-olds, although there appears to be a leveling off of labor force participation among men at this age. The youngest age at which a reversal clearly has taken place is 62, and it has occurred at older ages as well, up through 71. (To avoid cluttering the graph, we only show every third year of age, but participation rates among 55–61 year olds were essentially flat over the 1990s.)

The reversals shown in the figure will probably continue, for several reasons:

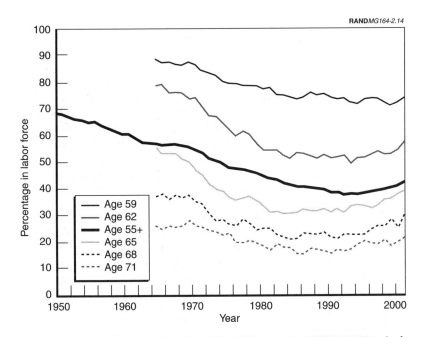

SOURCE: Age 55-plus series based on BLS (2003a), series LNU01324231; single years of age series based on unpublished tabulations of the 1965–2002 CPS, provided by the BLS.

Figure 2.14—Labor Force Participation Among Men Age 55-Plus and at Selected Single Years of Age, 1950–2002

- There is a trend away from defined benefit (DB) pension plans to defined contribution (DC) plans.[11] The fraction of workers covered primarily by a DB pension plan went from 38 percent in 1978 to 21 percent in 1998, whereas the fraction of workers with a DC plan as their primary pension went from 7 to 27 percent (DOL, 2002). In DB plans, workers typically face strong incentives to retire at the plan's early retirement age. During the 1990s, for about 30 percent of workers in the public and private sectors aged 51–69 with a DB plan, the early retirement age was 55 years,

---

[11]DB pension plans promise a lifelong guaranteed monthly benefit, typically based on years of service and the employee's earnings. In DC plans, such as 401(k) plans, employers and/or employees contribute to an account that the employee may draw down in retirement.

and for almost 90 percent it was age 62 or younger.[12] DC plans do not have such incentives.

- The normal retirement age for Social Security is currently being raised from 65 to 67. For workers who turn age 62 in 2003, the normal retirement age is 65 years and eight months. A higher normal retirement age implies a reduction of lifetime benefits. Changes in Social Security law between 1968 and 1979 increased benefits by more than 50 percent in real terms, which has been linked to younger retirement ages during the 1970s and 1980s (e.g., Hurd and Boskin, 1984). Lower lifetime benefits may thus induce delayed retirement.

- The Senior Citizens' Freedom to Work Act of 2000 eliminated the earnings test for Social Security recipients age 65 or older. The earnings test reduced monthly benefits in case of wage earnings in excess of a threshold. Even though the beneficiary would later be compensated with higher monthly benefits, such that the average effect of the earnings test on lifetime benefits was close to zero, the earnings test was perceived by older individuals as a disincentive to work.

- Social Security rules are currently changing to make delayed retirement more attractive. Workers who reached age 62 in 1986 could receive a 3 percent increase in monthly benefits for every year that they delayed claiming after the normal retirement age. This delayed retirement credit is being raised to a target of 8 percent per year. At 8 percent, the credit is approximately actuarially neutral—that is, over a lifetime, the higher monthly benefits approximately offset losses caused by fewer years of benefits. Workers who turn 62 years of age in 2003 are eligible for a 7.5 percent benefit increase for every year they postpone claiming after the normal retirement age.

- Our persistently low national saving rate may also have consequences for elderly labor force participation. High rates of return on stock holdings compensated for the low saving rates of the past two decades (Bureau of Economic Analysis [BEA], 2003), so that recent retirees entered retirement with sizable assets. For

---

[12]Based on data from the 1992–2000 Health and Retirement Study for respondents aged 51–61 in 1992 (Panis et al., 2002).

example, in the late 1990s the median and mean net worths of households just after retirement were $125,000 and $255,000, respectively (in constant 2000 dollars; Kapteyn and Panis, 2002). However, the much lower rates of return since 2000 may result in lower wealth holdings and thus less nonlabor income among the elderly, which in turn may induce them to delay retirement or to reenter the labor force after retirement.

In all, these changes are expected to reverse or at least slow the trend to earlier retirement. The BLS projects an increase in labor force participation among men age 65–74 from 14.8 percent in 2000 to 17.3 percent in 2010. This trend is already reflected in the projected growth rate of the labor force. However, that projection also assumed that the slow decline in labor force participation among men age 55–64 will continue, from 67.3 percent in 2000 to 67.0 percent in 2010 (Fullerton and Toossi, 2001). In light of the arguments above, we may actually experience a small increase.

Aside from the factors listed above, other trends may also affect the ability of men to continue working at greater rates than in the recent past. One consideration is whether men will be physically healthy enough to continue working past traditional retirement ages. One may point at the higher retirement ages of only a few decades ago and argue that, clearly, men are able to continue working longer than they do today. Moreover, male life expectancy at birth has been rising vigorously, from 46 years in 1900 to 66 years in 1950 and 74 years in 2000 (NCHS, 1998 and 2002b). Not only life expectancy, but also healthy life expectancy has been increasing (Manton, Corder, and Stallard, 1997). This implies that many workers are indeed physically able to work longer than before. Put differently, the 70-year-old of today looks a lot like the 65-year-old of a few decades ago.

Another factor that may influence labor force participation at older ages is the interaction between technological change and retirement from the labor force. As new technologies become available, older workers stand to benefit less from investing in new technology-driven skills as they have a shorter remaining work career over which to recoup their investment. To the extent that their skill levels are of an older vintage (e.g., their formal training occurred farther in the past), their skills may be less relevant in the face of new technologies and they may be more likely to be in jobs that would be eliminated.

On the other hand, if older workers or workers farther from the retirement decision do invest in new skills through on-the-job training or other mechanisms, it may extend the time they spend in the labor force.[13]

Several recent studies shed light on this issue. Bartel and Sicherman (1993) find that, in industries with unexpected increases in the pace of technological change during the 1970s and 1980s, older workers retired sooner because of the faster depreciation of their human capital. On the other hand, in industries with high permanent rates of technological change, workers retired later, especially in industries where a positive relationship exits between technological change and on-the-job training.[14] Using data for a more recent cohort of older workers, Friedberg (2001) finds that older workers who use computers on the job are 25 to 30 percent more likely to continue working over a four-year horizon. Overall, these studies suggest that interactions occur among technological change, training, and the labor force behavior of older workers.

Longer careers may also result from labor demand factors. Employers with difficulties recruiting workers are likely to make their wage offers, work conditions, or benefit schedules more attractive. Hurd and McGarry (1999) found that workplace flexibility and the employer's accommodation of older workers increased an older worker's anticipated work-life. The ability to make lateral career moves—here, a change of position in the company that is not a promotion and perhaps even involves less responsibility—may also contribute to delayed retirement. In Japan, for example, it is not uncommon for workers to retire from their company and subsequently be rehired, on renegotiated terms (Rebick, 1993). Phased retirement may also prove attractive to older employees. In 2000, 57 percent of respondents to the Health and Retirement Study who were close to retirement indicated that they would prefer to gradually reduce hours on the job, at the same hourly wage (Panis et al., 2002). Lofgren, Nyce, and Schieber (2003) reported that 16 percent of large employers

---

[13]This follows from the positive correlation between training and the slope of the wage profile. So more training leads to a steeper wage profile and a greater incentive to remain in the labor force and realize the eventual return (Bartel and Sicherman, 1993).

[14]Other research indicates that industries with higher rates of technological change make a larger training investment in their workers (Lillard and Tan, 1986; Bartel, 1989).

offered some form of phased retirement in 1999, up from 8 percent in 1997.

Labor Force Participation Among Women with Children

As discussed above, female labor force participation has been increasing steadily over the past four decades. The largest increase occurred among married women and, very recently, among never-married mothers. Figure 2.15 shows labor force participation rates for never-married, married, and other (separated, divorced, and widowed) men and women from 1970 to 2001 (U.S. Bureau of the Census 2002c). One contributor to the overall downward trend in labor force participation among men (see Figure 2.4) is the drop in participation among married men, a decline from 86 percent in 1970 to 77 percent in 2001. Participation among unmarried men actually rose slightly over the past three decades.

Women uniformly increased their labor force participation over the same period. In particular, participation among married women increased from 41 percent in 1970 to 61 percent in 2001, an increase of 20 percentage points. Never married women, whose participation was already the highest among all women, added 11 percentage points, whereas separated, divorced, and widowed women added 10 percentage points. Moreover, not only has the labor force participation rate increased among women, the average hours worked among women has increased slightly as well. By 1999, among mothers whose youngest child was under three years of age, the average work week was 30.9 hours. It was 33.4 hours among those whose youngest child was 3 to 5 years old, 35.6 hours for those whose youngest child was 6 to 17, and 38.0 hours among those without children under 18. All these work weeks figures have steadily lengthened since 1969 (BLS, 1999).

Figure 2.16 shows labor force participation rates among women with children at home by marital status and age of the youngest child (U.S. Bureau of the Census, 2002c). Among mothers, the married category is the largest (18 million married mothers at work versus 7 million unmarried) and therefore the most important for labor force composition. The labor force participation of married mothers increased strongly in the 1970s and 1980s and remains high. Until

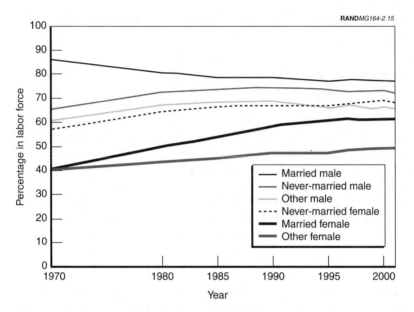

RAND*MG164-2.15*

SOURCE: U.S. Bureau of the Census (2002c), Table 568.
NOTE: Other = separated, divorced, or widowed. Population is those age 16 and above.

Figure 2.15—Labor Force Participation Rate by Sex and Marital Status, 1970–2001

recently, it was higher than that of unmarried mothers and had increased faster. The participation among unmarried mothers rose gradually and uniformly from 1980 to 1995, and faster after 1995. Never-married mothers with children under age six, in particular, surged from 53 percent in 1995 to 67 percent in 1998, and never married mothers with children age 6–17 from 67 percent in 1995 to 81 percent in 1998. Participation increased somewhat more after 1998 but appears to have leveled off by 2001.

Why did participation among married mothers increase steadily since 1970, and why did it so suddenly accelerate in the late 1990s among single mothers? Leibowitz and Klerman (1995) focus on explanations for the increase among married mothers between 1971 and 1990. They noted that participation in the first three years after a birth is significantly related to maternal education, maternal age,

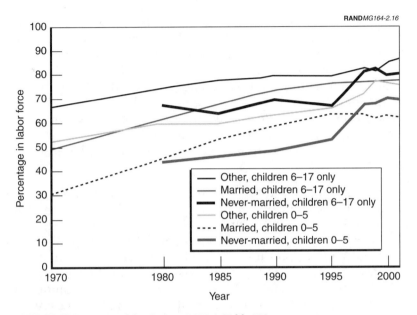

SOURCE: U.S. Bureau of the Census (2002c), Table 570.

NOTE: Other = separated, divorced, or widowed. Population is those age 16 and above.

Figure 2.16—Labor Force Participation Rate of Women with Children by Marital Status and Age of Youngest Child, 1970–2001

family size, and paternal age. During the 1970s and 1980s, the mix of women who were bearing children changed such that more of them returned to work within three years. Another important development was that women's wage prospects improved—in part because of increased investment in human capital—so that work became relatively more attractive to them. At the same time, men's wage prospects deteriorated, making women's work relatively more attractive to couples with a choice as to which partner worked. Changing demographic characteristics and wage prospects could explain almost one-half of the increased workforce participation.

The recent increase in labor force participation by unmarried women with children is generally attributed to the Earned Income Tax Credit (EITC) and welfare reform (Meyer and Rosenbaum, 2000; Grogger, Karoly, and Klerman, 2002). EITC credits increased twentyfold from

$1.6 billion in 1984 to $32 billion in 1998 (U.S. House of Representatives, 2000). Single mothers received about two-thirds of these EITC dollars (Meyer and Rosenbaum, 2000). In 2003, a single woman with two children who earns less than $13,730 is eligible for a 40 percent credit on dollars earned, up to a maximum of $4,204. Because tax credits may exceed the tax owed, and a mother of two with those earnings is not subject to any federal income tax, she will receive a check from the IRS for the credit amount. The credit becomes smaller with higher earnings and in 2003 is fully phased out at $33,692.

Welfare reform also introduced stronger incentives to work among single mothers. Until 1996, women with dependent children could receive welfare benefits under Aid to Families with Dependent Children (AFDC), a joint state-federal program. The Personal Responsibility and Work Opportunity Reconciliation Act (PRWORA) of 1996 replaced AFDC with Temporary Assistance for Needy Families (TANF). Among others, TANF's objectives were to promote job preparation and work. TANF mandated a 60-month lifetime limit for adult receipt of federally funded benefits. Many states took advantage of options in the law to implement shorter lifetime limits or intermittent limits, such as a maximum of 24 months of assistance in any 60-month period. Grogger (2003) found that time limits have had important effects on welfare use and work. Blank, Card, and Robins (2000) found that unmarried mothers not only participated more in the labor force but that their number of weeks worked per year also increased. Both increases started in 1994, before PRWORA but plausibly as a result of earlier state reforms.[15]

While the recent increases in labor force participation among mothers have been impressive, we should point out that not all are working. Unemployment among never-married women has always been high. For example, unemployment among never-married mothers with children under age 6 was mostly above 20 percent between 1980 and 1995 (U.S. Bureau of the Census, 2002c). Among other unmar-

---

[15]While most AFDC program parameters were set at the federal level, states could petition the U.S. Department of Health and Human Services (DHHS) to implement experimental, pilot, or demonstration projects they believed would result in a more effective welfare program. By 1996, DHHS had approved waivers for more than 40 states, many of them for statewide reforms (DHHS, 2000).

ried mothers, unemployment was lower but still mostly well above the national average and much higher than among married mothers. Unemployment among mothers dropped in the late 1990s but increased again after 2000, consistent with unemployment among other workers.

Workforce Participation: The Role of Child Care

How much further can workforce participation among women, particularly mothers, increase? Here again, it is instructive to compare the United States to other countries. Table 2.4 lists labor force participation rates among women age 20–64 in selected countries. Participation in the United States, at 72 percent, is above that of all countries except the Nordic countries. In those countries, the rates range from 71 percent in Finland to 75 to 76 percent in Denmark, Norway, and Sweden and 83 percent in Iceland.[16] Given certain conditions, it thus appears that female labor force participation in the United States could rise further.[17]

Table 2.4 also shows total fertility rates, i.e., the average lifetime number of births per woman. Raising children and working outside the home are competing activities, and one might intuitively expect a negative correlation between female workforce participation and fertility. Interestingly, fertility in the European Union (listed as the first 15 table entries) tends to be *higher* in member countries with higher female labor force participation. The correlation coefficient is 0.54 and statistically significant at the 5 percent level. (The significantly positive correlation does not hold up outside Europe.) The Nordic countries thus reap a dual economic benefit: High fertility rates help offset the population's aging and the attendant social welfare costs. High workforce participation means more fully utilized labor capacity.

---

[16]The Nordic countries have policies that permit long parental leaves after childbirth (e.g., 12–15 months in Sweden). While on leave, the parent is counted as in the labor force. Nordic participation is thus slightly inflated relative to countries with policies mandating shorter parental leave.

[17]The regulations and income taxes on which the Nordic countries largely rely to subsidize child care and create other labor market conditions suitable to work by women may introduce distortions in other areas.

Table 2.4

Female Workforce Participation (age 20–64) and Total Fertility Rate in 1999, European Union and Other Countries

Country	Female Workforce Participation	Total Fertility Rate
Austria	62.2	1.32
Belgium	57.8	1.61
Denmark	75.8	1.73
Finland	71.3	1.74
France	60.8	1.77
Germany	62.8	1.36
Greece	49.0	1.30
Ireland	54.9	1.88
Italy	46.0	1.19
Luxembourg	64.6	1.73
Netherlands	64.5	1.65
Portugal	66.8	1.49
Spain	48.9	1.20
Sweden	74.6	1.50
United Kingdom	67.5	1.68
United States	71.7	2.08
Canada	69.6	1.60
Mexico	42.1	2.62
Japan	63.8	1.41
Norway	76.3	1.80
Iceland	83.1	1.99

SOURCES: All female workforce participation from U.S. Bureau of the Census (2002c), Table 1335. Total fertility rate (TFR) in European Union from Council of Europe (2000); TFR in the United States, Canada, Mexico, and Japan from U.S. Bureau of the Census (2002c), Table 1312; TFR for Norway and Iceland from Central Intelligence Agency (2003).

NOTE: All rates apply to 1999 except 2001 TFR in the United States, Canada, Mexico, and Japan and estimated 2002 TFR in Norway and Iceland.

What factors generate a positive correlation between female work and fertility in the European Union? The answer is not yet known, but a common hypothesis is that it may be attributable to child care arrangements. In 1992, the European Union explicitly recommended that its "Member States gradually develop and/or encourage measures to enable women and men to reconcile family obligations arising from the care of children and their own employment . . . "[18] The recommendation listed nonfamilial public or private child care as the first such measure. Availability of affordable, high-quality child care indeed appears to increase female labor force participation. In 1986, Finland introduced a child home care allowance that enables parents to stay home for up to three years after the birth of a child, essentially reversing a trend toward more nonfamilial child care. In combination with an economic crisis that hit Finland, the new policy strongly affected Finnish women's labor force participation. Participation among mothers with children under age 12 fell from 76 percent in 1985 to 53 percent in 1991 (Salmi, 2000; Mahon, 2002). The lesson: Effectively increasing the price of nonfamilial child care drives down female labor force participation. Daly (2000) found that the more choice in child care arrangements a country's policies offered, the higher workforce participation among mothers with children from birth to age 10 was.

The same relationship has been found in the United States. Changing the market price of child care in one direction drives women's labor force participation in the other, and more so for the least-skilled women than for the most-skilled (Anderson and Levine, 2000; Blau, 2001). For example, Blau's (2001) estimate indicates that a 10 percent reduction in child care costs would lead to a 2 percent increase in the labor force participation rate among mothers with young children, an estimate that is within the range of those provided by other studies (see the reviews by Blau, 2001, and Anderson and Levine, 2000). Anderson and Levine's (2000) analysis indicates that the sensitivity of labor force participation to child care costs is larger for less-educated women compared with their more-educated counterparts. Their estimates imply, for example, that a 10 percent reduction in the price of child care would increase labor force participation by 4 percent for women with less than a high school education compared with a 3 percent increase for those with more than a high school education.

Another recent study indicates that child care costs can affect not only the propensity to work but also the intensity of work effort as measured by weeks worked per year or hours worked per week. Gel-

---

[18]Quoted from the Council of the European Union (1992).

bach (2002) finds that enrollment in public kindergarten—which provides essentially free child care during school hours—leads unmarried mothers whose youngest child is age 5 to increase their labor force participation by 4 percentage points, their annual weeks worked by 3.6 weeks, and their hours worked per week by 2.2 to 2.7 hours per week. Similar but somewhat smaller effects are found for married mothers. Gelbach's result suggests that the movement by some states toward providing universal pre-kindergarten programs for children as young as age 3 and 4 may serve to boost labor force participation of women with young children in the United States, although the size of the effect on the overall participation rate may be modest.

Workforce Participation Among the Disabled

Not surprisingly, labor force participation among people with a disability is lower than among those without. In 2002, workforce participation among the disabled and nondisabled age 16–64 was 28.6 and 81.5 percent, respectively (U.S. Bureau of the Census, 2003a). Obviously, the main reason for their inactivity in the workplace is their physiological impairment. In addition, there may be institutional disincentives to work (such as rules of the Social Security Disability Insurance [DI] program) and practical impediments in the workplace. Is there scope for increased workforce participation among the disabled in the twenty-first century?

First we need to define what we mean by a disability. There is no universally applicable definition of disability. For example, to be eligible for DI, an applicant must be unable "to engage in any substantial gainful activity by reason of any medically determinable physical or mental impairment that can be expected to result in death or that has lasted or can be expected to last for a continuous period of not less than 12 months." This definition includes both a medical and an economic element. A surgeon who cannot perform surgeries because of Parkinson's disease but is still able to earn a living as a teacher is thus not disabled for DI purposes. Most other definitions place less emphasis on economic considerations. A common definition of disability is based on individuals' own responses to the question "Do you have a health problem or disability which prevents you from working or which limits the kind or amount of work you can do?" By that definition, the surgeon with Parkinson's disease would be considered disabled. Other commonly used definitions rest on self-reported difficulties with activities of daily living, such as walking across the room, dressing, using the toilet, etc.

Depending on the definition, the measured prevalence of disability can vary widely. The participation figures above are based on a definition developed by the U.S. Bureau of the Census that combines seven factors asked in the CPS, including a self-reported work limitation, receipt of federal disability benefits, job separation because of poor health, etc. By that definition, 10 percent of individuals age 16–64 were disabled in 2002, amounting to 18 million individuals. The prevalence of disability increases with age: among individuals age 16–24 and 55–64, the rates were 3.6 and 22 percent, respectively. Almost regardless of the definition, workforce participation among the disabled is lower than among the healthy.

Figure 2.17 shows workforce participation among disabled men and women between 1983 and 2002. The data are based on two sources with different definitions of disability. For 1983–1994, the rates are based on the National Health Interview Surveys (NHIS) (Trupin et al., 1997). For 1995–2002, the rates are based on the CPS (U.S. Bureau of the Census, 2003a). The NHIS-based definition is less restrictive than the CPS-based definition, resulting in correspondingly higher labor force participation rates among the disabled. The series are internally consistent but may not be compared to one another.[19] Between 1983 and 1994, workforce participation among disabled men and women decreased and increased, respectively, just as it did among the population at large. Disabled men age 16–64 slightly decreased their workforce participation, whereas disabled women increased their participation fairly rapidly (Trupin et al., 1997). Overall, workforce participation among the disabled slightly increased

---

[19]The two series are internally consistent in the sense that the NHIS and CPS questions remained the same from 1983 to 1994 and from 1995 to 2002, respectively. However, the respondents' interpretation of the questions may have changed, corresponding to, for example, the definition that the Social Security Administration applied for its DI program. From 1996, DI benefits are no longer available to individuals whose disability was based on drug addiction or alcohol abuse. Such individuals may have been more likely to classify themselves as disabled before 1996 than after 1996.

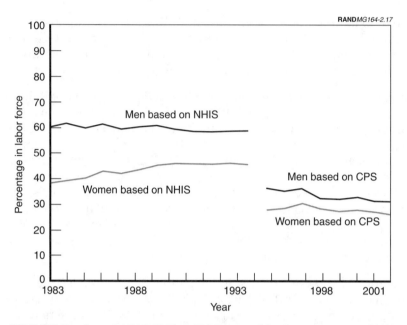

SOURCES: Trupin et al. (1997), Table 2; U.S. Bureau of the Census (2003a), Table 2.
NOTE: Population is those age 16 to 64. 1983–1994 based on NHIS data, 1995–2002 based on CPS data. The series are internally consistent but cannot be compared to one another.

**Figure 2.17—Labor Force Participation Among the Disabled,
by Sex, 1983–2002**

between 1983 and 1994. From 1995 to 2002, workforce participation decreased among both disabled men and women. Using the stricter definition, in 2002 workforce participation was 31 percent among disabled men and 26 percent among their female counterparts (U.S. Bureau of the Census, 2003a).

While workforce participation among the disabled has been slightly declining recently, several technological and institutional developments are under way that may reverse this pattern. First, medical technology is undergoing rapid change, so that some disabilities may be cured, prevented, or rendered more manageable in the future. Second, progress in IT may help the disabled perform tasks that they currently cannot. The new ability may be enabled by technology itself, such as speech recognition that replaces the need to type manually. It may also be enabled through organizational change, such as remote work from home. Burkhauser et al. (1999) showed that employer accommodation of individuals with disabilities significantly delays application for DI. (See Chapter Three for these and other technological developments.) Third, the Social Security Administration (SSA) is aiming to induce more DI recipients to return to work, using among others such tactics as removing disincentives to work. In particular, its Ticket to Work program allows DI recipients to return to work with maintained Medicare health insurance coverage for more than eight years and with the option to reenroll in DI without delay should the work effort fail (Ticket to Work and Work Incentives Improvement Act of 1999). The SSA is also required by law to experiment with a reduction of DI benefits by $1 for each $2 that a beneficiary earns over a certain amount, as opposed to the current entire elimination above the substantial gainful activity threshold.

Countering these developments, however, is the prospect that the prevalence of disability may be on the rise. Other things being equal, population aging and rising prevalence of disability with age imply that a greater fraction of working-age adults will be disabled in the future than today. Moreover, Lakdawalla et al. (2003) found that the incidence and prevalence of diabetes, asthma, and obesity, three major precursors to disability, are rising in the United States among persons under the age of 60. In other words, age-specific disability rates may also increase. However, this finding and its implication that the recent trend toward less disability among the elderly will reverse is still controversial (Manton, 2003).

Immigration Policy as a Lever to Influence Further Workforce Growth

As we noted earlier, immigration currently accounts for much of the growth of the U.S. population and the workforce. The size and composition of immigrant flows are largely a function of federal policy, thus implicitly or explicitly immigration policy has been used in the past to influence the size and composition of the population and the workforce. In particular, immigrant visas are issued for several reasons (see Figure 2.18). For 1994–2001, 13 percent of immigrants obtained a visa on the basis of employment. This includes so-called priority workers (in professions with a shortage in the United States), professionals with advanced degrees or with exceptional ability, and skilled workers. It also includes spouses and children of workers; only 6 percent of immigrants obtained a visa on the basis of own employment.[20] By far the most common category (66 percent) of immigrants were family members of other immigrants or U.S. citizens, including former immigrants who have become citizens. Refugees and asylum seekers constituted 12 percent of the new immigrant population, and 9 percent were admitted for various other reasons.

Immigrants and temporary foreign workers are heterogeneous in terms of their country of origin, English-language proficiency, and education levels. The level of education, on average, is highest for those admitted for economic reasons. For example, H-1B visas require that the beneficiaries possess at least a bachelor's degree (or

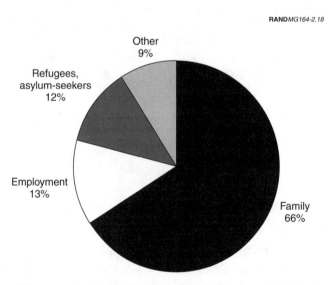

RAND*MG164-2.18*

SOURCE: Authors' calculations based on INS (2003a), Table 4.

Figure 2.18—Basis for Obtaining Immigrant Visas, 1994–2001

[20]Based on personal communication with Michael Hoefer, Director, Office of Immigration Statistics, Bureau of Citizenship and Immigration Services.

equivalent degree) and that the jobs they fill require a bachelor's degree. In 2001, indeed 98 percent of H-1B visa holders held a bachelor's degree and 42 percent had a master's degree or higher. Most (58 percent) were in computer-related professions. While employment-based immigrants and H-1B visa holders are well-educated, immigrants in other categories tend to have more limited educational attainment or English language proficiency (Schoeni, McCarthy, and Vernez, 1996). Their admission is currently largely a matter of social policy, based on family reunification or political hardship. While not admitted on the basis of employment, many of these immigrants work for pay, or they may support participation in the labor force by other family members (e.g., grandparents who provide unpaid child care in support of employment of the parents).

The extent to which immigration and temporary work visas offer alternatives for future workforce participation growth in general, or for targeted growth among higher skilled workers, is a matter of federal immigration policy. During the economic expansion of the 1990s and under pressure from employers with a need for skilled IT personnel, Congress raised the legal maximum number of H-1B visas that could be issued. As a result, the number of newly issued H-1B visas more than tripled from 52,000 in fiscal year 1995 to 162,000 in 2001 (U.S. Department of State, forthcoming).[21] Intracompany transfers followed the trend with roughly one L-1 for every two H-1B visas issued. The number of new H-1B visas declined to 118,000 in fiscal year 2002. However, while Congress permitted adjustment of the flow of temporary work visas to economic conditions, employment-based permanent immigration followed a different path. The number of employment-based immigrants fluctuated from 123,000 in fiscal year 1994, to just 57,000 in 1999, to 179,000 in 2001 (INS, 2003a).

Beyond the use of temporary work visas to alleviate shortages of skilled workers, immigration more generally is not always perceived to bring net benefits to the U.S. economy. Compared with the native born, immigrant households are relatively heavy users of some government services, such as schools and income-conditioned transfer programs but relatively light users of other government services such

---

[21]Statistics on H-1B approvals have only been available since 1999. The number of admissions also more than tripled between 1995 and 2001.

as Social Security and Medicare. For example, all 1995 government benefits amounted to $22,021 for native and $25,943 for immigrant households (Smith, 1998). In short, immigration touches many aspects of society and its policies have many implications beyond economic ones.

CHANGING DEMOGRAPHICS ALSO SHIFT DEMAND FOR GOODS AND SERVICES

Most of this chapter has focused on the implications of demographics for labor supply—i.e., for the size and the composition of the workforce. This section addresses an indirect effect of demographics on the future workforce, namely the effects that shifting population patterns have on the goods and services consumed in the United States. A changing mix of goods and services will induce different employment opportunities with some sectors hiring new workers and others shedding staff. In other words, as we emphasized in our conceptual framework in Chapter One, population shifts affect not only labor supply but also labor demand.

The two main demographic shifts of the past that will continue into the foreseeable future are the aging of the population and the increased participation of women in the workforce. The elderly consume a different basket of goods and services than do the young, and dual-earner couples are likely to purchase goods and services that single-earner couples may produce at home.

Young and Old Spend Their Money Differently

The Consumer Expenditure Survey affords a glimpse into the spending patterns of various age groups. Figure 2.19 shows the fractions of total consumption spent on various categories, by age group for 2001. There are some clear differences between young and old. Starting at the bottom of the figure, expenses on health care increase with age. Households headed by an individual age 55–64 spend 6.5 percent of their total outlays on medical care, compared with 11.2 percent at age 65–74 and 14.7 percent at age 75 or older (BLS, 2003b). This understates the true health-care expenditure difference between an older and a younger society because it includes neither

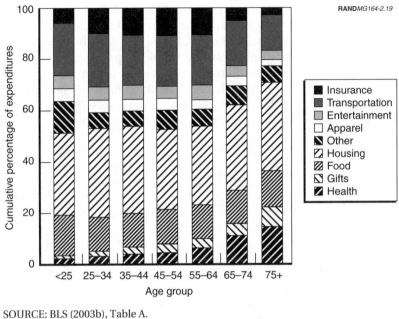

SOURCE: BLS (2003b), Table A.
NOTE: Insurance includes worker pension contributions.

Figure 2.19—Composition of Expenditures, by Age Group

social expenditures on the virtually universal health insurance of the elderly through Medicare, nor means-tested benefits through Medicaid. The elderly spend considerably less on insurance (including pension contributions) than the young and somewhat less on transportation and entertainment. Only minor differences appear in the share of food, housing, apparel, and miscellaneous goods and services.

As the number of elderly in the United States increases, demand for health care goods and services can thus be expected to expand. For the workforce and workplace, the implication will be that the pharmaceutical and medical technology industries will demand more workers that are highly skilled in their areas. Already, the aging—and more obese—U.S. population is driving strong demand for high-tech implantable devices to treat heart disease, orthopedic complaints, and other conditions (Wharton School, 2003). Nanotechnology is particularly promising for more precise and less invasive surgical procedures than those practiced today. Meanwhile, genomics hold the promise for a quantum leap in the treatment of various diseases, mental disorders, and such behavioral disorders as substance abuse. The main question is one of timing: how long will it take before nanotechnology and gene therapy will move from the research into the production stage? While this is difficult to predict, the aging of the population is likely to provide strong incentives for continuing innovations in medical technology.

Demand for such health-related services as long-term care will also change the mix of prospective workers. For example, BLS projects a 30 percent increase in the number of nursing, psychiatric, and home health aides in the first decade of the twenty-first century, to 2.7 million workers in 2010 (Hecker, 2001; Moncarz and Reaser, 2002). Demand for registered nurses is expected to rise by 26 percent over this period, to 2.8 million by 2010. Over the longer term, the baby bust that followed the baby boom may fuel even stronger growth. Married individuals and individuals with children are far less likely to enter a nursing home than childless widows and widowers (Lakdawalla et al., 2003). The future elderly will have fewer children, on average, than the current elderly, who are the parents of the baby boom generation. In other words, not only the number of elderly will increase, but the rate of institutionalization will also likely increase.

Working Households May Outsource Many Home Production Activities

Female labor force participation has risen considerably, especially among married women and women with children. These were the traditional homemakers, with primary responsibility for the household and children. As they enter the labor force, their homemaker responsibilities must be transferred to others or be accomplished outside work hours. To some extent, these responsibilities, particularly for child care, are shifted to such other family members as parents and parents-in-law—the grandparents of children whose mother enters the labor force. This type of assistance may become less available in the future, as grandparents themselves may still be working. Demand for paid child care is likely to increase as well, although the movement in many states toward universal preschool programs may lessen this demand to some extent.

Beyond child care, households "outsource" many formerly home-produced activities, substituting such market purchased goods and services as prepared meals, cleaning services, gardening, home improvement services, and so on. Among the occupations projected to have the largest job growth between 2000 and 2010 are food preparation and serving workers (including fast food—673,000 new jobs), waiters and waitresses (364,000 new jobs), and landscaping and groundskeeping workers (260,000 new jobs) (Hecker, 2001). These occupations typically require little formal education. Further, since these services are not internationally tradable, the jobs that they create are not subject to competition from less expensive unskilled labor abroad.

DEMOGRAPHICS AND THE FUTURE OF WORK

The future shifts in the U.S. population and labor force participation rates have important implications for the size and composition of the U.S. workforce. Most notably, the growth rate of the future labor force is expected to be slower in coming decades compared with the past. At the same time, the composition is shifting toward a more balanced age distribution, a higher proportion of women and minorities, and a workforce with more responsibilities outside work for younger and older dependents. In anticipation of our discussion of the importance of technology and globalization in the chapters ahead, we also focused on the importance of skill as a key attribute of the future labor force. While the United States produces a highly educated workforce judged by years of schooling, that preparation does not necessarily translate into higher skills for the workforce, especially compared with other developed countries.

These shifting demographic patterns have a number of implications for the future of the workforce, workplace, and compensation. We explored in more depth in this chapter the potential for increases in labor force participation and immigration to raise the growth rate of the future labor force. Other implications of the demographic trends are often interrelated with those that follow from expected advances in technology and further globalization. We take up those forces independently in the following two chapters and, in the last, the implications of all three together for the future workforce and workplace. We here preview those implications as they relate to worker numbers, skills, and other aspects of the workplace and compensation:

- *Who is in the labor force.* While this chapter has focused on the size and composition of the future workforce, future outcomes may deviate from current projections to the extent that decisions regarding labor force participation change from the recent past, or immigration patterns shift due to future policy. Technology, for example, may interact with workers' decisions about when and how long to work, or biomedical breakthroughs may affect the health and individual functioning in ways that alter labor force behavior. The disabled, in particular, may benefit from breakthroughs in technology. Changes in workplace arrangements or employer-provided benefits may also influence work decisions.

- *Skill requirements for the workforce.* Future technological advances and greater economic integration of the U.S. economy with other world economies are expected to increase the demand for a more highly skilled workforce. Shifts in the nature of business organizations and the growing importance of knowledge-based work also favor strong nonroutine cognitive skills, such as abstract reasoning, problem-solving, communication, and collaboration. Some evidence indicates that young people are responding to the economy's demand for higher skill levels by attending college in greater numbers, and employment-based visas could continue taking up some of the demand for high skills. Technological change and globalization are also expected to lead to less stable employment relationships, highlighting the importance of lifelong learning to facilitate transitions from less competitive sectors of the economy to more competitive sectors.

- *Nonstandard work arrangements.* Technology and other factors are expected to lead to and support future increases in the fraction of workers in nonstandard work arrangements that offer more flexible forms of employment, whether through part-time work or self-employment or through such distance work as telecommuting. These arrangements may be particularly attractive to future workers who seek to balance work and family obligations or such workers as the disabled and older persons who would benefit from alternative arrangements. Nonstandard work arrangements are likely to place additional weight on workers' personal responsibilities for keeping up with technological developments, arranging for health insurance, providing for retirement, etc.

- *The composition of compensation.* The changing composition of the future workforce has implications for workers' preferences over the types and nature of employer-provided benefits, and their willingness to trade-off wages, benefits, and working conditions. Older workers, for example, may prefer a different package of benefits compared to what younger workers would prefer, while those with family responsibilities may place more weight on those that address the balance between work and family life. Technology may allow a shift toward more personalized benefit structures, although workers in nonstandard work arrangements may need access to benefits through sources that are not based on employment.

Chapter Three

THE INFORMATION AGE AND BEYOND: THE REACH OF TECHNOLOGY

By the end of the twentieth century, the U.S. economy was shifting from one based on production to one based on information. New technologies had spawned new products and industries and had transformed the way firms in established industries were organized and labor was employed. In the coming decades, technological advances promise to further shape what is produced; how capital, material, and labor inputs are combined to produce it; how work is organized and where it is conducted; and even who is available to work.

To anticipate the future consequences of technology for the workforce and workplace, we begin this chapter by highlighting the remarkable pace of change in the incorporation of information technologies into the U.S. economy. Computing power and capacity, data transmission speed, and network connectivity have increased dramatically, while hardware costs have fallen rapidly. At the same time, increased user-friendliness of new software has led to rapid adoption of computer systems, with levels of business investment in computer hardware during the mid- to late 1990s reaching several times the level of previous years. Physical limitations may eventually slow the rate of technological progress after the current decade, but meanwhile, we can expect further increases in computing and data transmission speeds.

Technological progress has not been limited to the information technology (IT) and communications realm of computers, video-conferencing, and cellular phones, however. A wide array of technological advances, such as biotechnology and nanotechnology, are expected to have equally profound consequences for the U.S. economy in the next several decades. In the health care sector, for example, recent progress against a variety of diseases will be married to molecular-genetic advances spawned by the Human Genome Project to yield "personalized medicine," in which drugs might be individually tailored. Nanotechnology—the manipulation of matter at the atomic scale—could spur even more drastic revolutions in products, services, and quality of life over the next half-century. Possible applications include molecular electronics, photovoltaics, materials able to withstand extreme stresses, and manufacturing technologies.

In the second half of the chapter, we identify how the technological advances in the late twentieth century have influenced the workforce and workplace. The demand for IT professionals has grown explosively, but IT has also influenced the size and specialization of the workforce in other sectors. Job skill requirements have been shifting across all sectors, as the ability to program routine activities has reduced the demand for less-skilled workers while increasing the demand for those with problem-solving and communication skills. Not surprisingly, the demand differentials have been driving up the salary premium paid to workers with higher education levels. IT has made it easier for firms to vertically disintegrate and outsource non-core activities to realize savings. IT also promotes measurement and communication within firms and thus facilitates the evolving management emphasis on continuous quality improvement. In addition, technology facilitates telecommuting and the flexibility that it brings to workers' lives and workplace organization. Finally, technology has great potential to support the education and training of the workforce prior to labor market entry and as a part of lifelong learning. This is all finally beginning to affect the bottom line. After a long period in which it seemed that the information revolution was having no impact on worker productivity, an acceleration of the annual rate of productivity increase began in 1995 and has not been slowed by the post-2000 economic downturn. All this experience provides the basis for developing an understanding of how technology is likely to shape the world of work in the next 10 to 15 years, a subject we briefly anticipate at the end of this chapter before expanding on it in the final chapter.

THE ADVENT OF THE INFORMATION AGE

Among recent technological advances with a major impact on the way work is organized and conducted, IT arguably ranks at the top of the list. IT, broadly defined, includes technologies associated with communications (e.g., telephones, fax machines), computer hardware and related peripherals, and computer software. While such communications technology as the telegraph and then telephone played a role in the earlier industrial revolution, computer hardware and software mark the transition to an information-based economy. That transition has occurred in a relatively brief period. Stocks of computer equipment and peripherals in the nonresidential sector first appear in data produced by the Bureau of Economic Analysis in 1963. By 1980, these stocks had yet to reach 1 percent of the level attained by 2001, and as of 1990, the stock of computer equipment and peripherals was less than 10 percent of the level it would reach within a decade. Even the language associated with the information age has been rapidly absorbed into the popular lexicon. While the typical new word takes 10 to 20 years to move from small group usage to official recognition in English language dictionaries, words like "dot-commer" have made the cut in just five years (Tynan, 2003). In only a few decades, computers and other information technologies have altered product markets and transformed much of the workplace. That transformation will be a recurring theme in the second half of this chapter.

A Rapid Pace of Technological Advance

The greatest advances in computing technology have been manifested in processing speed, storage capacity, data transmission speed, the quality of user interfaces, and the reach of computer networks (Nordhaus, 2002b). The earliest electronic automatic computer was built in 1946, mainframes came on line in the late 1960s, and the microprocessor was invented in 1971. In 1965, Gordon Moore, the cofounder of Intel, predicted that transistor density on integrated circuits would double every 18 months. As seen in Figure 3.1, Moore's prediction has largely been borne out. The straight line (on a log scale) captures Moore's predicted rate of advancement, and the diamond symbols plot the actual pace of development. In just

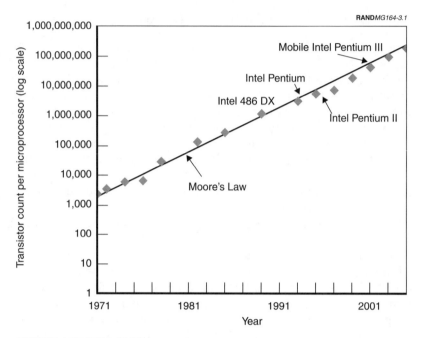

SOURCE: NSF (2002), Table 8.1.

NOTES: Line represents trend that defines Moore's Law. The data points are actual (1971–2001) and projected (2003–2005) data.

Figure 3.1—Moore's Law, Predicted and Actual, 1971–2005

three decades, transistor density on a fingernail-size wafer of silicon has increased from a few thousand to 44 million. At the same time that this exponential progression has occurred, the cost of 1 megahertz of processing power has fallen from $7,601 in 1970 to 17 cents as of 1999—i.e., by at least half every two years for three decades.[1]

Computing storage capacity has advanced at a similarly astounding pace, while cost per unit of storage has likewise plummeted. In 1970, the cost of one megabit of storage was $5,257, a figure that reached 17 cents as of 1999. Given these advances in processing speed and storage capacity at a lower real cost, the price of computers and peripheral equipment, adjusting for quality, has fallen dramatically

---

[1] These and other data are cited in Woodall (2000).

as illustrated in Figure 3.2.[2] The price decline reached an annual rate
of 21 percent between 1995 and 2001, even faster than the annual
average decline of 13 percent over the previous 15 years.

Another area of rapid progress has been the speed of transmitting
electronic information. Between 1990 and 2000, the capacity of a
single fiber-optic cable grew by a factor of 1,000, from 1 billion to 1

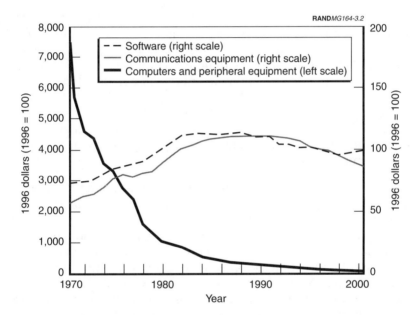

SOURCE: BEA NIPA Tables, Table 7.8 (http://www.bea.gov/bea/dn/nipaweb/
SelectTable.asp).

**Figure 3.2—Quality-Adjusted Price Indices for Information Technology,
1970–2001**

---

[2]The price index for computer hardware and peripherals is based on the use of
"hedonic" price measurement, a statistical technique that captures changes in the
price of such computer attributes as processing speed, memory, storage capacity, and
so on. For a discussion of this approach in the context of computer price indexes, see
CBO (2002). Other factors that explain falling computer prices include decreases in
quality-adjusted prices of other components aside from semiconductors and storage
devices and cost-saving technological advances in the computer-manufacturing process, such as building-to-order and contracting out (CBO, 2002).

trillion bits per second (NSF, 2002). As with the other dimensions of advancement, costs have fallen rapidly as well from $150,000 in 1970 to send 1 trillion bits of information to 12 cents as of 1999. Wireless communications have also taken root during this period, first with mobile phones and more recently with wireless Internet access through portable computers or mobile phones or other handheld devices.

Improvements in computer software accompanied the hardware advances. User-friendly interfaces have greatly expanded the capacity of individuals to harness the growing computing power and have thereby allowed computer use to infiltrate most sectors of the economy and all manner of workplace tasks. Of course, standardized software is ubiquitously used for administrative tasks and document processing. At the same time, specialized software has been developed for a wide array of complex functions in the business world, such as financial tasks, supply chain and inventory management, and human resource management.

Another major component of the growth of information technology has been the capacity for networking within and across firms, and between consumers and the producers of goods and services. The World Wide Web, introduced in 1989, is the ultimate example of this networking capability, with tremendous implications for the nature and costs of transactions. Connectivity began with remote terminals connected to a mainframe server, followed by the ability to connect individual personal computers to one another or central servers through local area networks. The reach of connectivity was extended as standardized file formats and such computer languages as hypertext markup language (HTML) allowed users with different systems to communicate across networks. In the business world, such networks are now employed to improve communication and data storage within firms, to facilitate interactions between businesses located around the world, and to provide information and transact sales between consumers and firms.

One feature of such networks is that their value to any given user depends on the number of other users. This relationship is expressed in Metcalfe's Law, which states that the value of a network grows in proportion to the square of the number of users: In other words, the network's value grows faster than the growth in the number of users.[3] This law can also explain the rapid adoption of a technology that exhibits network effects once a critical mass is reached. In the case of the Internet, the number of users has exploded in just a few short years. The number of Internet domain hosts has grown from just under 6 million in 1995 to almost 110 million by 2001 (NSF, 2002). As of September 2001, 143 million people in the United States, or 54 percent of the population, reported using the Internet, with 2 million new users added every month (NTIA, 2002). Worldwide, just over half a billion people use the Internet as of 2001, nearly double the number of users in 1999 (ITU, 2001).

While computing capacity and telecommunications have been the primary beneficiaries of more powerful, cheaper semiconductors, advanced microelectronic components have found use elsewhere. Microprocessors and other semiconductors have been incorporated into a vast array of such products as machine tools, aircraft and military equipment, automobiles and other durable goods (e.g., home appliances), consumer electronics, and children's toys, games, and learning materials. Estimates suggest that semiconductor shipments for noncomputer products accounted for 50 to 70 percent of worldwide semiconductor sales in the late 1990s (CBO, 2002).

Accelerating Investment and Diffusion

With exponential growth in capacity, expanding applications, and falling costs, U.S. businesses accelerated the pace of investment in information technologies, especially during the 1990s. Figure 3.3 illustrates the particularly dramatic increase in real investment in computers and related equipment during the latter half of the 1990s: Between 1995 and 1999, the average annual increase in investment spending on computer hardware exceeded 40 percent per year. Some of this was probably motivated by a desire to replace older computer equipment in the face of the Y2K transition (Gordon, 2002).[4]

---

[3]Network effects are also a characteristic of software and other technologies. For a discussion of the economics of networks, see Economides and Encaoua (1996).

[4]The Y2K transition refers to the inability of some computer software, largely written before the mid-1990s, to handle the transition from years "19XX" to "20XX."

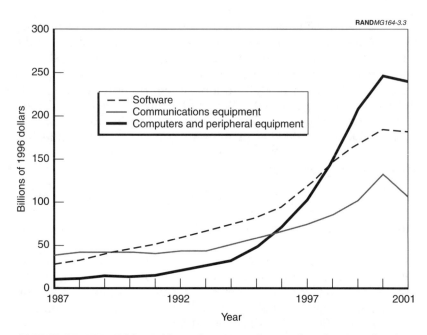

RAND*MG164-3.3*

SOURCE: BEA NIPA Tables, Table 5.9 (http://www.bea.gov/bea/dn/nipaweb/Select Table.asp).

Figure 3.3—Real Private Fixed Investment in Information Technology, 1987–2001

Investments in software and communications equipment increased at a somewhat slower pace over the same period.

Figure 3.3 also documents a downturn after 2000 in investment spending across the IT components, particularly for computers and peripheral equipment and for communications equipment. This pattern reflects a slowdown in investment spending in a weaker economy as firms have attempted to cut costs and extend the life of existing equipment. It may also reflect the lower need to upgrade equipment in the immediate aftermath of the pre-Y2K recapitalization.

While the revolution in IT has affected just about every corner of the U.S. economy, important differences can be found in the amount of investment in IT across major sectors. As Figure 3.4 demonstrates, the transportation, communications, and utilities (TCU) sector made the largest investment in IT up through the early 1990s, largely because of the obvious link between communications equipment and the telecommunications industry and related businesses. However, by the mid-1990s, the financial services sector had exceeded the annual level of IT investment by TCU, as the pace of investment in that sector increased rapidly in the latter half of the 1990s. It is notable that the sharpest decline between 2000 and 2001 in IT investment occurred for TCU, with a 19 percent decline for the communications component alone. IT clearly plays a considerably

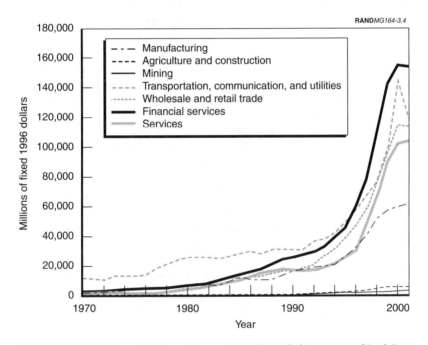

SOURCE: BEA Fixed Assets Tables—Nonresidential Detailed Estimates of Real Cost Investment (http://www.bea.gov/bea/dn/faseb/Details).

NOTE: Information technology defined as mainframe computers, personal computers, direct access storage devices, computer printers, computer terminals, computer tape drives, computer storage devices, integrated systems, prepackaged software, custom software, own-account software, and communication equipment.

Figure 3.4—Real Investment in Information Technology by Industry, 1970–2001

smaller role in agriculture, construction, and mining, as would be expected given the nature of the processes and products of these sectors.

These trends in IT investment reflect, among other things, the rapid rise in the use of microcomputers in the workplace since the advent of the personal computer (PC) in the 1970s. As of 2001, 53.5 percent of the U.S. workforce—72.3 million workers—reported that they use a PC on the job (Hipple and Kosanovich, 2003). This is more than double the rate (25 percent) estimated for 1984 (Freeman, 2002). While use of the Internet and/or e-mail at work is somewhat lower than the rate of computer use alone, the rate of increase over time has been more dramatic, a 54 percent annual rate of growth (NTIA, 2002).

In ways that are to be expected, computer use in the United States varies with education level: There is a fivefold difference in rates between those with less than a high school education and those with a college degree (16.2 percent versus 81.9 percent) (Hipple and Kosanovich, 2003). The fraction using a computer at work varies little between ages 25 and 55, but utilization rates decline thereafter (Friedberg, 2001; NTIA, 2002). Utilization rates also vary with occupation: Nearly 80 percent of managerial and professional workers use a PC on the job, and use is only slightly lower for administrative support personnel and technicians. Yet, even in farming, forestry, and fisheries, one in five workers reports using a computer on the job (Hipple and Kosanovich, 2003). Computing hardware and software used in the agriculture sector, labeled "precision farming," allow small- and large-scale farming operations to improve yields and profits through precise geographically based information on inputs, outputs, and weather patterns, combined with data on market fluctuations.

While our focus is on technological advancements and their effects on the U.S. economy, it is important to note that the IT revolution is taking place worldwide. Indeed, the IT revolution is fundamentally intertwined with economic globalization, a subject we turn to in more detail in the next chapter. Whether the metric is research and development (R&D) associated with IT, production and trade in IT-related products, or network connectivity, the reach of technology extends across the globe.[5] The diffusion of new technologies is uneven, however. For example, more than three out of four Internet users live in high-income countries, representing just 14 percent of the world's population. Disparities in access to technology within countries are also striking. India, for instance, has a high concentration of both scientists and engineers—many in the technology hub of Bangalore—in a county where the average education level is just over five years of schooling. Of 46 high-technology hubs identified in 2000, 13 were in the United States; 16 in Europe; 9 in Asia; 2 each in South America, Africa, and Australia; and 1 each in Canada and Israel (Hillner, 2000).

Technological Advances on the Horizon

While the technological advances in IT experienced in the past several decades have been remarkable, the pace of change will almost certainly continue for the next decade or longer. In terms of integrated circuits, current estimates suggest that Moore's Law will continue to hold for another 8 to 15 years or so before the foreseeable limits of physics set in. Even that pace of change will be challenging, however. Design, materials, and production constraints affect future improvements in various types of semiconductors, including microprocessors, memory circuits, and other integrated circuits used in computers (CBO, 2002). For example, as leading-edge integrated circuits evolve to having transistors that number in the billions (current counts are in the hundreds of millions), fabrication processes must incorporate higher levels of control and precision, and power consumption rises, which in turn generates more heat.

Despite these challenges, there continue to be major breakthroughs in transistor design that promise to keep pace with Moore's Law at least through 2010. For example, in 2001, Intel announced a breakthrough in transistor design that will lead to the "TeraHertz transistor"—equal to 1,000 gigahertz—as early as 2005 (Iwata, 2001; Intel, 2001). The new chip is projected to have upward of 1 billion transistors—almost 25 times the number of transistors on the Pentium 4—

---

[5]These figures and others in this paragraph are found in United Nations Development Programme (UNDP, 2001).

and 10 times the speed of the Pentium 4, with no additional power consumption. IBM has since announced an even smaller working transistor with equally dramatic implications for the speed of future computer chips (IBM, 2002c). While major hurdles still lie ahead in translating these designs into mass production, the designs demonstrate that Moore's Law should hold for the near term. Other advances continue to push the frontiers of memory access and data storage at the same time. For example, in 2002, IBM announced a new technology that would provide data storage density 20 times higher than the most dense storage device available today: "enough to store 25 million printed textbook pages on a surface the size of a postage stamp" (IBM, 2002a).

The practical implications of further miniaturization and other technical advances will include greater processing speed, higher storage capacity, and a wider array of applications. For example, advances in microprocessors will support a range of applications, such as real-time speech recognition and translation and real-time facial recognition. We can also expect greater use of wireless communications technology and increased capacity for data transmission speeds for sending larger and larger amounts of data (e.g., video streams) (Anderson et al., 2000). The fields of artificial intelligence and robotics are likely to advance further, with more sophisticated intelligent mobile robots linked together through wireless networks (Butler, 2003). The use of more intelligent robotics in manufacturing will support agile manufacturing—the ability to quickly reconfigure machines for the production of prototypes and new production runs—with implications for manufacturing logistics and inventories (Anderson et al., 2000).

Other new technologies exploit the continued miniaturization of computer chips and communications devices. For example, non-computing capabilities are being added to chips, notably microstructure technologies (MSTs) that will allow chips to function as sensors or actuators (NSF, 2002). A subset of these MSTs includes microelectromechanical systems (MEMS), which contain moving parts. MEMS and other MSTs could be used as chemical and environmental sensors, or "motes," which could communicate to wired and wireless networks. In the future, wireless sensors may be used in commercial or residential security applications, in agriculture to monitor climate and control irrigation efficiency, and for assessing the structural integrity of buildings and bridges (Roush, 2003). At an even smaller scale, these self-organizing sensors could reach the size of a few dust mites, capable of distribution on road surfaces, in building materials, and in fabrics. As another application, new high-technology radio identification tags the size of a pinhead are in development. Such devices, emitting a unique signal, could be attached to virtually every manufactured product to track it through factories, warehouses, transportation vehicles, retail outlets, and homes (Schmidt, 2001). When combined with a new Electronic Product Code and a Product Markup Language, such devices will be able to transmit signals to an Internet-based database to retrieve production information, instructions, and so on.

As computer networks grow and the volume of information to be transmitted expands (e.g., two-way video streaming), bandwidth for electronic transmission will need to advance in order to meet the need for communications capacity. New generations of fiber-optic technology (known as wavelength division multiplexing, or WDM) are expected to do just that (Hecht, 1999; Anderson et al., 2000). Already in use today, fiber-optic cables that once carried one wavelength of light can now carry multiple wavelengths each with a separate signal, thereby dramatically expanding the capacity of the existing network of fiber-optic cables. In just a decade, the capacity of fiber-optic cables has increased 1,000-fold. As the demand for bandwidth grows, this new technology is expected to further expand capacity. With expected growth in demand for more bandwidth and with expected price declines for the technology, WDM is projected to be affordable for individual consumers in their homes by about 2010.

As the information revolution proceeds, the economies of the United States and Canada are expected to continue to be on the vanguard of new technological developments and their applications in markets for products and services (Hundley et al., 2003). Leading positions will also be held by select countries in Europe and Asia. Countries expected to be on the leading edge of the technology revolution are those that have well-developed physical and regulatory/legal infrastructures, highly educated workforces (especially IT professionals), efficient capital markets, and economies and societies that are open, flexible, and adaptive to change. The preference for many European societies for more economic and social equity is seen as potentially inconsistent with the risk-taking and concomitant rewards associated with dynamic technological change. In Asia, the course of the IT revolution depends, in part, on the extent to which such countries as China, India, Malaysia, the Philippines, and Thailand become IT users as well as producers. The prospects for other countries in Asia, Africa, Latin America, and the Middle East that currently lag in the IT sphere are mixed. Economic growth and supportive policies may promote more-rapid adoption of IT, which in turn could support further growth and investment in a "virtuous circle" (IMF, 2001). Adoption of IT may even allow some low-income countries to "leapfrog" older technologies by replacing, for example, mechanical phone systems with advanced digital ones, bypassing analog technology. At the same time, many low-income countries lack the IT-promoting features listed above, which limits their potential for rapid IT adoption.

APPLICATIONS OF THE "NEW BIOLOGY"

The latter part of the twentieth century was marked by technological advances beyond the rubric of information technology. In the past several decades, the biomedical sciences made tremendous progress in the diagnosis and treatment of disease, from such life-threatening illnesses as cancer, heart disease, and diabetes to such degenerative diseases as Alzheimer's and Parkinson's to such mental health disorders as depression and schizophrenia. Researchers confronted the emergence of infectious diseases, such as AIDS, with gradual progress in the understanding of the virus leading to methods for prevention, diagnosis, and treatment. Across a wide range of diseases, new drug and treatment therapies evolved from basic research on the human body and its organs. The trend toward longer life spans, discussed in Chapter Two, may be expected to continue, in part, because of these investments in the biomedical sciences.

More broadly, tremendous progress has come in the area of biotechnology, defined as "techniques that use organisms or their cellular, subcellular, or molecular components to make products or modify plants, animals, and micro-organisms to carry desired traits" (Paugh and Lafrance, 1997). Perhaps the most visible scientific effort in recent years was the mapping of the human genome, published in draft form in 2001, which serves as an incomparable resource for understanding how the body works and the causes of disease (NIH,

2001). This milestone builds on previous efforts to genetically map other organisms and to identify the genetic basis for various human diseases, mental disorders, and behavioral health disorders (e.g., addiction). The field of genomics has been used to understand genetic differences in disease progression and how individuals respond to treatments. The human genome project relies heavily on the increased power and reduced cost of computing and data storage, as well as on improvements in scientific instrumentation. The same may be said of other biomedical advances, such as advanced imaging techniques and molecular diagnostic techniques. As a result, scientific research in the biomedical field now involves teams of researchers not only from biology and chemistry but also from such disciplines as imaging, computer sciences, mathematics, and informatics (NIH, 2001).

In the near future, progress in biotechnology will almost certainly generate medical advances that will further extend life expectancy and enhance the work capacity of those with work-limiting disabilities (National Intelligence Council [NIC], 2000; Antón, Silberglitt, and Schneider, 2001). As our understanding of the genetic variation in human populations advances, the field of medicine, especially pharmacology, is expected to evolve toward "personalized medicine" in place of "one size fits all" (Wortman, 2001). Based on slight genetic variation from person to person, drugs would be tailored to match the genetic makeup of individuals or groups of individuals to increase their effectiveness and reduce side effects. For example, a test is now being used to determine which of several chemotherapy doses is optimal for children with a particular form of leukemia. According to industry experts, this shift in the pharmaceutical industry will fundamentally alter the health care system toward "disease management packages" to treat diseases and even to design targeted interventions to prevent such ailments as cancer, heart disease, and dementia before they start. Scientists debate about whether there are biological limits to our ability to continuously extend the life span (e.g., Olshansky, Carnes, and Désesquelles, 2001; Oeppen and Vaupel, 2002). While that debate is not yet settled, it is clear that those limits, if any, will not be reached in the next few decades.

In addition to extending life, biomedical advances will also improve its quality for those with a chronic illness or disability, often in ways that will enhance their productive capacity in the workplace. For example, in the 1980s, cochlear implants, which convert sound into electrical impulses, were developed to improve the hearing of those with hearing impairments. Today, scientists are experimenting with artificial retinas that employ minuscule silicon chips to convert light into electrical signals transmitted to the brain (Stone, 2003). With further development, such devices could eventually provide artificial eyesight routinely for those who would otherwise be vision impaired. Likewise, there is hope that biomedical research and advances in organic and artificial replacement parts will improve the functioning of those who suffer heart attacks, liver disease, strokes, or paralysis, eventually replacing complex organs through tissue engineering (Garr, 2001). Early research in this area is developing techniques for joint replacement therapies based on injecting engineered tissue formed from polymers, cells, and growth stimulators (Goho, 2003). Some of these advances rely on the biomedical sciences alone, while others also exploit developments in computer sciences with respect to microchips and miniaturization.

The reach of the "new biology" has extended beyond the medical and pharmaceutical industries to touch even the primary sector: agriculture. Among the more controversial areas of progress has been the use of biotechnology to genetically modify crops and animals. The field of genetic engineering or bioengineering has extended what humans have done for centuries in breeding plants and animals for size, taste, and resistance to disease. To move beyond the limits of traditional breeding methods, new techniques for genetic cutting and splicing were developed in the late 1970s and early 1980s, followed by more-sophisticated methods later in the 1980s and in the 1990s (NAS, 1998). These technologies allowed scientists to introduce new genetic material, often from other species, into plant and animal DNA to enhance resistance to disease or confer other desirable traits. For example, one of the first genetic modifications was made to cotton plants by introducing the genes from the bacterium *Bacillus thuringiensis (Bt)* that created a protein toxic to insects. With this new genetic material, the modified cotton plant, commercially available in 1996, could generate enough of the required toxic proteins to make it resistant to insects (NAS, 1998). Other crops have been genetically modified to resist pests, diseases, and herbicides and, in the case of fruits and vegetables, to extend shelf life. These crops include cantaloupe, corn, papayas, potatoes, soybeans, squash, tobacco, and tomatoes (NAS, 2000).

The genetic modification of food crops and animals has tremendous potential for altering agricultural markets and world food supplies (especially in poorer countries), as well as broader consequences for other biologically based products (NIC, 2000). The agricultural sector is slated to become even more "high tech" as new crops are bioengineered to resist pests, disease, and herbicides. As the field advances, scientists are expected to produce crops more tolerant to salt or drought conditions and with properties—such as concentrations of micronutrients—desirable for human health (NAS, 1998, 2000). Other areas of likely advancement include bioengineering plants to produce new compounds, such as industrial oils, plastics, enzymes, drugs, and vaccines. Similar advances apply to animals as well, with application to the production of medicines and organs and tissues suitable for human transplantation (NAS, 2002). Bioengineering applications thus have the potential to both raise agricultural productivity and increase the demand for new agricultural products that generate uses beyond those available today.

The revolution in biotechnology, however, will be accompanied by significant concerns regarding ethical, moral, religious, privacy, and environmental issues (Antón, Silberglitt, and Schneider, 2001). Manipulation of the human genome, including the possibility of human cloning, has already raised significant concerns, and these issues are expected to remain highly visible as further scientific progress is made. Individual genetic profiling raises the specter of employers or insurance companies having access to information about an individual's genetic predisposition to diseases. Challenges in bioengineered agriculture include avoiding the evolution of pests or diseases resistant to the defenses of the new crops, minimizing the consequences of introducing genetically altered species into the ecosystem, and limiting the effects on food safety from genetically modified organisms. Restrictions on genetically modified crops in European countries already place limits on the markets for these products. Such controversies are likely to intensify and may ultimately modify the course of diffusion and adoption of the results of the "new biology."

NANOTECHNOLOGY:
REVOLUTIONARY TECHNOLOGY ON THE HORIZON

In looking to the future, the one area of technological innovation that has the potential to equal or exceed the influence of the twentieth-century advances in computing and information technologies is the emerging field of nanotechnology (NNI, 2003). Nanotechnology, the ability to measure, manipulate, and organize matter at the atomic scale, bridges the fields of biology, chemistry, physics, engineering, and computer science.[6] In addition to applications in information technology, nanotechnology is expected to lead to breakthroughs in pharmaceuticals and other aspects of biotechnology, energy technology, and aerospace and materials technology, among others. As a cross-cutting technology, nanotechnology will facilitate technological change that extends and enhances existing technologies—further computer power for semiconductors, for example—as well as more revolutionary applications—computers no bigger than a bacterium and new materials displaying paradoxical properties of strength and flexibility and performance in heat and cold. The earliest applications in the next 10 to 15 years are likely to be in the first category, while those in the second category may be further in the future.

In recent years, nanotechnology has moved from the realm of science fiction into the reality of laboratories at major technology companies and research universities, with early commercial applications in several product areas. R&D expenditures by the federal government in nanotechnology initiatives have climbed from $422 million in fiscal year 2001 to a proposed $847 million in fiscal year 2004 (Bond, 2003). The NSF has established six new nanotechnology centers, and the Department of Energy has established another five. Investments by large corporations and smaller startups financed by venture capital further add to the soaring investment in this area. In the United States, total investment in 2002 has been estimated at $1 billion, a level comparable to that of the semiconductor industry (NNI, 2003). Moreover, this investment is taking place worldwide, with advanced countries including Canada, Japan, and members of the European Union joined by rapidly developing China, Korea, Tai-

---

[6]For a brief summary of the field, see "Nanotech Executive Summary," 2001.

wan, and Singapore in the race to build their future economies around these technologies.

Looking ahead—in some cases decades into the future—nanotechnology promises both evolutionary and revolutionary changes. Consider the following areas of application (NSF, 2001; NNI, 2001, 2003):

- *Electronics and information technology.* To extend Moore's Law beyond current projections, nanotechnology offers the promise of molecular electronics in the not-too-distant future. The next generation of chips to exploit further miniaturization based on silicon devices is likely to use organic molecules to create integrated circuits (Rotman, 2001). Such semiconductor chips would create the capacity of today's supercomputers on a single chip or a memory chip with a million times the density of what is possible now. Molecular electronics of this type are already being fashioned at a rudimentary level in industrial and academic labs, and efforts are under way to bring the technology to market (IBM, 2002b). Further into the future, quantum computing based on using single electrons as switches offers the potential for even further scale reductions. Bioelectronics is another area in which the forecast is for revolutionary consequences, with proteins as building blocks for electronic circuitry. Visionaries in this field see "pervasive computing" or "electronics everywhere" at a scale almost impossible to imagine today.

- *Medicine and health care.* Applications in the fields of genetics, medical devices, and pharmaceuticals may revolutionize the diagnosis and treatment of disease and disability. Advances may include new methods for using magnetic, nuclear, and optical imaging techniques at the molecular level to enhance the detection of disease, such as potential cancerous tumors or areas of plaque buildup in the heart and neck arteries that can lead to heart attacks (Huang, 2003). The treatment of cancer is evolving toward "targeted therapeutics," whereby antibodies or other agents can find and destroy specific cancer cells. Other "smart drugs" will be able to target specific diseases—for example, drugs that release antibiotics only in the presence of infection. Human physical capabilities may be extended, with, for example, human organs restored or enhanced with nanoengineered tissue.

- *Energy and the environment.* Promising new energy solutions that will replace fossil fuels, such as highly efficient solar power and fuel cells, are likely to come from nanotechnology. Applications are expected to extend to energy generation and utilization, including new energy sources and approaches to energy efficiency and environmental protection. For example, within a decade or so, new advances in lighting made possible by nanotechnology could reduce worldwide energy consumption by 10 percent, with a corresponding reduction in carbon emissions. Nanoengineered photovoltaic material could produce inexpensive nano solar cells that are spread like paint or plastic wrap and applied to building materials or other surfaces (Scigliano, 2003).

- *Aerospace and transportation.* Airplanes, spacecraft, and other aeronautical applications require extraordinary materials that exhibit unique properties in order to perform in extreme environments. New materials made possible by nanotechnology will lead to lighter, faster, and safer vehicles. Roads, bridges, runways, pipelines, and rail systems are likely to benefit from more-durable and -reliable materials and construction methods.

- *Biotechnology and agriculture.* Extensions of current biotechnology with the new tools of nanotechnology are likely to further improve agricultural yields and allow for more-economical water filtration and desalination. Molecular biological building blocks, such as proteins and nucleic acids, may be manipulated to produce new chemicals and pharmaceutical products, as well as combined with synthetic materials to merge biological functions with other desirable material properties.

- *Materials and manufacturing.* New materials made possible by nanotechnology architectures, beyond what is possible with chemistry alone, may offer improved performance and reliability with applications to a tremendous array of products. Manufacturing methods developed through nanoscience and nanoengineering are expected to evolve to the nanometer scale, with the ability to precisely control nanoscale building blocks that are then assembled into larger structures. As a recent example, scientists announced the creation of a new designer material, self-assembled in three dimensions from two different types of particles in increments of less than 1 nanometer. The custom properties of the new material reflect those of the original components (IBM, 2003; Redl et al., 2003).

In the same way that 50 years ago it was not possible to imagine the full array of applications that would follow from the replacement of vacuum tubes by silicon, the far-reaching applications of nanotechnology in these and other fields are not completely knowable. NSF projections suggest that investments in the field of nanotechnology will reach more than $1 trillion annually by 2015 in the United States alone, with implications in the twenty-first century as significant as the combined effect of antibiotics, the integrated circuit, and synthetic polymers in the twentieth century (NSF, 2001). Thus, as we discuss below, we can expect these new technologies to continue to affect the products we produce and how they are made; the health and productivity of the workforce; the skill requirements for the workforce needed to make the scientific discoveries, bring them to commercial application, and produce the resulting goods and services; and the way the economy is organized to take advantage of the new technologies.

Yet while the potential for nanotechnology is vast, pioneers in the field are cautious about promising too much too soon (NNI, 2003). As with all technologies, considerable lags can occur between basic scientific discoveries and full-scale commercial applications. However, for the 10- to 15-year horizon, nanotechnology is almost certain to generate evolutionary technological change that enhances the capability of existing products and lowers costs. At the same time, like the revolution in biotechnology, many of the advances in nanotechnology also raise social, legal, and ethical implications, as well as national security concerns, that need to be addressed as the technologies evolve (NSF, 2001). If public acceptance of the new technologies is slow to materialize, their adoption and diffusion may not match the pace of discovery.

HOW TECHNOLOGY IS AFFECTING THE WORKFORCE AND WORKPLACE

The technological advances in the latter part of the twentieth century have had a wide-ranging influence on the economy and the labor market. Industries have emerged and expanded in both the goods and services sectors to provide the products and services associated with developing and implementing the new technology. For example, consistent with the process of investment and diffusion in the IT sector discussed above, the IT sector was especially dynamic during the 1990s. Between 1991 and 2001, the IT sector generated a 16-fold increase in the production of computers, semiconductors, and communications equipment.[7] Over the same period, employment in the services industries of the IT sector (measured by the number of such professional-level IT workers as computer programmers, computer systems analysts and managers, hardware and software engineers, and so on) more than doubled, from 1.2 million to 2.5 million, a growth rate five times faster than the rate of overall occupational growth (U.S. Department of Commerce [DOC], 2003). Technological advances have had a significant effect on overall U.S. economic performance as well as on the labor market. The IT sector alone, accounting for just 8 percent of GDP in 2000, is estimated to have contributed about one-third of all output growth between 1995 and 1999 (U.S. DOC, 2000).

These advances have been made possible by considerable investment in R&D. In information technology, for example, this includes R&D into the basic architecture of semiconductors, microprocessors, memory chips, and storage devices as well as the application to computer hardware and peripherals. The rapid pace of progress is manifested in the number of patents granted for IT applications. In absolute terms, annual patents for IT applications (e.g., communications, data processing, electrical computers) increased from about 1,400 per year in 1980 to over 18,000 per year in 2001. As shown in Figure 3.5, the share of all patents awarded for IT applications grew rapidly over the same period, from just more than 2 percent to about 10 percent, with a more rapid increase during the 1990s than in the previous decade.[8] The rate of growth in patents in the biomedical field (e.g., biotechnology, pharmaceuticals, medical electronics, and medical equipment) shows a similar profile (Hicks et al., 2001).

---

[7]This number is derived from industrial production data generated by the Federal Reserve, Table 2, available at http://www.federalreserve.gov/releases/G17/table1_2.htm.

[8]A leveling off of the upward trend occurred after 1999, which may have stemmed from the business cycle downturn or other factors.

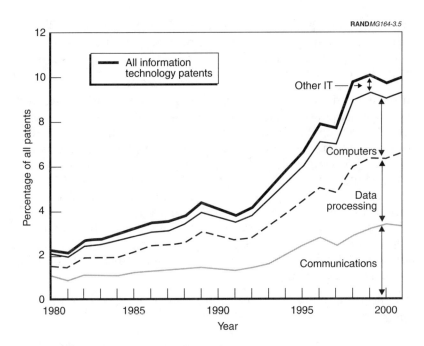

SOURCE: U.S. Patent and Trademark Office (2002a).

NOTE: Patent classes aggregated as follows: communications—classes 370, 375, 379, and 455; data processing—classes 700–707, 716, and 717; computers—classes 708–713; and other IT—classes 714 and 725.

Figure 3.5—Information Technology Patents as a Share of All Patents, 1980–2001

Aside from the direct effect of technology in terms of the industries that arise to produce and service the new technologies, new technologies are integrated into existing industries with consequences that are often subtle. Consider a case study of how progress in IT in the form of image processing of checks affected the structure of jobs in two departments of a large bank (Autor, Levy, and Murnane, 2000). In the deposit processing department, a subset of the tasks in the paper-based system typically performed by staff with a high school education were now performed by various computerized scanners and processing equipment. Of the tasks that could not be substituted for, jobs were reorganized to be more specialized, with a steeper pay gradient that increased with the degree of skill requirements. In the case of image keyers, since they now work with scanned check images, it is no longer necessary for them to be physically collocated with other check-processing staff. This permits the relocation of these jobs.

In the exceptions-processing department (dealing with checks that require individual attention, such as stop-payment or a check written on a closed account), in anticipation of the new technology and after its introduction, the structure of jobs was reorganized in a way that required greater problem-solving abilities. The result was a 28 percent reduction in the department's labor force, almost exclusively among those with a high school education only. With additional in-house training, the workers who remained in the exceptions-processing department could upgrade their skills, while recruiting focused on hiring more-skilled staff, particularly those with a college education who could better function in a department with ongoing process improvement.

This example illustrates several aspects of the way technology is influencing the nature of work:

- As a result of automation and the investment in new technology, the same tasks could be accomplished with a smaller workforce, which raises worker productivity.

- Some jobs are becoming more specialized and requiring greater analytic and problem-solving skills to perform tasks that cannot easily be automated. Often these skill requirements are manifested in increased demand for workers with higher education levels.

- Pay is tied to underlying skill capacities with a greater reward for those with the highest skills relative to lower-skill counterparts.

- With greater specialization and work products that can be digitized and distributed over electronic networks, it becomes possible to redistribute workers across geographically dispersed work sites rather than requiring workers to be collocated.

- The incorporation of new technologies requires the reorganization of work to account for the new responsibilities and level of decisionmaking required of workers in various occupations.

- Adapting to technological change often requires retraining workers so that they are able to work with the new technology and within new organizational structures.

Shifting from the microcosm provided by this example to the macrocosm of the U.S. economy, in the remainder of this section, we consider how technology more broadly—or, in some cases, IT specifically—has affected each of these dimensions of work: productivity, skill content of jobs, wage structure, geographic distribution of work, reorganization of the workplace, and delivery of workplace education and training.

The Missing Productivity Boost Has Been Found

Just as the technologies of the industrial revolution led to productivity gains measured by output per worker, it was anticipated by economists that the adoption of various information technologies throughout the economy would lead to a surge in productivity. Yet, the advent of the information age resulted in an immediate boost in neither economic output nor productivity despite high expectations that it would. As illustrated in Figure 3.6, from 1973 to 1995, labor productivity in the nonfarm business sector increased at an annual rate of about 1.4 percent. There was no dramatic upward shift as new information technologies took hold. As late as 1987, Nobel laureate Robert Solow remarked, "You can see the computer age everywhere but in the productivity statistics" (Solow, 1987).

As Figure 3.6 shows, however, the missing productivity growth—labeled "Solow's paradox"—has finally materialized.[9] Since 1995, the rate of productivity growth more than doubled to 2.9 percent per year, a return to the near 3 percent annual growth rate experienced from 1948 to 1973. The productivity gains were not limited to a few industries but applied to a range, including durable goods manufacturing and such services as wholesale and retail trade and finance

---

[9]Interestingly, the surge in productivity growth in the United States has not been experienced in other advanced economies that have made significant investments in IT (Australia is one exception). Studies indicate that, in many cases, other factors offset the productivity-enhancing effect of IT investments (IMF, 2001).

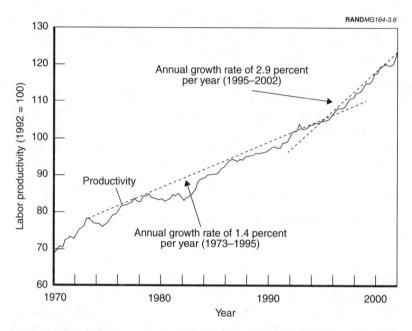

SOURCE: BLS Major Sector Productivity and Costs Index Tables (http://data.bls.
gov/labjava/outside.jsp?survey=pr).
NOTE: Labor productivity is measured as output per hour in the nonfarm business
sector.

Figure 3.6—Labor Productivity, 1970–2002

(Baily, 2002). During the peak of the 1990s business cycle, these
trends and others formed the basis for characterizing the "New
Economy." According to that paradigm, technological advances,
business process innovation, and sound government fiscal and
monetary policy were viewed as contributing to an economy with
low unemployment, low inflation, rising incomes, and steady gains
in productivity.

The acceleration in the rate of productivity growth since 1995 does
not appear to be solely a cyclical phenomenon. In fact, as indicated
in the latest data plotted in Figure 3.6, the growth in productivity has
remained at about 3 percent per year despite the economic slowdown that began in 2001 and a decline in investment spending
starting in 2000 (shown earlier in Figure 3.4 for IT but mirrored in the

data for all nonresidential investment). Analyses by economists indicate that the rise in economywide productivity can be attributed to growing productivity within the IT sector itself, as well as increased productivity in other sectors of the economy (see Box 3.1).

Thus, it appears that the increase in productivity growth has been largely the result of firms' employing labor and capital more efficiently in producing goods and services, potentially as a result of the increased investment in IT over the period. Recall from Figures 3.2 and 3.3 that the late 1990s were characterized by fast declines in quality-adjusted prices for computer hardware and rising rates of investment in computers and peripherals. Moreover, the productivity improvements were not limited to the "New Economy" sectors but appear to have been experienced across many goods- and services-producing sectors of the economy (Nordhaus, 2002a; Triplett and Bosworth, 2002). Indeed, Baily and Lawrence (2001) report that productivity growth was fastest in the later half of the 1990s in industries that made the heaviest investment in IT, although the direction of causality is not certain (Baily, 2002).[10] Analysis of service sector productivity gains also suggests that greater use of intermediate inputs, presumably in the form of contracting out for the purchase of material and services inputs, contributed significantly to productivity growth in some industries, such as business services, insurance agents and brokers, and transportation services (Triplett and Bosworth, 2002).

As discussed earlier in this chapter, all indications are that the pace of technological change experienced in the past several decades will continue virtually unabated for the next 5 to 10 years or more. It is even possible that new technological breakthroughs will quicken the pace of change. Although the exact path of future developments is difficult to predict, IT innovations are almost certain to add further capability while continuing to reduce cost. Along with advances in computer hardware and software, the Internet is viewed as a growing resource for business-to-business and business-to-consumer transactions (Lucking-Reiley and Spulber, 2001; Bakos, 2001).

---

[10]Baily (2002) summarizes various case studies of industry trends demonstrating that productivity improvements arise from other sources as well (e.g., organizational improvements) and that some sectors that invested heavily in IT did not experience rapid productivity gains (e.g., banking).

Box 3.1

Explaining the Increase in Productivity

Economists have carried out several studies in an effort to identify the sources contributing to the rise in productivity since 1995. An analysis by the Council of Economic Advisors (CEA) indicates that, through the first three quarters of 2002, all of the increase in the annual rate of labor productivity growth since 1995 was structural rather than cyclical (CEA, 2003). The acceleration of structural productivity growth since 1995 is attributed to

- *capital deepening in the IT sector (about 23 percent of the increase),*

- *an increase in total factor productivity in the computer sector (about 8 percent), and*

- *an increase in total factor productivity (TFP) in all other sectors of the economy (62 percent).*

TFP is the residual source of productivity gain after accounting for increases in capital or labor inputs. For example, a gain in TFP would follow if a firm boosts output by redesigning its production processes while still using the same level of inputs of capital, labor, and other materials.

Other growth accounting studies reach similar conclusions, although the percentage shares attributable to these three components vary (see CBO, 2002; Baily, 2002; Triplett and Bosworth, 2002; and Oliner and Sichel, 2002, and the studies cited therein). Among the various studies on this topic, the CEA analysis provides one of the larger estimates of the share of productivity growth since 1995 attributable to TFP in other sectors. In contrast, Gordon (2000) estimates that, excluding durable goods manufacturing, all the productivity gains are attributable to the computer industry alone, in the form of both capital accumulation and growth in TFP in the sector.

Economists searched for explanations not only for the original slowdown in productivity growth after 1973 but also for the failure of productivity growth to return to pre-1973 levels following more widespread use of IT. Although the paradox has yet to be fully resolved, a range of explanations has been considered. For example, computer prices or output may have been mismeasured in service-producing sectors; the capital investment in computers may not have been sufficiently large to have an effect; and the effect of computers might have had to await firms' adopting new practices to exploit

Box 3.1—continued

the hardware and software advances (Triplett, 1999). The rebound in productivity growth that has now occurred suggests that expectations that computers would have an earlier effect were overly optimistic, given that computing equipment at the time represented a relatively small fraction of the overall capital stock (Oliner and Sichel, 2000). Furthermore, many of the benefits in such areas as new business processes and new organizational structures go unmeasured in the national accounts (Brynjolfsson and Hitt, 2000).

Given that these new technologies have yet to reach saturation in the economy, most analysts expect the boost to productivity from the IT revolution to continue for the near term. Typical forecasts and "educated guesses" are in the range of 2.0 to 2.8 percent per year for the near term, close to the more recent experience.[11] Litan and Rivlin (2001) forecast that the Internet alone has the potential to add 0.2 to 0.4 percent per year to productivity in the next several years. There is, of course, uncertainty around this consensus estimate, including the possible longer-term consequences of the September 11 attacks and the increased resources devoted to security measures that are not reflected in output data.

Some economists are more pessimistic about the longer-term sustainability of the recent surge in productivity. Gordon (2002) for one argues that the 1990s were characterized by a set of events—the invention of the Internet, the Y2K transition bug that compressed the replacement cycle, the dot-com and telecom bubbles—that are unlikely to be repeated in the future. He also contends that, because of diminishing returns to more numerous and more powerful computers given a fixed endowment of human time, a limit exists to the demand for new computers with added capacity, even if prices continue to fall. Comparing them with the great inventions of the nineteenth and twentieth centuries, such as electricity, the internal com-

---

[11]See, for example, Baily, 2002; Jorgenson, Ho, and Stiroh, 2002; and Oliner and Sichel, 2002, and the studies cited therein. The Bureau of Labor Statistics (BLS) forecast for 2000–2010 in Su (2001) is at the top of the range.

bustion engine, telecommunications, and urban sanitation infrastructure, Gordon concludes that the Internet and other IT advances will fail to measure up over the longer run (Gordon, 2000).

Technology Is Shifting the Skill Requirements of Jobs

In theory, technology could be either a relative complement or substitute for skilled labor.[12] Much of the process of industrialization in the late nineteenth and early twentieth centuries replaced highly skilled artisans with capital equipment operated by less-skilled workers (Goldin and Katz, 1998). Consider the example of automobile manufacturing, which was initially carried out in large shops with highly skilled craftsmen who hand-fitted the various components. Eventually, technological improvements led to assembly line production using standardized and interchangeable parts assembled by less-skilled workers. Later still, robotized assembly lines required fewer less-skilled assembly line operators and instead employed more-skilled machine operators. Thus, as this example illustrates, the initial technological advances substituted for skilled labor, while later technology displaced unskilled labor.[13] The more recent experience has led to the common perception that technology and skills are relative complements, at least for the technological advances of much of the twentieth century and beyond (Bresnahan, Brynjolfsson, and Hitt, 2000; Acemoglu, 2002; Autor, Levy, and Murnane, 2002).

For a more recent example, consider the case of computer systems. Computers automate routine tasks and those that can be well defined (e.g., clerical tasks and related bureaucratic activity), thereby substituting microprocessors and software for human labor that is not highly skilled. In some cases, the substitution may replace all tasks previously performed by a given worker (consider, for example, automated teller machines replacing bank tellers, telephone operators replaced by automated switching machines). In many others,

---

[12]When new technologies increase (decrease) the demand for more-skilled labor relative to less-skilled labor, technology and skill are relative complements (substitutes) (Goldin and Katz, 1998).

[13]In a more systematic analysis across industries in the manufacturing sector from 1909 to 1940, Goldin and Katz (1998) trace the origin of contemporary capital-skilled labor complementarity to the transition from factories to continuous-process and batch methods that increased the relative demand for skilled workers.

computer automation substitutes for a subset of tasks. At the same time, business computer systems generate demand for highly skilled labor in the form of technical staff who operate and repair the equipment, develop and install the software, and build and monitor the networks. Outside the increased need for highly skilled IT staff, computer systems often generate more data that may be profitably analyzed, thereby increasing the demand for the analytical and problem-solving skills of workers, managers, and other professionals. At the same time, technology may also change the skill requirement of mid- to low-level occupations (Burtless, 2000). Consider, for example, the use of scanning technology by sales or inventory clerks, which may reduce some of the skill requirements for those jobs, such as key punching. At the same time, the scanning technology generates new data for inventory control, reordering, and accounting, which increases the value added of the tasks performed by such lower-skilled workers.

While the recent technological advances may favor either skilled or unskilled workers, depending on the application, the overwhelming evidence is that on balance, recent technological advances favor more-skilled workers, a phenomenon known as "skill-biased technical change." Figure 3.7 illustrates the economywide trend over the past four decades in the average skill content of jobs based on data analyzed by Autor, Levy, and Murnane (2002). The skill content of a job is defined by five skill categories based on whether the job involves routine or nonroutine tasks, and cognitive or manual skills. Each skill category is indexed to zero (no change) in 1959.

Figure 3.7 shows that, in the past four decades, there has been a steady rise in the share of jobs requiring nonroutine cognitive analytic (problem-solving) and interactive (communication) skills, especially during the 1980s and 1990s. At the same time, the share of jobs requiring routine cognitive and manual skills, after rising during the 1960s, fell steadily in the next three decades consistent with the timing of the rise of the computer era. The share of nonroutine manual skills represented in the occupational mix fell steadily over the entire period. In analyzing the drivers of these economywide trends by industry, occupation, and education groups, Autor, Levy, and Murnane (2002) find that computerization is associated with the

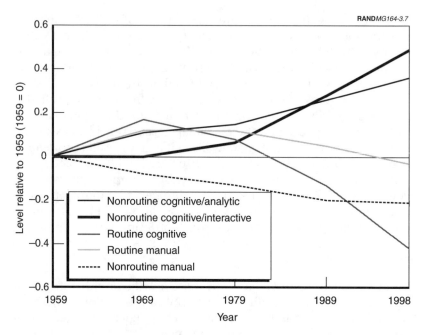

SOURCE: Autor, Levy, and Murnane (2002), Table 3.

**Figure 3.7—Economywide Measures of Occupational Task Input,
1959–1998**

reduced relative demand for routine manual and cognitive tasks and
the increased relative demand for nonroutine problem-solving and
complex communications tasks. This should not be surprising
because routine tasks, both cognitive and manual, are those most
amenable to computerization. The clear, repetitive nature of these
tasks can be defined by rules codified in computer software and
performed by computers or other machines. Nonroutine skills, such
as those requiring flexibility, creativity, problem solving, and complex communications—whether cognitive or manual—are not as
readily translated into programmable rules.

In a related study of changes in the relative quantities and wages of
workers by education level, Autor, Katz, and Krueger (1998) conclude
that relative demand for skilled labor (college equivalents) grew more
rapidly in the United States between 1970 and 1995 compared with

the 1940 to 1970 period. In the 1980s, demand accelerated only in manufacturing, with the greatest degree of skill upgrading taking place in industries with intensive computer investment.

Firm-level analyses provide a complementary source of information on the relationship between technology and the demand for labor. For example, in the manufacturing sector, Berman, Bound, and Grilliches (1994) documented large increases during the 1980s within detailed industries in the use of higher-skill nonproduction workers at a time when wages for skilled workers were rising. They also found a positive correlation between the rising demand for skill and investment in computers and R&D across both manufacturing and nonmanufacturing industries. More recently, in a sample of approximately 400 large U.S. firms, Bresnahan, Brynjolfsson, and Hitt (2000, 2002) found that firms with larger investments in IT and IT intensity increased their demand for human capital and workforce skills.

Taken together, the evidence points to the growing importance of cognitive skills in the workplace, whether in the manufacturing sector, where production line employees now program and repair complex machine tools, or in the services-producing sector, where workers increasingly are responsible for managing, interpreting, validating, transforming, communicating, and acting on information generated by new technologies. More and more, the term "knowledge workers" is applied to workers who go beyond just providing information to now being responsible for generating and conveying knowledge needed for decisionmaking (Reich, 2001). With the ease of online stock trading, for example, brokers are no longer needed to carry out transactions. Instead, they must now be a source of knowledge about the future course of markets and the investment needs of their clients. Knowledge work requires the capacity for abstraction to make sense of patterns and symbols, the ability to view problems in the context of complex systems, an aptitude for experimentation to understand how systems behave, and the capacity to work collaboratively with others to solve difficult problems (Thornburg, 2002). This type of transformation in the skill requirements of the workplace has already affected a wide range of occupations and industries, and many more are likely to be influenced with further technological advances.

Technology Is Changing the Wage Structure

To the extent that technology is changing the demand for labor of various skill levels, economic theory would lead us to expect that the demand shifts have implications for the wage structure as well. Indeed, much of the recent empirical literature has tried to explain the very substantial increase in the skill premium that accompanied the period of growth in IT. The skill premium, as typically measured, captures the wage differential between low- and high-skilled workers defined by education level. For example, Figure 3.8 plots the trend in the median real average hourly wage by education level since 1973.[14] Over the entire period, high school dropouts and those with only a high school diploma experienced real wage declines of 18.5 and 4.1 percent, respectively. At the same time, those with a college or advanced degree benefited from a 15.9 and 19.5 percent real wage gain, respectively. (Those with some college were about even, with real wage growth of just 1.4 percent.) The premium for a college degree compared with a high school diploma increased 30 percentage points, from 46 percent to 76 percent. Compared with a high school dropout, the college premium increased even more sharply (from 67 percent to 138 percent). The widening wage gap is even more pronounced when 1979 is used as the base because a slight narrowing of the wage gap occurred during the latter part of the 1970s. More generally, over this period, wage dispersion grew because of the increase in wage differentials by education level as well as increased wage dispersion within education groups (Murphy and Welch, 1992; Gottschalk, 1997; Katz and Autor, 2000).[15]

---

[14]These data are based on the CPS and include all wage and salary workers. BLS has maintained a similar series since 1979, also based on the CPS, for median weekly wages of full-time wage and salary workers by education level. The data for full-time workers from 1979 to 2001 show a pattern over time in the education premium similar to that reported in Figure 3.8 based on median hourly wages for all workers.

[15]The real wage trends plotted in Figure 3.8 are adjusted for inflation using the Consumer Price Index (CPI-U-X1). There is evidence that the CPI overstates the true rate of inflation, although the extent of the overstatement is subject to debate (see the articles in the December 1993 issue of the *Monthly Labor Review,* and Moulton, 1996). Correcting for the overstatement would increase the rate of growth of real wages for each education group, but it would not affect the trend in the wage differential between education groups.

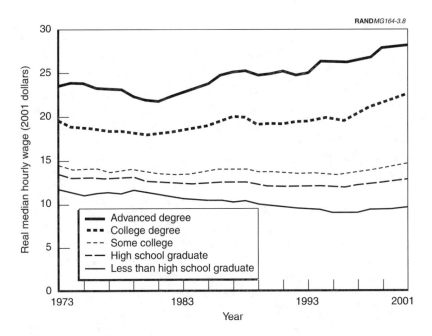

SOURCE: Mishel, Bernstein, and Boushey (2003), Table 2.17.

Figure 3.8—Real Median Hourly Wage by Education Level, 1973–2001

This increase in the college-education wage premium during the
1980s and 1990s came at the same time that the supply of college-
educated workers continued to increase, suggesting that demand
must have been increasing even faster. In seeking an explanation for
these trends, researchers have considered a range of supply,
demand, and institutional factors. Among the demand-side factors,
skill-biased technical change has consistently been identified as one
of the drivers behind the growing wage gap by skill level, although
studies vary in the magnitude of the effect attached to this explanation. Evidence in favor of this hypothesis comes in several forms, but
researchers consistently found that technological progress that
increases the demand for more-skilled workers explains a sizable
portion of the rise in the wage differential by education level since
the 1980s (see Box 3.2).[16]

---

[16]For recent reviews of this literature, see Johnson (1997) and Acemoglu (2002).

Box 3.2

The Contribution of Technological Change to the Changing Wage Structure

An extensive literature has developed to explain the growing wage inequality in the United States in the past several decades.[17] In reviewing the cumulative evidence from this literature, Acemoglu (2002) concludes that "an acceleration in [skill-biased technical change] during the past few decades appears to be the main cause of the increase in [wage] inequality" (p. 9).

One set of early studies considered the growing education wage gap in the context of a standard labor supply and demand model, which posits that changes in relative wages by skill group must stem from changes in relative supplies or technological change. Applying this approach, studies by Bound and Johnson (1992), Katz and Murphy (1992), and Murphy and Welch (1992) concluded that skill-biased technical change was the only factor capable of explaining the large increase in the college-education wage premium during the 1980s, after accounting for the role played by changing relative supplies. Thus, in these studies, evidence in favor of a technology explanation is indirect: a residual unexplained factor attributed to technical change (Card and DiNardo, 2002a, 2002b).

Other studies look for more direct evidence on the relationship between various measures of technology and the wage structure. In an early study, Mincer (1991) modeled the time-series changes in the male college-to-high-school wage differential and the experience premium for high school and college workers. His regression analysis, showing a positive effect of R&D expenditures per worker and capital equipment expenditures per worker on the education premium, supports his hypothesis of technology-skill and capital-skill complementarities. In a more recent study at the industry level, Allen (2001) finds a positive relationship between various

---

[17]Studies of wage or earnings inequality generally examine annual measures. Because individual earnings may rise or fall over time, researchers have also examined patterns of wage mobility and the distribution of longer-run measures of earnings (see Gottschalk, 1997, for a review). These studies generally find that, while there is mobility in the earnings distribution and less inequality can be found in longer-run earnings measures, earnings mobility has not increased over time. Thus, taking mobility into account does not change the trend toward greater inequality in earnings.

Box 3.2—continued

measures of technical change (e.g., R&D intensity, the capital-labor ratio) and the schooling wage gap within industries between 1979 and 1989. These results are consistent with the related evidence from industry- and firm-level studies cited above that show the sectors experiencing more rapid technological change increased their demand for more educated workers (see, for example, Berman, Bound, and Grilliches, 1994; Autor, Katz, and Krueger, 1998; Bresnahan, Brynjolfsson, and Hitt, 2000, 2002).

A more controversial source of evidence comes from Krueger (1993), who documents that workers who use computers on the job enjoy a 15 percent wage premium compared with those who do not use computers. Given the positive correlation between education levels and computer usage, he calculates that growing computer use can explain one-third to one-half of the rise in the college wage premium between 1984 and 1989. That is, a higher demand for workers capable of performing computer-intensive tasks is driving up the returns to a college education. Updated estimates by Autor, Katz, and Krueger (1997) through 1993 support a similar conclusion. However, as DiNardo and Pischke (1997) argue, these estimates are biased by selection of those who use computers on the job. If computer users are more skilled in ways not measured by the analyst, the higher returns to computer use will simply reflect a return to unobserved ability rather than to the ability to use the technology.

While most studies conclude that technological change played a role in widening wage differentials by education level, it is not clear that skill-biased technological change provides a consistent explanation for the various dimensions of the changing wage structure in the past several decades (e.g., the rise in wage inequality within education groups and the slowdown in the rise in wage inequality in the 1990s) (Card and DiNardo, 2002a, 2002b). Rather than a unicausal explanation, a confluence of factors likely played a role in affecting the wage structure. In the next chapter, we return to this literature to consider the effect of another demand-side factor—globalization—on the wage structure. Other factors that can explain the rise in wage inequality include a slowdown in the increase of college-educated workers, rising immigration, declining unionization rates, a falling minimum wage, and economic deregulation (Katz and Murphy,

1992; DiNardo, Fortin, and Lemieux, 1996; Freeman, 1996; Fortin and Lemieux, 1997; Topel, 1997; Card and DiNardo, 2002a, 2002b).

Technology Is Altering How Firms Are Organized

In addition to the effects on the labor force and wage structure, the new information technologies adopted in recent decades have had implications for other aspects of the production process, from the capital equipment used in the goods-producing sectors to the ways firms across all sectors are organized and conduct their business. Machine tools and other equipment have become increasingly sophisticated through the incorporation of computer chips and software that allow greater automation, improved accuracy, and faster retooling. Business processes have been revamped to exploit information-based software that allows better management of human and physical resources, business-to-business relationships, and business-to-customer relationships.

Such changes have taken place in "old economy" goods-producing sectors, such as the steel and machine tool industries, as well as services-producing sectors, such as retailing, trucking, and banking. An example from the banking industry was provided above. From the manufacturing and retailing sectors, the textile and garment industry illustrates how new technologies are transforming long-standing industries. In the textiles and apparel sector, as in much of retailing, the use of bar code and related information technologies supports "lean retailing"—the use of accurate and timely information, from the supply chain to sales results, to efficiently manage inventories and rapidly respond to changing demand (Abernathy et al., forthcoming). These technologies have been accompanied by an explosion of diversity in product lines that allows producers and retailers to offer more variety to consumers and ensure that stocks of specific items are available at individual retail outlets to meet demand. Order fulfillment takes place in a matter of days based on frequent but smaller orders compared with the infrequent bulk orders of the past. Shipments are processed through distribution centers on their way from suppliers to retail shops, rather than being warehoused.

While it is difficult to measure and quantify the ongoing changes in business organization, a number of signs point to the changes under way in terms of the organization of firms, business practices, compensation systems, and the nature of employer-employee relationships. In terms of the organization of the firm, the hierarchical, vertically integrated corporation was the dominant organizational model for much of the twentieth century (Malone and Laubacher, 1998). Vertically integrated firms could enjoy economies of scale and scope and thereby produce goods more efficiently than less-integrated firms. Vertical integration provided the means to control and coordinate the various stages of production performed by large and often geographically dispersed groups, especially in an era when markets were underdeveloped and supply networks were more uncertain. While this model has by no means disappeared and revenues and production volumes may be as large as before, some sectors of the economy are moving toward more specialized, vertically disintegrated firms do. With vertical disintegration, firms increasingly specialize broadly in products and services that define their core competencies while outsourcing other functions ranging from industrial design and manufacturing processes to back-office work, human resources, and computer and other information services to janitorial and cafeteria services (Appelbaum, 2003; Postrel, 2003). This trend is facilitated by the power of information technologies and their associated networks to coordinate and control across organizations and within organizations in a more decentralized manner.

As noted earlier, the increased use of intermediate inputs appears to have contributed to productivity gains in some segments of the services sector and may explain part of the productivity gains in the goods-producing sector as well. This type of outsourcing presumably allows firms to contract out for those aspects of the production process that can be accomplished less expensively by another firm, potentially because of greater efficiencies on the part of the contractor (Abraham and Taylor, 1996). Contractors may also be able to perform work less expensively if they provide less-generous fringe benefits packages than the contracting firm or face lower labor costs if they are not unionized. Finally, firms are expected to have less loyalty to the employees of their subcontractors, thereby allowing them to more readily adjust employment levels in the face of changing business circumstances.

Technology may also shape firms' decisions about how to organize production within the firm—particularly the role of workers with more-extensive skills and decisionmaking authority versus those with fewer skills and less autonomy—and how to structure the compensation system to motivate workers at various levels of the organization. Evidence has been found that firms have made adjustments in employee decisionmaking and incentive structures toward more participatory, "high-performance" work systems to reap the benefits of more-sophisticated technology and improved business practices (Appelbaum, 2003). For example, as of 1997, upward of three out of four establishments report using quality circles, while nearly half report practicing job rotation (Kruse and Blasi, 1998). Such practices invest greater authority and problem-solving responsibilities in frontline employees rather than managers. Jobs become more flexible and broadly defined, employees work in collaborative teams requiring a high degree of information sharing and communication, and outcomes focus on timeliness, quality, and customer service. Companies that adopt such practices also invest more in training for their workers (Lynch and Black, 1995). A related development is the increased reliance on performance-based pay to improve employee motivation. Production-based pay, profit-sharing, and stock-option plans allow employees to share directly in the profitability of their employers. As of 1997, roughly two in five establishments report having profit sharing or stock options for their employees, not only for executives but also for other personnel (Kruse and Blasi, 1998).

Many of these practices were initiated in the early 1980s—predating the period of major investment in IT—largely in response to competition from Japanese firms that appeared to benefit from alternative management styles. A growing literature points to the beneficial effects of these workplace practices and compensation systems in terms of productivity and employee morale, particularly when participatory practices are combined with financial incentives, worker training, and employment security (Ichniowski et al., 1996). However, only a small minority of firms—about 10 percent, according to data in 1997—combine the workplace, compensation, and other practices associated with "high-performance" workplaces (Kruse and Blasi, 1998).

Case studies and firm-level data suggest a correlation between these changes in business organization and the extent of investment in IT (Bresnahan, Brynjolfsson, and Hitt, 2000, 2002). IT adoption is associated with better measurement and communication within the firm, which will change the optimal organizational structure of the company. Thus, IT investment and reorganization of the firm are posited to be complementary innovations, along with changes in products and services. Bresnahan, Brynjolfsson, and Hitt (2002) argue that together these innovations provide a more complete explanation for the skill-biased technical change discussed above because they go beyond simple automation and substitution to include the complementary changes in workplace practices.[18]

There is also speculation that IT may be changing the nature of employer-employee relationships, with firms in the "new economy" relying more heavily on "alternative" or "contingent" workers in place of traditional employees. As of 2001, just over 9 percent of the workforce was classified in alternative work arrangements, the largest group as independent contractors (6.4 percent), followed by on-call workers (1.6 percent), temporary help agency workers (0.9 percent), and workers provided by contract firms (0.5 percent) (BLS, 2001). Contingent workers, those who do not expect their job to last or who are in temporary jobs, represented 4.0 percent of total employment as of 2001.

The share of employment in alternative work arrangements shows little change since 1995, when BLS first began collecting nationally representative data on such work arrangements. The fraction in contingent work has actually declined somewhat, from a high of 4.9 percent as of 1995. Other studies suggest little change since the mid-1980s as well (Kruse and Blasi, 1998). Utilization of such work arrangements is generally lower in industries classified as high tech or in IT industries, with the exception of contract firm employment (Neumark and Reed, 2002). At the same time, such alternative and contingent employment relationships are more prevalent in "high-tech" cities (those with a high concentration of high-tech employment) and in high-growth industries. One explanation for these patterns is that reliance on alternative or contingent workers is a temporary phenomenon as firms in high-growth sectors adjust their workforces.

---

[18]This view is consistent with the banking case study discussed above (Autor, Levy, and Murnane, 2000).

Technology Facilitates Work at a Distance

In the same way that technology can facilitate the vertical disintegration of firms and contracting out, within a given organization IT also has implications for the physical location of the workplace (Autor, 2001). Some segments of the workforce, such as those in sales or transportation, have always been mobile on the job and new technologies offer them less-expensive, more-reliable methods for staying in touch with their home office and their customers. For other workers previously confined to an office, when equipped with a phone, fax machine, PC, and Internet connection, they may be able to perform many or all of their functions from an office in their residence or another site. In many cases, the activities of off-site workers, such as telephone call center employees or other workers who perform much of their jobs using computers and other communications devices, can be electronically monitored.

Reliable data on current telecommuting patterns are hard to come by and estimates of the telecommuting workforce today vary because no common definition of "telecommuting" or "telework" exists. As of 2001, data collected by the BLS indicate that nearly 20 million workers, or 15 percent of the workforce, usually did some work at home (at least one day a week) as part of their primary job (BLS, 2002a). About half these teleworkers were wage and salary employees who took work home on an unpaid basis, while another 17 percent had a formal arrangement to work at home. The remainder, about one-third, were self-employed. As might be expected, most of those who work at home are in positions of authority or those with more autonomy in their work. In fact, about four of five workers who worked regularly at home were in managerial, professional, or sales positions. Such workers also have more education and higher incomes, on average. Because of changes in questionnaire wording, gauging changes over time in the prevalence of home-based work is difficult, but some evidence suggests that it is on the rise (NSF, 1998; Kuenzi and Reschovsky, 2001).

Using a broader definition of off-site work, about four out of five workers either work off site themselves or work with others who work at a distance (ITAC, 2003). Thus, technology allows greater communication and work activities interdependent with those located at a distance. For example, IT allows even greater physical separation between workers performing such tasks as "back office" functions (e.g., accounts processing), performance monitoring, and telephone-based operations (Autor, 2001). With greater task specialization and work products that rely on digitized information that can be coordinated over electronic networks, staff performing different functions may be physically separated to take advantage of local labor market conditions or other factors that affect firm performance. As we discuss more in the next chapter, this physical separation may extend from U.S.-based workers operating in different states to work performed by foreign workers overseas.

Technology Is Changing the Delivery of Workplace Education and Training

As technology operates to increase the demand for more-skilled labor, workers often need to undergo retraining to take advantage of how new technologies are employed in the workplace or to operate within new organizational structures. At the same time, technology has great potential to support the education and training of the workforce prior to labor market entry and as a part of lifelong learning. Technology-mediated learning—the use of computers and other information technologies as an integral part of the learning process—is gaining ground through such applications as computer-based instruction, Internet-based instruction, and other methods for customized learning (American Society for Training and Development [ASTD], 1998). Information technologies potentially allow access to instructional materials any time, any place, reducing the costs associated with bringing instructors and students to a central location as in traditional classroom settings. The technologies also allow ready access to training and instructional manuals in workplace settings through personal computers or wireless devices. Most important, the technologies support individualized learning programs.

A number of examples of technology mediated learning are used in civilian and military workforce applications today. As of 2000, corporate distance learning was a $1.2 billion business and growing at a rate of 80 percent per year (Moe and Blodget, 2000). In addition, the U.S. Department of Defense (DoD) has embraced technology-mediated learning methods. Distance learning offers the opportunity for instruction among the DoD's far-flung personnel. One application, DANTES (Defense Activity for Nontraditional Education Support), provides distance-learning opportunities for off-duty DoD employees around the world. Among other supports, DANTES allows DoD personnel to participate in distance-learning courses to fulfill undergraduate and graduate degree requirements and to receive certification for civilian occupations that match their military specialty.

The next generation of technology-enabled learning is being developed through the U.S. Advanced Distributed Learning (ADL) Initiative, a public-private collaborative sponsored by DoD to go beyond proprietary Web-based learning systems.[19] The ADL Initiative's objective is to reduce barriers to and costs of e-learning by establishing specifications that allow the interoperability, accessibility, and reusability of training components and curriculum on a worldwide basis. This effort encompasses such features as wireless and personal digital assistant (PDA)–based training, simulation-based training, assessments of individual and team performance, and tracking of online learning activities, all based on open architecture that is usable across platforms. Already the resources developed have been adopted in a variety of settings.

More generally, new technologies in the next 10 to 20 years offer tremendous potential to revolutionize the way education and training are delivered in order to improve efficiency and effectiveness in learning. Just as individualized medicine is envisioned as an outgrowth of biotechnology, individualized learning programs optimized for a given person's knowledge base and learning style are expected for the future.[20] Such learning programs will become increasingly sophisticated over time with advances in hardware and software, including artificial intelligence, voice recognition, and natural language comprehension. They will also benefit from improvements in intelligent tutoring systems that allow self-paced, interactive learning based on "learning objects"—independent, reusable

---

[19]Information about this joint effort involving academia, industry, and government can be found at http://www.adlnet.org/index.cfm?fuseaction=abtadl.

[20]For a wide range of perspectives on future learning scenarios and technologies, see U.S. DOC (2002).

software modules stored in "learning libraries" that can be used in combination with one another to create customized learning (ASTD, 1998).

For example, one application that goes beyond traditional distance learning is the use of electronic performance support systems, typically wearable computer devices that provide real-time access to information needed on the job to perform increasingly complex, dynamic tasks. Examples include the development of systems by the military and such private companies as General Motors to provide mechanics with information needed to repair and maintain even the most sophisticated equipment or machinery (ASTD, 1998; Hibbard, 1998). These devices allow hands-free voice-controlled access to all types of job-related information displayed on nearby computer screens or devices mounted on the user's head, thereby embedding training in workplace processes and supporting and reinforcing traditional training. The software may be tailored to match the user's level of experience and the complexity of the problem and can allow employees to work on a wider range of tasks given real-time access to reference material. Such systems may also be used in factory or other plant settings to provide managers with real-time access to operational data needed for decisionmaking. They may also be used to collect information discovered while employees work, feedback that can improve procedures and training and reference materials.

In other applications, workers may be trained using simulation technologies, best known now for their use in training pilots in civilian and military contexts. As simulation technologies develop further, their use in training of complex skills and for ongoing monitoring of performance levels will grow (U.S. DOC, 2002). Such devices will not be exclusive to high-tech occupations or industries. For example, simulation technologies may be used with sales personnel to train and evaluate performance in interacting with customers. Other visions for the future role of technology in learning include virtual laboratories linking individuals at multiple sites; tele-immersive environments that visualize and simulate three-dimensional spaces; and automatic translators that bridge language barriers between participants in education and training programs.

Advances in the cognitive sciences that improve our understanding of how individuals of all ages learn are expected to complement the capabilities of new learning technologies. These approaches may be especially fruitful for individuals with learning disabilities and other handicaps and should be complementary with biomedical advances in treatment regimes to improve physical and mental functioning.

TECHNOLOGY AND THE FUTURE OF WORK

Viewed together, the converging and interdependent trends in information technology, biotechnology, and nanotechnology, as well as other areas of technological advance, have led technology experts to conclude that the pace of technological change will almost certainly accelerate in the next 10 to 15 years (Antón, Silberglitt, and Schneider, 2001). Synergies across technologies and disciplines will generate advances with wide-ranging applications in terms of research and development, production processes, and the nature of products and services.

Just as the IT revolution in the past two decades has reshaped the world of work, we can expect the accelerating pace of technological change to have wide-ranging implications for the future of the workforce and the workplace. We have alluded to some of those changes in this chapter, and we revisit these issues in a more extensive discussion in the concluding chapter. To preview that discussion, we highlight here some of the most salient implications:

- *Who is working.* Advances in diagnosis and treatment of disease and disability may further extend the life span and improve health and functioning as people age. This will have implications for participation in the labor force and productivity at older ages. The prospect of curing progressive or permanent disabilities suggests a shift toward remediation for, rather than accommodation of, individuals with disabilities and improved prospects for labor force activity. Greater economic productivity through the life span may outweigh the likely increase in the cost of medical care that will accompany new medical technologies. At the same time, access to technology and training opportunities may affect career trajectories at older ages.

- *Skill requirements for the workforce.* The evolutionary and revolutionary technologies in the coming decades will sharply increase the demand for a skilled workforce to undertake the basic

R&D, develop the applications and production processes, and bring the resulting products to the commercial market. Technologies that change the way work is conducted—continued advances in IT and other knowledge-based industries, and production processes associated with nanomanufacturing among others—are also expected to shift demand toward a more skilled workforce. The traditional education and training system may need to respond to the changing workforce requirements, and potential workforce shortages in key occupations may need to be addressed. At the same time, technology can facilitate distance or distributed learning in order to support ongoing worker training and lifelong learning.

- *How work is organized.* Information technologies facilitate the move toward more decentralized forms of business organization, both the vertical disintegration of firms evident by increased specialization and the organization of work within firms. Further technological advances that support agile manufacturing and rapid change in response to market shifts may further extend these trends. Some sectors may consist of "e-lancers," businesses of one or a few workers linked by electronic networks in a global marketplace for products and services. Shifts in business organization in turn have implications for compensation structures, including wages and employee benefits.

- *Where work is conducted.* Our discussion of the various technological advances, particularly in IT, suggest that for many occupations in the future, where work is conducted will not be tied to a given physical location to the same extent as the past. Particularly when work products can be exchanged and monitored electronically, it becomes less essential that workers be physically collocated with coworkers engaged in related tasks. Flexibility with respect to the physical location of where work is performed may allow workers to better balance work and family obligations, to save time commuting, and to generally be more productive. At the same time, if workers are in jurisdictions different from their employer's—say a different state or even a different country—it may raise issues for the applicability of regulations and benefit programs (e.g., fringe benefits, social insurance) that vary across geographic space.

- *Further integration of the world economy.* The technology revolution is taking place on a global scale, albeit unevenly distributed across regions and countries. Nevertheless, the United States must compete with other countries investing in these new technologies and be poised to supply the workforce capable of providing the associated goods and services. Information technologies and distributed work make possible global teams that draw on the best skills available in a worldwide labor market.

In many cases, these implications, derived from the perspective of the forces of technological change, will also be shaped by the demographic and globalization forces discussed in Chapters Two and Four. These interactive effects are the focus of Chapter Five.

Chapter Four

A NEW ERA OF GLOBAL INTEGRATION

It is now commonplace to hear the world today described as being increasingly integrated, interconnected, or interdependent. Whether the metric is the extent of cross-national trade in goods and services, the mobility of investment capital across borders, the flow of human migrants from one country to another, or the number of Internet users across the globe, many see the economies and peoples of the world tied together even more so than in the past. The outbreak of Severe Acute Respiratory Syndrome (SARS) in late 2002 demonstrates the extent to which even the germs that infect humans can jump from continent to continent in a matter of hours. Some have argued that we have entered a new era of global integration that has had and will continue to have wide-ranging economic, political, social, and cultural implications.

The phenomenon of globalization can be viewed from a number of perspectives; there is no single agreed upon definition (World Bank, 2000). In this chapter, we are most interested in the economic aspects of globalization as reflected in various cross-border transfers: flows of goods and services, direct investment and other capital flows, the transfer of knowledge or technology, and the movement of people. From the perspective of the United States, the era of economic globalization affects the size of the markets we produce for, the mix of products we consume, and the nature of the competition in the global marketplace. It also has implications for the labor market that U.S. workers compete in and the sources of domestic and international labor available to U.S. firms. In addition to the economic dimension of globalization, it also has political, social, and cultural dimensions, such as the balance of power across nations and the transmission of culture across national boundaries. While these issues are important and may have implications for the future of global integration, we devote less time to them because they are not expected to be as directly influential in shaping the future U.S. world of work.

We begin by highlighting the key characteristics of the era of economic integration that is under way. This era has been marked by dramatic increases in trade. Total trade activity (exports plus imports) has increased from about one-tenth of U.S. GDP in 1960 to a quarter now. Meanwhile, the sectoral distribution of trade has changed; trade in services has grown from 18 to 30 percent of the total over the last 20 years. One important aspect of increasing trade has been further disintegration of production, as some production steps have been outsourced overseas. This includes not only manufacturing jobs but also higher-skilled jobs in the services sector, such as IT and business processing services. Capital flows have also become globalized in recent decades. U.S. acquisition of foreign assets increased sixfold between 1980 and 2000, and foreign acquisition of U.S. assets grew even more. Globalization has extended to labor and capital skills, as worldwide migration has doubled in the last quarter-century, resulting in greater mobility of workers, not only the less-skilled but also the highly skilled. At the same time, IT advances have enabled highly skilled workers on different continents to collaborate without physically relocating.

Next, we discuss the forces that underlie the current wave of economic globalization. We identify two principal sets of driving forces. First, over the past 50 years, communication and information transmission costs have declined precipitously. Second, multilateral trade agreements have reduced import and export barriers, while the move to flexible exchange rates in the early 1970s increased capital mobility. Globalization has given rise to a backlash driven by concerns about job loss, environmental degradation, and other perceived social impacts. Nevertheless, on balance, we believe the trend towards a globally integrated economy is likely to continue, driven by further IT advances and reductions in barriers to trade.

We then consider the consequences of greater economic integration with the rest of the world for the U.S. economy, workforce, and workplace, drawing on research that measures the effects of globalization in the recent period. The consensus among economists is that globalization has had and will likely continue to have, at the aggregate level, a favorable effect on income, prices, consumer choice, competition, and innovation in the United States. The gains, however, will not be evenly distributed. Some industries facing greater competition will lose jobs. Most workers displaced by competition quickly find other jobs, but displacement effects can be greater during business cycle downturns and permanent earnings losses can be significant. More-educated workers tend to be reemployed more rapidly than their less-educated counterparts and their relative earnings losses tend to be smaller, presumably because their skills are more transferable from one job to the next. This suggests that, while painful, future job loss associated with higher-skilled services sector employment may not be as costly in terms of unemployment and permanent wage loss compared with earlier waves of blue-collar trade-related job displacement.

Globalization has also been linked to the relative decline in real earnings among less-skilled workers over the last few decades. Research suggests that, while trade made a modest contribution to the trend, other factors, such as technology and immigration, are more important, and it must be kept in mind that many less-skilled workers are employed in nontradable services. A potential benefit from trade is a reduction in wage and employment discrimination against women and minorities caused by the more highly competitive markets associated with industries more open to trade. Some evidence suggests that globalization may weaken implicit employer-employee understandings that insulate workers through the internal labor market from market pressures once workers are hired.

We conclude by previewing some implications for the future that we will discuss further in Chapter Five. Among those are the following: that global competition will challenge not only the less-skilled workers but also the highly skilled; that a highly skilled workforce will be essential for the United States to maintain its competitive position in the world economy; that more workers may need to retrain and switch sectors to sustain employment; and that further vertical disintegration of production will result in more telework, including business conducted intercontinentally.

THE PHENOMENON OF ECONOMIC GLOBAL INTEGRATION

In many respects, the phenomenon of an increasingly interconnected world was not entirely new to the second half of the twentieth
century. Consider these two quotes:

> [T]he period was one of rapid globalization: capital and labor
> flowed across national frontiers in unprecedented quantities, and
> commodity trade boomed in response to sharply declining trans-
> port costs. (O'Rourke and Williamson, 2000, p. 5)

> Named the Russian flu, this worldwide influenza epidemic . . .
> begins in Central Asia in the summer . . . , spreads north into Russia,
> east to China and west to Europe. It eventually strikes North Amer-
> ica, parts of Africa and major Pacific Rim countries. (http://www.
> msnbc.com/site_elements/blank.htm)

The first description applies to the international economy in the late
nineteenth century, while the second recounts the spread of the
worldwide "Russian flu" epidemic in 1889 to 1890 in which hundreds
of thousands died. In terms of economic activity, all the growth in
trade between World War II and the mid-1970s merely returned trade
as a share of the economy to the level the country experienced on the
eve of World War I (Krugman, 1995; Frankel, 2000). Indeed, the aber-
ration in the twentieth century was the decline in trade activity
between the two world wars as protectionist pressures, world con-
flict, and political instability reduced the degree of openness of most
of the world's economies (Williamson, 1998).[1]

While trade's share of the economy is not that different today from
what it was 100 years ago, other important differences can be found
between the earlier era of globalization and the one we are in today
(Krugman, 1995; Bordo, Eichengreen, and Irwin, 1999):

- The flowering of trade at the end of the nineteenth century primarily involved more-developed countries in the Atlantic economy, whereas trade today increasingly takes place between
  more-developed and less-developed economies.

---

[1] For an even longer historical view of globalization, see Taylor (2002).

- The current era of globalization is characterized by rapid mobility of all factors, especially information and capital flows which travel at high speeds across digital networks.

- A growing share of trade consists of services—many of them related to such technological innovations as IT, discussed in Chapter Three. The array of industries subject to international competition has thus grown more diverse.

- Goods-related trade is no longer limited to raw materials and final goods but increasingly consists of intermediate goods which are themselves inputs into the production of other intermediate or final goods. Thus, the process of vertical disintegration and growing specialization of the firm discussed in Chapter Three is extended to the international level as the vertical disintegration of trade.

In the remainder of this section, we discuss these differences in the context of trade in goods and services, capital and foreign direct investment, and labor and intellectual capital. We also briefly discuss aspects of global health and security in the context of a more integrated world.

Growing Trade, Especially in Services and with More Diverse Countries

From a global perspective, in the last 20 years, total world merchandise trade export volume has increased about 2.5 times, considerably faster than the increase in total world production (see Figure 4.1). This relative growth of merchandise trade primarily arises from a rapid increase in the volume of trade in manufactures, by a factor of almost 3.5 since 1980. In contrast, over the same period, world trade in mining products and in agricultural products roughly kept pace with world production.[2] Compared with merchandise trade, there has been an even more rapid growth in trade in services since 1980,

---

[2]Compared with world production in their respective sectors, trade in agricultural and mining productions have both increased faster than production since 1980, indicating that share of production traded has increased within each sector.

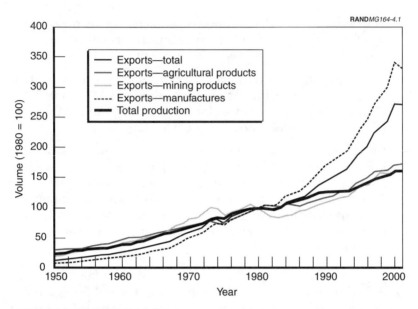

SOURCE: WTO (2002), Table II.1.

Figure 4.1—Volume of World Merchandise Exports, 1950–2001

according to available data (see Figure 4.2). While the value of merchandise exports increased by a factor of 3 since 1980, services exports increased by a factor of more than four. The absolute dollar level of trade in services is even now only about one-quarter the level of merchandise trade, however ($1.5 trillion in 2001 for services versus $6.4 trillion for merchandise trade).

This pattern of growing export activity, with a relatively faster growth of services trade is mirrored in the trade patterns for the United States. Four decades ago, trade accounted for less than 10 percent of the U.S. economy, compared to more than 20 percent by the advent of the twenty-first century (see Figure 4.3). The sum of exports and imports as a share of GDP—a measure of total trade activity—topped out at 25.5 percent in the business cycle peak year of 2000.[3] In every

---

[3]Other business cycle peak and trough years are also marked in the figure, based on business cycle dating by the National Bureau of Economic Research (see http://www.nber.org/cycles/).

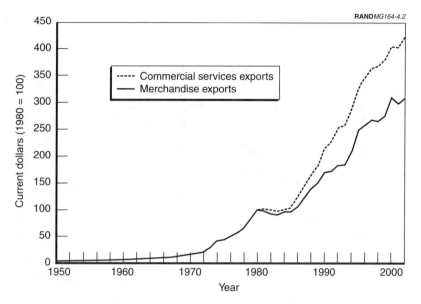

SOURCE: WTO Trade Statistics Historical Series Tables (http://www.wto.org/english/res_e/statis_e/statis_e.htm).

NOTE: Commercial services data begins at 1980.

Figure 4.2—Value of World Merchandise and Services Exports, 1950–2002

year since 1976, the level of imports has exceeded exports, indicating a deficit in U.S. trade in goods and services. The sequence of current account deficits is financed by capital inflows (i.e., the acquisition of U.S. assets by foreigners), so that economic ties between foreign countries and the United States have increased substantially.

The growth of U.S. trade in services (e.g., travel and transportation, telecommunications services, education, financial and business services, technical services, and royalties and license fees) is especially evident for exports. Since 1980, services have gone from 18 percent of all U.S. export activity to 30 percent (see panels A and B in Figure 4.4). At the same time, a 19-percentage-point decline occurred in the share of exports consisting of foods, feeds, and beverages and industrial supplies and materials (including petroleum and other energy products). Shifts in the other categories were more modest. Overall,

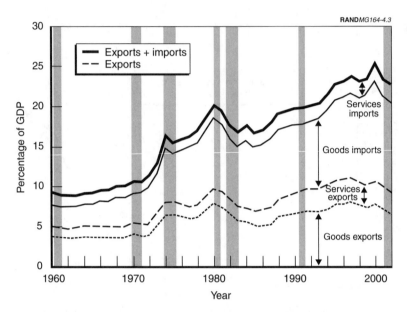

SOURCES: BEA U.S. International Transactions Accounts Data, Table 1 (http://www.bea.gov/bea/international/bp_web); BEA NIPA Tables, Table 1.1 (http://www.bea.gov/bea/dn/nipaweb/SelectTable.asp); and NBER Business Cycle Expansions and Contractions (http://www.nber.org/cycles/).

NOTE: Gray shading marks business cycle recessions (from peak to trough).

Figure 4.3—U.S. Exports and Imports as a Share of GDP, 1960–2002

by 2002, the share of services exports was the same as the share of capital goods exports (exclusive of automotive products). Nevertheless, the services share of exports, at 30 percent, is not proportionate to the overall share of services in the U.S. domestic economy, a share that reached 67 percent in 2001.[4] This reflects, in part, the fact that many services are location-specific and not readily tradable across international boundaries.

The sectoral composition of trade shown in Figure 4.4 reveals another important dimension of change: higher volumes of intrasec-

---

[4]Based on data from the Bureau of Economic Analysis, National Income Product Accounts, for 2001 (see http://www.bea.doc.gov/bea/dn1.htm).

RAND*MG164-4.4*

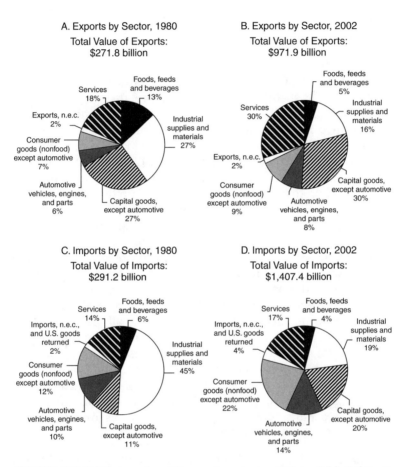

SOURCE: BEA U.S. International Transactions Accounts Data, Table 2 (http://www.bea.gov/bea/international/bp_web).

NOTES: Data for 2002 are preliminary. n.e.c. stands for "not elsewhere classified."

Figure 4.4—Distribution of U.S. Exports and Imports by Sector, 1980 and 2002

tor trade—i.e., flows of both exports and imports within the same industry. For example, in 2002, automotive vehicles, engines and parts constituted 8 percent of U.S. exports and 14 percent of imports (see panels B and D in Figure 4.4). In some cases, these trade flows represent exchanges of intermediate products or inputs into the production of more complex goods, which themselves are destined for world markets. For example, the U.S. imports semiconductors that are then assembled into computers, which are subsequently exported.

This key feature of contemporary trade patterns—referred to as "vertical trade," "slicing up the value chain," "disintegration of production," or "multinationalization of production"—means that finished products may be composed of inputs produced and assembled in stages in different countries (Krugman, 1995; Feenstra, 1998; Hummels, Rapoport, and Yi, 1998; Bordo, Eichengreen, and Irwin, 1999; Hummels, Ishii, and Yi, 2001). Multinational firms no longer limit production to a single country but carve up the production process into stages implemented in multiple countries through subsidiaries or contractors. This allows more labor-intensive stages of the production process to be located in lower-wage settings, as opposed to stages that are more capital-, knowledge-, or technology-intensive, which are located in higher-wage settings. This pattern of specialization extends on a global scale the vertical disintegration of the firm discussed in the prior chapter in the context of technological change. U.S. firms outsource not only domestically but also internationally, thanks to IT innovations that allow greater coordination and monitoring of production and to greater trade flows caused by declining tariffs as well as falling communication and transportation costs (discussed further below). Just as firms specialize in a particular stage of the production process, countries are moving toward specializing in a particular stage of production as well (Hummels, Rapoport, and Yi, 1998; IMF, 2002).

Feenstra (1998) illustrates this phenomenon in the case of Mattel, a U.S.-based firm with a large U.S. presence in terms of design and marketing functions. Yet, as of 1996, Mattel's Barbie doll was assembled in Indonesia, Malaysia, and China out of raw material (hair and plastic) from Taiwan and Japan, and molds and paint from the United States. As another example, Grossman and Helpman (2002) cite the case of a particular "American" car with just under two-thirds of the production value originating from abroad. German design contributes 7.5 percent, Japanese components and advanced technology 17.5 percent, minor parts from Taiwan and Singapore 4 percent, Korean assembly 30 percent, British advertising and marketing 2.5 percent, and data processing from Ireland and Barbados 1.5 percent. This leaves 37 percent of the production value attributable to the United States.

Aside from such examples, systematic data on the extent of such vertical trade is not routinely produced. One set of estimates from 1990 indicates that 7 percent of total trade for U.S. goods-producing industries was vertical—defined as the use of imported intermediate parts in the production of goods that are later exported. The share was highest in office and computing machinery (16.7 percent), followed by petroleum and coal products (15.5 percent), nonferrous metals (12.2 percent) and aircraft (11.6 percent) (Hummels, Rapoport, and Yi, 1998). Other large developed economies, such as Germany and Japan, also have low shares overall, while such countries as the Netherlands, Ireland, and Korea have shares in the range of 25 to 35 percent. This same study estimated that the growth of vertical trade accounted for more than 25 percent of the increase in the export share of output in several OECD countries up through 1990, although the United States was below the average.

As trade flows have increased and production has become more internationalized, the United States has altered the mix of trading partners toward countries with lower wages (see Figure 4.5, which is limited to data on exports and imports of goods). Canada remains the United States' largest trading partner, with 20 percent of total trade in goods in 2002, nearly the same as the share in 1980 when it was 18 percent. While Japan held the second ranking position as of 1980 with 11 percent of trade activity, Mexico has assumed that ranking as of 2002, growing from 6 percent in 1980 to 13 percent of total U.S. goods trade activity.[5] Total goods trade activity with Mexico reached $233 billion in 2002, about 62 percent of the activity with Canada in the same year, compared to 33 percent of the level of Canadian activity as of 1980.

The growing importance of Mexico as a U.S. trading partner is indicative of a shift in trade activity—notably goods imports—with a

---

[5]Mexico became the United States' second largest trading partner as of 1999 (Chomo, 2002).

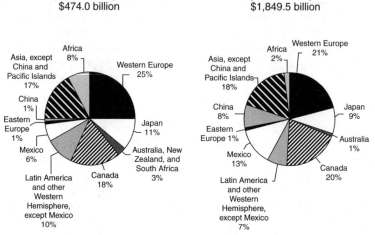

RAND*MG164-4.5*

A. Goods, Exports, and Imports
by Region, 1980

Total Value of Goods
Exports and Imports:
$474.0 billion

B. Goods, Exports, and Imports
by Region, 2002

Total Value of Goods
Exports and Imports:
$1,849.5 billion

SOURCE: BEA U.S. International Transactions Accounts Data, Table 2 (http://
www.bea.gov/bea/international/bp_web).

NOTES: In 2002, New Zealand is included in "Asia, except China, and Pacific
Islands" and South Africa is in "Africa." Data for 2002 are preliminary.

**Figure 4.5—Distribution of U.S. Goods Exports and Imports by Region,
1980 and 2002**

number of newly industrializing countries, particularly in Asia. For
instance, one dramatic shift in the last several decades is the
increased share of goods imported from China. As of 1980, Chinese
goods imports amounted to less than four-tenths of 1 percent of total
U.S. goods imports. As of 2002, that share reached nearly 11 percent,
or $125 billion, a figure that exceeded the level of Japanese goods
imports for the first time. Goods imports from the four "Asian tigers,"
namely Hong Kong, the Republic of Korea, Singapore, and Taiwan,
totaled another $91 billion in 2002, or nearly 8 percent of U.S. goods
imports. This share has remained relatively unchanged since 1980 in
contrast to the rising share from China. Meanwhile, trade with
countries having very low incomes is still limited, largely because the
size of their economies relative to the United States is low: the 49

countries designated by the United Nations as least developed are responsible for less than 1 percent of total U.S. trade.[6] Instead, the bulk of U.S. trade activity continues to take place with other industrialized countries, i.e., with Canada, Japan, Australia, New Zealand, South Africa, and the countries in Western Europe. These countries made up 53 percent of goods exports and imports in 2002, a small decline from the 56 percent share in 1980.[7]

The Convergence of Trade and Technology in IT-Enabled Services—Outsourcing Overseas

While a century ago imports from low-income countries primarily involved agricultural commodities, today the bulk of imports from such countries as Mexico and those in east and south Asia involve labor-intensive manufactured goods (Bordo, Eichengreen, and Irwin, 1999). Increasingly, however, trade in services is flowing to lower-income countries as well, as U.S. companies outsource various service functions to foreign-owed subsidiaries (i.e., offshoring) or to foreign contractors (i.e., outsourcing). Rising education and skill levels in lower-income countries, coupled with lower wages, allow U.S. firms to save money while still meeting their need for quality. Advances in communication technologies and falling prices associated with voice and data transmission further facilitate the shift of IT-enabled services from the United States to overseas locations. More generally, the movement of white-collar jobs overseas is linked to the broader trends in IT discussed in the prior chapter. Since the work products in many information-based and knowledge-based industries can be readily transmitted over high-speed computer networks, the physical location of the workforce is increasingly less relevant.

---

[6]Based on data for 2002 from the U.S. Bureau of the Census Ft900 International Trade in Goods and Services series (see http://www.census.gov/foreign-trade/www/press.html#current), aggregated for the 49 countries currently classified by the United Nations as least developed (see http://r0.unctad.org/en/pub/ldcprofiles2001.en.htm).

[7]These percentage shares differ from those evident in Figure 4.5 due to rounding and the grouping of South Africa and New Zealand with other countries in their region as of 2002 rather than with Australia as was the case in 1980.

During the early 1990s, a number of Silicon Valley technology companies began outsourcing software-coding jobs to companies in India. Lower-skill data entry jobs were also transferred to countries overseas. More recently, a broader range of IT jobs have been outsourced—as have business-process operations (e.g., back-office work and call center operations), typically to countries with English-speaking, educated workers, such as India. For example, computer programmers in India now routinely perform high-skilled software development while Indian engineers design microchips, jobs previously limited to higher-paid workers in more advanced economies (Engardio, Bernstein, and Kripalani, 2003). Various large U.S. corporations, including General Electric, American Express, and Conseco, have established back-office facilities in such countries as China, India, Jamaica, and Mexico with estimated cost savings of 30 to 40 percent (Wharton School, 2002a).

In terms of call center operations, Delta Air Lines is the first airline to contract with companies based in India to handle some of its customer reservations made over the telephone. And, welfare recipients in several dozen U.S. states who call for assistance with balances on their electronic benefits cards or other matters reach operators based in Bombay and elsewhere in India (Waldman, 2003).[8] Because these workers overseas are coached to lose their native accents, adopt U.S. idioms, and even take on Americanized names, U.S. consumers who call an 800 number are often unaware that they are speaking to someone in another country (Carmichael, 2003).

The examples extend even beyond IT and business processing tasks to other higher-skill jobs. For example, transmitting blueprints over the Internet and teleconferencing allows one U.S.-based architectural firm to farm out the preparation of detailed architectural plans to staff based in Shanghai, China (Goodman, 2003b). Staff in China are paid a fraction of their U.S. counterparts, and the work effort continues over a 24-hour cycle. Workers based in China, Costa Rica, Hungary, India, Ireland, the Philippines, and other countries engage in a range of white-collar jobs, such as evaluating health insurance claims, preparing tax returns, analyzing financial data, and conduct-

---

[8]In at least one state, the shift of state-financed social services support functions overseas has resulted in controversy as we discuss further below.

ing financial market research (Engardio, Bernstein, and Kripilani, 2003; Goodman, 2003b; Sharma, 2003; Waldman, 2003). Here again, the cost savings can be considerable. Graphic artists who can contribute to movie special effects earn $5,000 per year in India, while top business school graduates in India command $12,000 per year, both tiny amounts compared to their U.S. counterparts (Sharma, 2003). Cost is not always the only consideration motivating the outsourcing of jobs overseas. Boston's Massachusetts General Hospital now has CT scans analyzed by Indian radiologists to relieve stress for its own radiology staff, particularly during night shifts when the work can be conducted in the daytime in India (Sharma, 2003).

Data to estimate the extent of these international outsourcing trends in the services sector are not readily available, but some estimates suggest that the movement is relatively modest to date but growing. A recent survey conducted by the Information Technology Association of America (ITAA) in 2003 indicates that 6 percent of all U.S. firms have moved IT jobs overseas (ITAA, 2003). Among firms specializing in IT products and services (e.g., computer hardware and software, communications, and semiconductors), that fraction jumps to 12 percent compared with 3 percent of non-IT firms. A slightly larger fraction in each category plans to move IT jobs offshore in the next 12 months. The types of jobs being moved include such higher-skilled jobs as programming or software engineering (67 percent), network design (37 percent), and web development (30 percent). The migration of IT jobs to other countries is more common among larger U.S. IT firms (more than 1,000 employees) presumably because they already have operations in multiple countries. An estimated cumulative total of 473,000 computer-related jobs are expected to migrate overseas by 2015 from a base of 27,000 as of 2000 (McCarthy, 2002). In total, a projected 3.3 million IT-sector jobs are expected to have migrated overseas by 2015, compared with 400,000 to date (Greenhouse, 2003).[9]

In terms of back-office outsourcing, recent estimates indicate that about 5 percent of large U.S. firms (revenues from $100 million to $4 billion) were currently outsourcing or had plans to outsource por-

---

[9]Another recent analysis suggests the flow could be even higher, a project 500,000 jobs by then end of 2004 (Morello, 2003).

tions of the back-office operations overseas (Wharton School, 2002a). In India alone, recent estimates forecast $21 billion in revenue by 2008 associated with call center and business processing operations (Rai, 2002). Associated employment is projected to increase tenfold, from approximately 100,000 to 1.1 million employees. India's dominance in this field may soon be eclipsed by competition from China, Ireland, and the Philippines among others. At the higher end of the skill spectrum, a recent forecast projects 500,000 financial-services jobs will be outsourced to India in the next five years (Sharma, 2003).

As companies gain experience with offshore operations and contracting and the associated needs for monitoring and quality assurance, the range of jobs that can be outsourced expands (Sharma, 2003). This has been the recent pattern with outsourcing services-related functions overseas, as lower-skill data entry and computer programming tasks have given way to jobs entailing accounting, finance, research, and higher-level programming. One such example is India's move into medical services, where early experience with transcribing dictation of U.S. doctors provided a foundation for advancing to the analysis of CAT scans using three-dimensional computer models (Sharma, 2003). In the future, companies may choose to blend onshore and offshore models to offer greater flexibility as well as the capacity to work around the clock. To date, India has been one country to gain from the growing experience of U.S. firms with offshore functions, but other countries are likely to gain market share over time as well. The education of the workforce, language skills, reliability of the economic infrastructure (e.g., electricity, telecommunications), security of sensitive information (personal or proprietary), and political stability are important considerations in decisions about when and where to outsource functions abroad.

The Internationalization of Capital Flows

The phenomenon of economic globalization also encompasses increased mobility of capital across international borders, and trade and financial integration often move together (IMF, 2002). Such capital flows may take two forms:

- Direct investment (i.e., a firm in one country uses capital to establish a plant in another country or to purchase a large equity stake in a company in another country, also known as foreign direct investment [FDI])

- Portfolio investment (i.e., purchases by residents or firms in one country of bonds, small amounts of equity, or other financial instruments in another country).[10]

On a worldwide basis, there has been a substantial increase in such capital flows, particularly when measured on a gross basis (i.e., counting both inflows and outflows). Among high-income countries, gross private capital flows as a share of GDP increased more than threefold between 1990 and 2000, from 11 to 34 percent (World Bank, 2002b). Low- and middle-income countries also experienced an increase, though a smaller one, over the same period (from 7 to 11 percent of GDP).

From the perspective of the United States, the last several decades were marked by increased capital flows. During the 1990s, capital inflows (foreign acquisition of assets in the United States) increased to a peak of 10 percent of GDP in 2000 (see Figure 4.6). Capital outflows (U.S. residents' acquisition of assets abroad) also increased sharply over the same period, although capital outflows since 1983 have always been below inflows, indicating the consistent annual net indebtedness of the United States to the rest of the world. In terms of the stock of assets, the United States shifted from being a net creditor since the late 1920s to a net debtor by the end of the 1980s. Preliminary data for 2002 show U.S. assets owned by foreigners exceeded the value of foreign assets owned by U.S. residents by $2.4 trillion (at current cost), or 23 percent of GDP.[11]

These international capital flows play an important role in the internationalization of production and trade. The boundaries of the firm are not limited to the geographic borders of its home country; direct investment in companies overseas provides the means to control production and expand into new markets. The level of activity on a

---

[10]In addition to these two main categories of capital flows, there are also loans and other residual transactions.

[11]Based on data collected by the Bureau of Economic Analysis at the U.S. Department of Commerce available at: http://www.bea.doc.gov/bea/di1.htm.

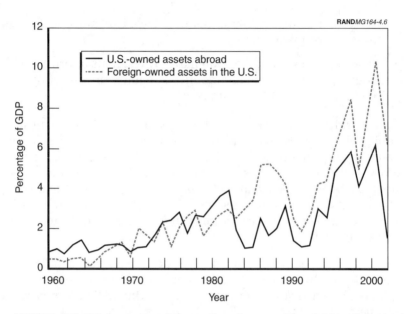

SOURCE: BEA U.S. International Transactions Accounts Data, Table 1 (http://www.bea.gov/bea/international/bp_web)

Figure 4.6—U.S. Capital Flows as a Share of GDP, 1960–2002

worldwide basis is substantial. For example, as of 2000, approximately 65,000 multinational corporations (i.e., parent firms that control assets abroad) were involved in international production worldwide with about 850,000 affiliates (UN Commission on Trade and Development [UNCTAD], 2002). Among the world leaders are such U.S.-based companies as General Electric, ExxonMobil Corporation, and General Motors, which ranked in the world's top 10 multinational corporations in 2000 by foreign assets. Together, U.S.-based multinational parent corporations accounted for 56 percent of U.S. goods exports and 35 percent of goods imports in 2000 (Mataloni, 2002). Even so, most activity for U.S.-based multinational corporations remains within the United States: among U.S.-based parent companies and their majority-owned foreign affiliates, 75 percent of their combined production, capital expenditures, and employment were concentrated in the United States as of 2000, a rate about the same as a decade earlier in 1989.

With the growing internationalization of production, concerns have been raised in the past about the operations of foreign-owned multinationals located in the United States. Available data indicate that FDI in the United States on the part of foreign multinationals is an important source of job creation: foreign affiliates in the United States accounted for nearly 16 percent of employment and 18 percent of sales in the manufacturing sector as of 1999. They also contributed 15 percent of economywide R&D expenditures. The evidence also indicates that foreign-owned companies in the United States pay wages comparable to U.S. firms in the same industries (Landefeld and Kozlow, 2003). Foreign multinationals operating in the United States also represent a source of technology transfer and often invest in the human capital of their U.S. workers (Feldstein, 2000).

Based on recent experience, the trend suggests even greater internationalization of production in the years ahead, although such flows are sensitive to the business cycle. Between 1991 and 1995, worldwide FDI inflows and outflows increased nearly 20 percent per year and the rate of growth nearly doubled in the second half of the decade. Most investment flows are expected to continue to concentrate among the more developed countries. For example, when U.S. multinationals do invest abroad, their investment is concentrated in countries with large, prosperous markets rather than in countries with low wages: Three out of every four dollars invested by U.S. multinationals is in other developed countries (Landefeld and Kozlow, 2003). Consistent with the growth in trade in services, a growing share of U.S. FDI is in services such as banking, finance, insurance, wholesale and retail trade, utilities, and other services (Bordo, Eichengreen, and Irwin, 1999). At the same time, FDI flows are beginning to shift toward lower-wage countries, both developing countries and those in central and eastern Europe. For example, developing countries increased their share of worldwide FDI inflows from an average of 18 percent between 1986 and 1990 to 28 percent as of 2001 (UNCTAD, 2002). However, the 49 least developed countries received only one-half of one percent of FDI inflows in 2001, almost no change from the late 1980s.

The Globalization of Labor and Intellectual Capital

In the same way that goods, services, and capital move across borders in an increasingly integrated world economy, international migration is another aspect of globalization. Data recently released by the UN (2002) for 2000 reveal that 175 million people worldwide live in a country other than where they were born. Although this is less than 3 percent of the world's population, the number of migrants has more than doubled since 1975. The majority (60 percent) of these migrants live in the developed world (41 million in North America, for example), so that about one in 10 persons living in developed countries is a migrant. This contrasts with one in 70 persons in developing countries. In addition to migrants, another 16 million people worldwide are classified as refugees, most of whom are in Asia (9 million) and Africa (4 million). Long lists of individuals are also awaiting decisions on asylum applications (Hatton and Williamson, 2002). Migrants from many low-income countries retain close ties back home, providing substantial flows of remittances that can exceed 10 percent of GDP (examples include El Salvador, Jamaica, Nicaragua, and Yemen).

As discussed in Chapter Two, the annual inflow of migrants to the United States has approximately tripled since 1970 (see Figure 2.6). North America as a whole absorbed a net of 1.4 million migrants annually between 1995 and 2000, followed by Europe with 800,000 net migrants per year. Efforts to limit the migrant inflow are not entirely successful: illegal immigrant flows into the United States equal about 300,000 per year while flows in western Europe reach 400,000 to 500,000 annually (Hatton and Williamson, 2002). In the United States, immigrant flows represent potential labor market entrants with both low and high skills. Indeed, as discussed in Chapter Two, where insufficient domestic supply of highly skilled labor in specific occupations exists, U.S. companies can turn abroad. For example, in 2001, more than 330,000 temporary work visas were issued for specialty occupations, mostly computer-related jobs (INS, 2003a). In high-tech centers such as California's Silicon Valley, immigrants make up substantial portions of the scientific and engineering workforce (about one-third in the case of Silicon Valley as of 1990) (Saxenian, 1999). Their contributions extend to entrepreneurship as well: as of 1998, Chinese and Indian immigrant engineers led one in four high-technology Silicon Valley firms. With greater numbers of foreign nationals in corporate leadership positions, many firms have adopted a more global orientation in terms of their business strategy (Feldstein, 2000).

The outflow of skilled individuals from low-income countries, a repeat of the brain drain of the 1960s, is of increasing concern for developing countries (Bhagwati, 2003). For example, graduates of elite engineering schools and other universities in China, India, Korea, and Taiwan come to the United States to receive Ph.D.s in science and engineering and many stay after completing their degree. Current estimates suggest 70 percent of foreign-born U.S. Ph.D. recipients do not return to their country of origin (Bhagwati, 2003).

While international labor migration captures one dimension of the globalization of labor, communications and information technologies increasingly support another approach to global integration of the workforce: the use of global work teams. Relevant for such primarily knowledge-intensive projects as new product development, numerous examples of multinational firms drawing on top talent from an international pool of labor can be cited. Among the examples provided by Marquardt and Horvath (2001) is IBM's creation of a five-site, five-country global work team in 1997 to develop a series of small software components for use in a larger application. In the offshore sites—Beijing (China), Bangalore (India), Minsk (Belarus), and Riga (Latvia)—and the U.S. coordinating site (originally Seattle, later Raleigh), staff worked around the clock to reduce the time to develop and test the new software components. The teams and their work products were connected by the Internet, shared coordination software, and other collaborative technologies. Costs of the offshore site activities were reduced by 10 percent compared with similar operations in the United States, and the time-to-market was reduced from three months to less than one month. IBM also created a strong presence in each of the emerging markets where the staff were based. This example illustrates how global teams are used to reduce costs and gain economies of scope, tap specialized skills around the world, solve complex problems, increase operational speed, and gain understanding of local markets.

Such global teams are not limited to those formed by multinational corporations. The development of the Linux operating system, first posted on the Internet in 1991 as a simple Unix-based operating system developed by a computer-science student in Finland, provides an example of self-generating global teams (Malone and Laubacher, 1998). The original Linux author encouraged other programmers to access the software for free and make modifications. These enhancements were in turn posted for other programmers to work with. Within three years, an informal configuration of thousands of individuals around the globe, without benefit of a formal management structure or oversight, had developed a highly-rated Unix operating system.

While no systematic data suggest patterns and trends in the usage of such global teams, a growing set of resources has been designed to support them.[12] The phenomenon is another dimension of the FDI and vertical trade trends discussed earlier that allow multinational firms to draw on a global labor pool. More generally, these technologies facilitate a continuum of long-distance work relationships within and between companies or even individuals, located half a world away from one another. Future technological advances in the IT field discussed in Chapter Three, including real-time translation devices, would further support more cross-national collaboration.

The internationalization of labor is also tied to the greater ease with which new knowledge and technologies are transferred across international boundaries. FDI is one such source of technology transfers as multinational companies invest in plants, equipment, and people in lower-wage settings (IMF, 2000). Investments in R&D on the part of multinational firms can be considerable as well. Although data are limited and great variability occurs across countries, estimates indicate that foreign affiliates account for close to two-thirds of all R&D expenditures in a number of countries, including Ireland, Hungary, and Taiwan (UNCTAD, 2002). Return migration or circulatory migration is another mechanism for international knowledge flows, turning the "brain drain" into "brain circulation" (Saxenian, 1999, 2002). For example, immigrant engineers in Silicon Valley, through their language skills, cultural knowledge, and technical expertise are equally adept in the business world in their home countries as they are in the United States. Their cross-national networks and pursuit of

---

[12]See, for example, the list of web resources in Appendix B of Marquardt and Horvath (2001).

business opportunities both in their country of origin and in the United States promote more rapid global integration through the transfer of capital, skill, and knowledge.

In some cases, the technology transfer may be viewed as a negative aspect of global integration. In a recent case, engineers at Boeing threatened to strike at the end of 2002 if the company did not reduce its corps of engineers based in Moscow (Holmes, 2003). While Boeing's strategy for an increased presence in Russia aimed to create a 24-hour worldwide workforce and to increase sales of Boeing planes in that country, U.S. staff feared the loss of technology and competitive advantage to their Russian counterparts along with the reduction in jobs because of outsourcing. Similar concerns have been voiced over the investment in the services-related IT sector in India. As another example, after years of relying on foreign companies for high-technology products and knowledge, China is beginning to exert its influence as the world's most populous country by developing its own technology standards in such areas as high-definition television and the next generation of mobile phone technology (Goodman, 2003a). This would provide China with a dominant position domestically and could even lead to adoption of the technology in other countries to the benefit of Chinese firms.

The ease with which knowledge and technological know-how can traverse national boundaries has focused attention on the role of intellectual property rights in the worldwide marketplace. Systems of patents, trademarks, and copyrights evolved to allow investors to reap the returns of their efforts exclusively for a period of time, thereby providing incentives for costly R&D. These national institutions are now embodied in international agreements designed to establish common rules through such measures as the World Trade Organization's (WTO's) 1994 Trade-Related Aspects of Intellectual Property Rights (TRIPS) agreement. Even with such agreements, disparities between countries in their economic bargaining power can affect access to technology and disputes over intellectual property rights remain central to many trade-related disagreements (UNDP, 2001). This becomes particularly important when a substantial public interest is associated with a technology that must be weighed against ensuring private rewards for innovators. Providing access to drugs at lower cost for treating the HIV/AIDS pandemic in parts of

Africa and Asia is but one example where public and private interests may collide.

Other Dimensions of Global Integration

The concept of globalization is increasingly taking on other meanings beyond the economic integration of countries around the world through trade, capital, and labor linkages. For example, since the terrorist attacks in New York and Washington, D.C., on September 11, 2001, concerns over homeland security in the United States, as well as security abroad, have become salient. In recent decades, terrorist organizations have evolved from localized threats to worldwide networks of individuals, interconnected through the same information technologies that are spurring economic integration (Hoffman, 1998; Arquilla and Ronfeldt, 2001). With their global reach and potential access to deadly biological, chemical, nuclear, or conventional weapons, the threat posed by terrorist organizations is alarming. Concerns about international terrorism, as well as political instability more generally, may have implications for the extent to which U.S. firms engage in direct foreign investment overseas or outsource operations to companies abroad. For example, the surge of outsourcing of services-related functions to India discussed above may be threatened by the military tensions between India and Pakistan, two countries with nuclear arsenals (Schroeder, 2003a).

Likewise, the outbreak of SARS put a spotlight on global health security issues, particularly the potential for new and recurring infectious diseases to spread quickly in a world where people move rapidly from place to place. From a first case in November 2002 in Guangdong province in southern China, SARS spread within a few months to infect more than 4,800 people in 26 countries in Asia, Africa, Europe, Australia, and North America (Lemonick and Park, 2003). The costs of the SARS outbreak have been estimated to equal at least $30 billion as a result of lost tourism, falling retail sales, and market turmoil, among other things. At the same time, as a result of a global effort by scientists, health professionals, and others to identify the disease, develop diagnostic tests, and assess options for treatment and prevention, the outbreak was brought under control. The SARS experience illustrates both the potential for infectious diseases to spread globally as a result of increased world integration and how information technologies and global networks can marshal the resources to treat such diseases and curtail their spread.

FORCES BEHIND GLOBAL ECONOMIC INTEGRATION

World trade and financial flows are the two dominant components of global economic integration. Their growth can be attributed to a number of factors, among them declining costs of transporting goods, falling communication and information-transmission costs, and reductions in tariffs and other barriers to international exchange. In many cases, these factors have influenced both trade and capital flows.

Declining Communication and Information-Transmission Costs

During the nineteenth century, the growth in trade was fueled by declining transportation costs following the establishment of navigable waterways (e.g., the Erie Canal), the debut of the steamship, the introduction of the railroad, and the development of mechanical refrigeration (O'Rourke and Williamson, 2000). In the latter half of the twentieth century, a key driver of the growth of trade and capital flows has been declining costs associated with transporting "weightless" communications—data and other information content. For example, the shifting trade and investment patterns of the last few decades have been facilitated by the advances in telecommunications and computer technology and the rapidly declining prices of that technology that were discussed in the previous chapter. As Figure 4.7 illustrates, a call from New York to London that would have cost $1 in 1950 cost just 6 cents as of 1990, and the call is essentially free today using the Internet (although the quality may not be as good). Through voice, video, and electronic communications, firms can work with subsidiaries or suppliers in other countries and ensure the quality and timeliness of product delivery necessary to meet their own production processes. The quality of communications has improved as well, and that has facilitated the transfer of such functional areas as call centers from the United States to countries overseas. For example, telecommunications speed has improved between the United States and India as near-instant communications

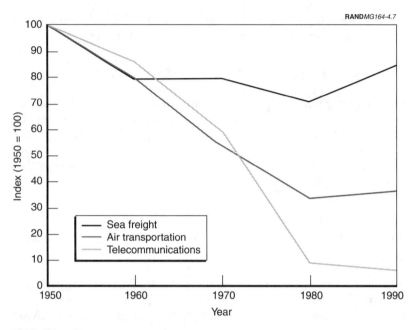

SOURCE: Hufbauer (1991).

NOTES: Average ocean freight and port charges per short ton of import and export cargo. Average air transportation cost per passenger mile. Cost of a three-minute telephone call from New York to London.

Figure 4.7—Transportation and Telecommunications Costs, 1950–1990

through undersea fiber optic cables replaced satellite communications, which entailed a three- to four-second delay (Wharton School, 2002b).

In addition to lower communication costs, the revolution in information technologies also provides a mechanism for rapid transmission across electronic networks of inputs and outputs in the IT-enabled services sector. The technologies also provide the means for supervising work products, monitoring quality, and improving service links between production locations in such areas as transportation and insurance. Other technological innovations support increased scope for inexpensive customization of components and parts (IMF, 2002). Just as the development of these technologies led to the vertical disintegration of firms domestically and outsourcing to

U.S.-based contractors, these same technologies enabled firms to consider outsourcing on an international scale to take advantage of lower costs overseas.

Reductions in transportation costs have also played a role in the expansion of trade in goods in the last half century, but the price declines have not been as dramatic as those affecting communication costs (see Figure 4.7). The most important innovations in the past half-century have been the use of containers for ocean transport and the advent of jet engines and cargo aircraft. While transportation costs for sea freight transport have been relatively stable since 1960 and air travel since 1980, shipping times have fallen markedly as transportation methods have shifted to faster ocean vessels and jet aircraft. For example, between 1965 and 1998, the share of U.S. imports arriving by air increased from 6 to 25 percent (IMF, 2002). The increased reliance on air delivery has allowed greater trade in perishable food and related items (e.g., cut flowers), and inputs into just-in-time processes. Trading potential remains limited in many less developed countries due to their more limited transportation infrastructure (e.g., roads, airports, and container ports) which results in higher costs. Transportation costs and times may rise in the future, particularly in the container shipping business, due to additional security measures designed to thwart international terrorists.

Falling Barriers to Trade and Capital Flows

Since the end of World War II, the increased volume of trade and financial flows has also been propelled by a series of bilateral and multilateral agreements, as well as unilateral reforms, that have reduced impediments to global integration.[13] The general pattern involved reducing barriers to trade, followed by removing impediments to capital market integration. Initial progress was made among developed economies in the 1960s and 1970s. Liberalization

---

[13]While there are parallels between the late nineteenth century and the period after World War II in terms of falling transportation and communications costs (albeit with different technologies), the same can not be said of trade barriers. The growth of world trade in the late nineteenth century cannot be attributed to more liberal trade policy. No overall decline in tariffs in the Atlantic economies occurred between the 1870s and World War I (O'Rourke and Williamson, 2000).

among developing economies followed in the 1980s and 1990s (Krugman, 1995; IMF, 2002).

After World War II, the General Agreement on Tariffs and Trade (GATT) was established as an international organization devoted to promoting greater world trade. A series of multilateral trade negotiations, among the more recent the Uruguay Round completed in 1994, produced steady declines in tariffs. Other regional trade agreements, such as the North American Free Trade Agreement (NAFTA), which went into effect in 1994, promoted greater trading activity with specific U.S. trading partners. In the case of the NAFTA trading partners, Mexico and Canada, trade barriers have been reduced substantially. All goods traded between the United States and Canada are now duty-free, while Mexican tariffs have fallen below 2 percent on average and two-thirds of U.S. exports to Mexico are now duty-free (USDA, 2001). Between 1994 and 2002, total U.S. goods trade activity with Canada and Mexico combined increased 75 percent, from $346 billion to $607 billion.[14] Finally, specialized agreements have focused on particular categories of products. For example, the 1996 Information Technology Agreement eliminated most tariffs on trade in semiconductors, computers, software, telecommunications equipment, and other high-technology products (Destler, 1999). Transportation costs have been further reduced by the expanded use of open-skies agreements, which eliminate restrictions on airline service to and from different countries.[15]

With trade flows increasing as trade barriers declined, the move to flexible exchange rates in the early 1970s resulted in a tremendous growth of international capital mobility, prompted by the desire for greater portfolio diversification (i.e., risk pooling) (Obstfeld, 1998). The end of fixed exchange rate regimes allowed countries to relax regulations and restrictive capital controls in the late 1970s and early 1980s while maintaining autonomy in the setting of monetary policy. Such new financial instruments as global equity mutual funds emerged as well to promote international portfolio investments.

---

[14]Based on data collected by the Bureau of Economic Analysis at the U.S. Department of Commerce available at http://www.bea.doc.gov/bea/international/ bp_web/list.cfm?anon=131&registered=0, Table 2.

[15]For information on such agreements, see the State Department website at http:// www.state.gov/e/eb/tra/c661.htm.

In addition to relaxed capital controls that affect currency and financial markets, barriers to FDI have also been eroding over time. For example, between 1991 and 2001, the number of annual regulatory changes favorable to FDI on a worldwide basis grew from 80 affecting 35 countries to 194 applicable to 71 countries (UNCTAD, 2002). The Asian and Pacific region accounted for 43 percent of the changes in 2001 alone. Such changes include more liberal entry and operational conditions, sectoral liberalization, and guarantees. Other changes promoting greater FDI include bilateral investment treaties, double taxation treaties, and various strategies to promote export-oriented investment (e.g., general marketing, image-building, and so on). Singapore is viewed as one of the early movers in the area of investment promotion, with efforts that date back to the late 1960s.

The growing internationalization of production, represented by the increase in FDI, has thus benefited from the economic and technological forces that have promoted greater trade, as well as growing liberalization of FDI policies. Indeed, trade and capital liberalization are increasingly viewed as complementary (Hummels, Rapoport and Yi, 1998). For example, greater incentive exists for FDI when trade barriers are lowered, as the effects of even low trade barriers, such as tariffs, are compounded by the multiple cross-border transactions associated with each segment in the production chain. Likewise, when barriers to FDI are reduced, firms have greater incentive for vertical specialization in trade because they can invest directly in the various stages of the production process.

While the trend has been toward increased trade liberalization, substantial barriers to trade still exist for many countries. For example, average trade-weighted tariffs in 2001 were 28 percent in India, 14 percent in China, and 9 percent in Argentina, compared with 2.8 percent in the United States (World Bank, 2003b). Such tariffs are generally higher in developing countries, but they are high as well in other developed countries for selected imports (e.g., food products and textiles in the United States and agricultural goods in Japan and the European Union) (WTO, 2003). Other impediments to further trade in goods and services include quotas, product-specific technical regulations or standards (e.g., on agricultural products or sophisticated equipment), and government subsidies of export-oriented industries. Agricultural subsidies remain notably prominent among major industrialized countries and serve as a barrier to increased imports, especially from low-income countries (WTO, 2003).

Future Forces Should Foster Further Globalization

The future course of economic globalization in the U.S. economy is difficult to predict with much certainty. It depends not only on economic conditions in the United States but also on economic conditions in our major trading partners, as well as on future developments in international trade and investment agreements and other liberalization efforts. Clearly the path in the last half-century has been one of the growing importance of trade and capital movements on a global scale, and, in all likelihood, that path will continue albeit with cyclical swings above and below that trend line. Future growth in worldwide trade will be spurred by further reductions in telecommunications costs, driven by many of the technological changes discussed in Chapter Three. Technological advances in IT in particular will further support the trend toward internationalization of production, including the shift of IT-enabled services to overseas firms. Surveys of multinational corporations indicate plans for continued FDI in the next several years, with great potential for higher investment in developing countries with plentiful labor, flexible economies, and open trading regimes (UNCTAD, 2002).

The projections of future trade activity for the United States through 2010 prepared by BLS show exports increasing at an average annual rate of 7.8 percent between 2000 and 2010, while imports are projected to increase 7.9 percent per year (Su, 2001). For exports, this is an acceleration over the trend from 1990 to 2000 (a 7.0 percent annual rate of change), while for imports it is a lower rate of growth compared with the prior decade (a 9.3 percent annual rate of change). The combined effect is to raise the combination of exports plus imports to 44.2 percent of GDP by 2010, compared with the recent peak of 25.5 percent in 2000 (see Figure 4.3). It is important to note that these projections, published in November 2001, did not take into account the potential effects of the September 11, 2001, terrorist attacks.

Even if the share of exports and imports in the U.S. economy reaches nearly 45 percent by 2010, the U.S. economy would not achieve the hypothetical state of "perfect economic integration." Frankel (2000) points out that since the U.S. economy represents about one-fourth of gross world product, if the United States were equally likely to buy goods and services from foreign sources as domestic ones, the U.S. import-to-GDP ratio would equal 0.75. This is about six times the level of the current ratio of about 0.12. The two other large economies, Japan and the combined European Union, also exhibit ratios comparable to the United States. In contrast, the economies of most other countries are considerably smaller, constituting on average about one-half of one percent of world output. In a perfectly integrated world, the average country would thus buy or sell 99.5 percent of their output overseas. Only Singapore and Hong Kong attain this level of integration today. Among the factors cited by Frankel (2000) that restrain further economic integration are differences in currencies, languages, and political systems, along with the effects of distance, borders, and other geographical and trade-policy factors.

Of course the projections for the future level of trade in the U.S. economy depend critically on policies with respect to tariffs and other trade and capital flow barriers, both in the United States and abroad. While major trade agreements were negotiated in the two decades between 1973 and 1994, future negotiations on major agreements involving the United States were stalled by the failure to renew "fast-track" negotiating authority in 1994 during the Clinton administration (Destler, 1999). Such authority, available to every U.S. president since Gerald Ford, streamlines the process of negotiating international trade agreements.[16] As of August 2002, this authority—now labeled "trade promotion authority" (TPA)—was reestablished through the Trade Act of 2002.[17]

With this law, the outlook for greater openness of the U.S. economy looks quite promising. It is expected that new bilateral trade agree-

---

[16]Specifically, fast track committed the Congress to vote on trade agreements within a fixed period (90 days) with no amendments. This reduced concerns among negotiating partners that Congress would fail to act on or would modify an agreement, once negotiated (Destler, 1999).

[17]Trade promotion authority is set to expire again on June 1, 2005. The Act also included a number of other provisions renewing and enhancing several existing agreements with countries in South America, the Caribbean, and Africa (Mewhirter and Fullerton, 2002).

ments will be negotiated in the near term (e.g., agreements with Chile and Singapore have recently been finalized). Meanwhile, negotiations will resume in full force for more-complex multilateral agreements, such as the Free Trade Area of the Americas, which has been in process since late 1994 (Mewhirter and Fullerton, 2002). Negotiations pursued under TPA will proceed according to a set of principles that cover goals for agricultural products, industrial goods, and services, as well as objectives with respect to labor, the environment, intellectual property rights, and child labor, among others. The WTO, established by the Uruguay Round ending in 1995, provides further institutional support for negotiating new trade agreements among the 148 member countries and for enforcing the provisions of existing agreements.

Advancement of trade liberalization cannot be assumed to be inevitable, however (Frankel, 2000). It is conceivable that further liberalization will fail to progress at a pace consistent with the recent past, as already appears to be the case with the current Doha round of WTO negotiations (Leonhardt, 2003). However, while a stall in progress is not out of the question, it seems less likely in the current climate that the liberalization experienced to date will be reversed. Yet, it is constructive to consider the experience of the late nineteenth and early twentieth centuries. Historical analysis by economists suggest that the unfavorable distributional consequences of the wave of globalization more than a century ago resulted in the previously mentioned trade (and immigration) backlash that occurred in the interwar period (see the review by Williamson, 1998). One recent analysis of workers in Great Britain suggests that workers' perceptions of job insecurity are higher the greater the amount of foreign direct investment in the industry within which they work. This suggests a direct link between globalization in an industry and worker insecurity (Scheve and Slaughter, 2002). Such insecurity, along with other concerns about the consequences of globalization, may contribute to a backlash against international integration.

Most analysts expect that, in the United States at least, the protectionist pressures of the past are unlikely to emerge to the same degree. However, there may be efforts to link further trade liberalization with particular countries or regions to concerns over labor standards, the environment, human rights, the existence of democratic institutions, or the protection of property rights (Destler, 1999). Just as blue-collar workers in the manufacturing sector protested over the movement of jobs overseas in the past two decades, a new wave of concern centers on the movement of white-collar jobs overseas (Engardio, 2003). For example, when a New Jersey state senator learned that a U.S.-based contractor to the state was outsourcing work overseas, a bill was introduced in the state assembly requiring workers on state contracts to be U.S. citizens or legal aliens (Schroeder, 2003b). Several other states are considering similar laws. A total of nine jobs were affected in the New Jersey situation, yet this case drew considerable attention and has broader implications for workers employed with public funds as well as private-sector workers.

There are also signs that other countries, especially low-income nations, are more reluctant to seek further trade liberalization without the major industrialized countries relaxing some of their remaining barriers (e.g., subsidies for agricultural products, patent protections on pharmaceuticals) (Leonhardt, 2003). If so, this may limit the pace of expansion of trade between the United States and developing countries.

HOW ECONOMIC GLOBALIZATION IS AFFECTING THE U.S. ECONOMY, THE WORKFORCE, AND THE WORKPLACE

The phenomenon of economic globalization creates both opportunities and challenges for the United States. One the one hand, increased global economic integration produces a range of benefits from expanded markets for U.S. products to lower prices and greater variety of goods and services to consume. Economists have long argued that countries engaged in cross-border trading benefit from increased specialization in the production of goods and services in sectors in which they have a comparative advantage based on available labor, capital, and natural resources (Helpman, 1999; Frankel, 2000). With open markets, countries produce and export those goods and services for which its costs are relatively less and import those goods and services that can be produced relatively less expensively in other countries. Such specialization and exchange results in a more efficient use of resources and raises living standards in both sending and receiving countries. Trade is also theorized to promote more efficient production through economies of scale and to spur innovation as domestic firms have access to and compete in the global marketplace. Open capital markets allow investors in different countries to pool risks, they provide opportunities for borrowing abroad to finance investment, and they guard against unsound fiscal and monetary policies on the part of governments (Obstfeld, 1998).

On the other hand, while greater integration in world trade and capital markets can enhance welfare at the national level and over the long term, there can be short-term and longer-term consequences for particular segments of the U.S. economy and workforce as labor, capital, and other inputs are reallocated to their most efficient uses. Certain firms and industries may find that in a global marketplace they cannot compete with lower-priced imports and will go out of business. Workers in affected industries and firms must be reabsorbed into other sectors of the economy—perhaps in sectors more insulated from foreign competition—or they may drop out of the labor force. Even when reemployed, workers may experience long-term wage reductions as a result of displacement because human capital they acquired is less valuable upon reemployment. Markets open to trade can also experience longer-lasting effects on the wage structure to the extent that the prices for different productive inputs (e.g., labor of different types) become more equal across trading partners.

As globalization expands to integrate new industries and segments of the workforce previously insulated from global economic pressures and integrates more of the world's population into the global marketplace, what can we expect in terms of the future of work? To address that question, in this section we consider what we know about the consequences of globalization in the last several decades—both the aggregate and distributional effects—as the share of trade in the U.S. economy has more than doubled, and capital, labor, and knowledge have flowed more freely among countries. While the level and nature of economic globalization can be expected to evolve in ways that have been described above, many of the implications of further globalization can be inferred from recent experience. In particular, we focus on the implications of the growing importance of global trade and capital integration in the U.S. economy in terms of overall economic performance, followed by the effects on competition and innovation, employment, wage levels and the wage structure, and employment relationships.

While our discussion in the remainder of this section focuses on the United States, a related issue concerns the consequences of globalization for other countries. As economic globalization has proceeded, great interest has focused on whether the results are good or bad for developing countries. Research on this issue generally finds that when developing countries become more economically integrated with the rest of the world, they too benefit in the aggregate in terms of higher economic growth (see Box 4.1). Worldwide, the distributional consequences are manifested in the growing gap between industrialized nations and other countries, primarily those with the lowest incomes, which have not participated in the latest wave of global integration.

Strong Economic Performance Accompanied Increased Globalization

The consensus among economists is that, at the aggregate level, the increased integration of the U.S. economy in the past half-century has had a favorable effect on incomes, prices, consumer choice, competition, and innovation (Burtless et al., 1998). In terms of long-run growth, Figure 4.8 illustrates that, at the same time that trade's share of the U.S. economy more than doubled, real GDP per capita—a measure of U.S. standard of living—did so also. While there have been the inevitable dips and rebounds associated with the business cycle (the shaded areas mark periods from the business cycle peak to trough), the long-run trend has been one of increased standards of living.[18] Trade contributes to long-run income growth by allowing U.S. workers to specialize in the production of goods and services that are our comparative advantage, while gaining access to goods and services overseas that can be produced at lower cost.

---

[18]When compared with other major industrialized economies, the United States has maintained the highest standard of living since the early twentieth century (see the comparative data series prepared by BLS on GDP per capita available at: http://www. bls.gov/fls/). While the economies of Japan and Germany grew faster after the end of World War II, they did not continue to close the gap with U.S. living standards at the same pace after the early 1970s. Per-capita GDP in the two countries has stagnated at about 80 percent of the U.S. level as of the late 1990s.

Box 4.1

The Consequences of Globalization for Other Countries

An extensive literature in economics explores the consequences of trade and financial liberalization on economic growth and well-being. In terms of developed economies, the conclusions are much the same as the ones we reach above in discussion of the benefits and costs of trade for the United States. The benefits and costs of more openness in developing countries have also been explored through case studies and analyses of data for multiple countries, industries, and firms over time (IMF, 2002; Baldwin, 2003). A general finding from that literature is that developing countries, on the whole, benefit from trade integration in terms of higher income per capita, increased productivity, and higher rates of economic growth provided that lower trade barriers are accompanied by appropriate exchange rate, monetary, and fiscal policies.

Financial crises, such as external debt defaults and currency crises (e.g., an exchange rate depreciation), have been more common in the last 25 years among developing countries with relatively low openness to trade, rather than among those that have been more globally integrated (IMF, 2002). Over the long run, there is also evidence that greater financial integration reduces volatility in national output (GDP), as well as rates of inflation and exchange rate shocks. At the same time, higher rates of growth associated with greater openness do not appear to affect the distribution of income within countries, although the poverty rate can fall because of rising incomes on average.

While economic globalization appears to benefit those countries that open their product and financial markets, the income gap between rich and poor countries has grown. Considering the twentieth century as a whole, per-capita GDP increased sixfold for the richest quarter of the world's population, while the poorest quarter experienced less than a threefold increase (IMF, 2000). By and large, those low-income countries that did not see their incomes converge toward those of higher-income countries were those that did not successfully integrate into the world economy—nations in sub-Saharan Africa, the Middle East, and the former Soviet Union (World Bank, 2002a).

Box 4.1—continued

Broader measures of welfare, such as life expectancy and other social indicators, show more convergence across countries than what is found forper-capita incomes, in part because technological breakthroughs in agricultural and medical technology were made available despite these countries' low incomes. Further diffusion of technological advances offers the potential for stimulating economic growth and human development in a virtuous circle beyond what would otherwise be possible (UNDP, 2001). Market forces are unlikely to be sufficient to achieve this goal for a variety of reasons. Instead, further progress is likely to depend on international private- and public-sector initiatives to advance the development of and access to appropriate technologies for the world's poorest countries.

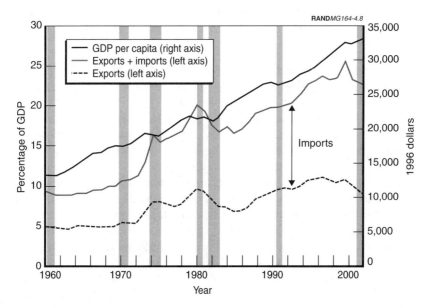

SOURCES: BEA U.S. International Transactions Accounts Data, Table 1 (http://www.bea.gov/bea/international/bp_web); BEA NIPA Tables, Tables 1.1 and 8.7 (http://www.bea.gov/bea/dn/nipaweb/SelectTable.asp); and NBER Business Cycle Expansions and Contractions (http://www.nber.org/cycles/).

NOTE: Gray shading marks business cycle recessions (from peak to trough).

Figure 4.8—U.S. Trade and GDP Per Capita, 1960–2002

In a completely closed economy, U.S. consumers would consume only goods and services produced with inputs of materials and labor available within our borders. We would neither enjoy Chilean fruits in the middle of the North American winter nor savor the taste of a French Bordeaux wine with dinner. We would not drive Japanese cars, play with toys made in China, or wear athletic shoes assembled in Indonesia. From the perspective of U.S. consumers, trade will typically expand the range of choices available and may also result in the reduction of prices for some goods when foreign suppliers can produce them at lower cost. In their buying decisions, consumers face more choices, including imports priced lower than similar domestically produced items. For example, between 1980 and 1996, the price of imports to the United States rose less rapidly than the price of exports, and both rose considerably less than prices overall in the U.S. economy (Burtless et al., 1998).[19] Such price competition requires U.S. producers to adopt more efficient methods and reduce their costs of production.

As economic globalization has proceeded in recent decades, other countries have experienced strong rates of growth with levels of economic integration that exceed those of the United States today. For example, Ireland, known as the "Celtic tiger," consistently ranks as one of the most globally integrated countries, with a number-one ranking on two recent indexes, based on the extent of economic integration, use of technology, and other factors.[20] Between 1991 and 2001, Ireland's annual growth rate averaged 7 percent per year and unemployment fell dramatically (World Bank, 2003a). Fueled by an open policy with respect to FDI, strategic investment in the telecommunications sector, and investment in the technical education of its relatively young labor force, Ireland's export growth since 1994, primarily in services and high-tech industries, has been the highest in the OECD (Burnham, 2003). While the United States is unlikely to achieve the levels of trade experienced by Ireland simply

---

[19]Import prices benefited from the strong U.S. dollar during parts of the period. When the dollar value is high relative to other currencies, it reduces the costs of imports to the United States, although it makes U.S. exports less competitive.

[20]See the Globalization Index published annually by *Foreign Policy* together with A. T. Kearney (available for 2003 at http://www.foreignpolicy.com/wwwboard/g-index.php) and the index generated by Andersen and Herbertsson (2003).

because of the size of the U.S. economy relative to other countries, the example of Ireland and other countries illustrates that economic globalization can be accompanied by strong economic performance.

Global Integration Expands Markets, Intensifies Competition, and Spurs Innovation

For U.S. firms, a more open world economy expands the size of the market they can sell to, elevating sales and possibly reducing costs and raising productivity through economies of scale. Larger world markets can increase the return from fixed investment in R&D (e.g., in the pharmaceuticals industry). In markets characterized by network effects (recall Metcalfe's Law discussed in Chapter Three), such as telecommunications, expanded world markets increase product value. U.S. producers also gain access to expanded markets for capital goods and intermediate inputs, which can reduce the costs of final goods. At the same time, the increased openness of U.S. markets, both through export competition and import competition, pressures U.S. firms to remain competitive in the global marketplace. Firms must compete not only with potential rivals in the domestic market but also with those overseas or transplanted to the United States through FDI. The expectation is that such market forces will require U.S. firms that face import competition, or that export products to other countries, to improve their performance over time or risk going out of business. Such forces will spur innovation and adoption of technologies and production processes that can reduce cost. Trade also provides access to foreign technology and ideas (e.g., business organization practices), which further allow productivity gains for U.S. firms.

Consistent with these expectations, one recent study concluded that, of nine industries examined in the United States, Germany, and Japan, those that faced greater international competition were the most productive primarily as a result of adopting innovative manufacturing design methods and best-practice organizational methods (Baily and Gersbach, 1995). The U.S. automotive industry is one example considered in the study. As long as U.S. auto companies did not directly compete against Japanese auto firms, they would not risk making the innovative, automation-related changes, such as agile manufacturing and design for manufacturing, that would lead to productivity gains. Faced with competition, U.S. auto manufacturers began adopting many of the innovations used by Japanese auto firms.

Likewise, many of the changes in firm organization discussed in the context of technological change can be tied to globalization as well. Increased competition in import-competing or export-competing industries can lead firms to adopt innovations in production processes and management practices to boost productivity and lower costs. Thus, the trend toward vertical disintegration of the firm through outsourcing and the shift to high-performance workplace practices and associated compensation systems can be linked to globalization. While the technologies discussed in Chapter Three enable these changes in firm organization and employment relationships, global competition provides the impetus for their adoption.

In looking ahead, a critical challenge in the face of continued global competition will be for the United States to maintain its predominant position in the high-technology field. Recent experience indicates that U.S. leadership cannot be taken for granted. The United States was the world's leading producer of high-technology products (specifically aerospace, computers and office machinery, communications equipment, and pharmaceuticals) with about one-third of world production from 1980 to 1995.[21] During the 1980s, however, U.S. producers faced substantial competition from Japan. Much of U.S. firms' world market share lost during that period was subsequently recovered during the 1990s as U.S. high-technology firms were forced to innovate and reduce costs. With recovery in the latter part of the 1990s, the U.S. share of the world market for high-technology products reached 36 percent as of 1998. Among U.S. high-technology industries, aerospace was the only one to lose world market share in both the 1980s and 1990s, although that was also the sector in which the United States had the largest world market share to begin with.

In terms of exports, the U.S. high-technology sector had nearly 20 percent of the world total in 1998, yet this represents a decline from the 1980 peak of 26 percent as a result of competition from such

---

[21]The results reported in the remainder of this section draw on an analysis of trade data prepared by the NSF (2002).

newly industrializing countries as Singapore and Taiwan. The United States was also the export leader in all the component high-technology industries except for pharmaceuticals. These shares, however, were also lower than they had been in 1980 (with the exception of those for communications equipment). In the future, such countries as China are likely to emerge as significant competitors in various segments of the high-technology market. For example, as noted above, China is currently challenging the lead of U.S. and European companies in the development of the next generation of cellular phone technology. In emerging areas, such as nanotechnology, the United States is viewed as a leader in R&D, yet other countries including Japan are making major investments in the area and could eclipse the U.S. advantage (NNI, 2003).

The United States also currently leads the way for knowledge-intensive services industries—those incorporating science, engineering, and technology in their services or delivery of their services—with about 40 percent of world revenues between 1980 and 1998. In each of five sectors—communications, financial, business, educational, and health—the United States was the leading provider of services as of 1998. The U.S. share of the world market as of that year reached 53 percent for financial services (Japan was second at 6 percent) and 36 percent for business services (France ranked second at 17 percent). It was 37 percent for communications services (followed by Britain with less than 18 percent). The United States has also consistently maintained a dominant position in trade in intellectual property, including royalties and fees. In the future, U.S. leadership in these fields depends on continued advances in technology, as well as having a skilled workforce capable of producing knowledge-intensive services.

Trade Alters the Mix of Jobs, with Displacement in Some Sectors Matched by Growth in Others

Perhaps the most talked-about aspect of foreign trade is the movement of jobs from the United States to other countries as a result of increased specialization. Newspaper accounts abound regarding the closure of U.S. manufacturing plants with the jobs transferred overseas to be performed by workers receiving lower wages. With the increased pattern of vertical trade, manufacturing jobs in lower-wage countries may include intermediate products as well as final products. More recently, as discussed earlier in this chapter, there is movement of higher-skilled jobs and white-collar jobs overseas—either through outsourcing or offshoring—as countries with lower wages invest in education and training, including in the technology field. With increasingly skilled workers in low-wage countries, the cost-quality trade-off in shifting work overseas is not as stark as it used to be. As noted above, one recent estimate projects 3.3 million U.S. services-related jobs, or about 2 percent of employment, will be outsourced to such low-wage countries as China, India, Russia, and the Philippines by 2015 (McCarthy, 2002).

These examples, viewed in isolation, raise concerns that trade has been and will continue to be responsible for net job loss, whether in manufacturing or in services. While it is true that some jobs previously performed by U.S. workers are now performed by workers overseas, it is also true that trade generates new jobs for U.S. workers in domestic exporting industries. As of 1999, an estimated 11.6 million jobs in the United States were supported directly or indirectly by goods and services exports, representing about 9 percent of employment.[22] With continued growth in exports relative to GDP, that share is likely to expand. In two industries—computers and electronic products and primary metals—more than one-third of jobs were tied to exports as of 1997 (U.S. DOC, 2001). Other sectors, like agriculture, also rely heavily on foreign markets for the goods they produce. On balance, research suggests that the employment-generating effect of expanding exports exceeds the employment-reducing effect of increasing imports (Kletzer, 2002) (see Box 4.2). Thus, the consequence of trade for overall employment levels is, at most, small, and there is little reason to expect this pattern to differ as the United States becomes more integrated into the global economy.

Although the overall effect of trade on economywide employment levels appears to be relatively small, the increased openness of the U.S. economy does result in job losses in some sectors, while other sectors experience gains, a feature that can be expected in the future

---

[22]These data are cited by the Office of the U.S. Trade Representative, available at http://www.ustr.gov/outreach/statemap.shtml.

as well. In the same way, technological advances will displace workers in certain occupations that are no longer required, while raising the demand for workers in other occupations. Kletzer (1998, 2000, 2002) considers the link between trade and job displacement by examining patterns of job displacement in manufacturing industries facing import competition from the mid-1970s to the mid-1990s.[23] In U.S. industries with increasing foreign competition, such as footwear, leather products, watches and clocks, and toys, more jobs have been lost over the period studied and the adjustment burden on workers displaced in those sectors could have been substantial. At the same time, other industries facing import competition (e.g., office machines, photographic equipment) have experienced rates of displacement below the economywide average. Still others with higher job displacement (e.g., space vehicles, health services supplies) faced little or no import competition. Kletzer's assessment is that, while trade can be clearly linked to job loss in some import-sensitive sectors, the economywide effect of trade on job displacement is small.

As a result of trade-related displacement that will occur in the future, workers in the shrinking industries and occupations may face spells of joblessness, and they may experience permanent wage losses. Recent experience with economywide job displacement, due to any number of factors, provides some perspective on the expected consequences. During 1997 and 1998, 1.9 million workers with long tenure (at least three years) permanently lost their job because of a plant move or closing, a position that was shifted or abolished, or insufficient work.[24] That represented 2.5 percent of all long-tenured

---

[23]Job displacement in this context is typically defined as an involuntary (to the employee) job loss resulting from an employer's operating decisions (e.g., plant closure, position elimination, etc.).

[24]This discussion is based on a special analysis of the displaced worker supplement to the February 2000 CPS, a biennial survey of displaced workers (see Helwig, 2001). Data from the January 2002 CPS displaced worker supplement show 4.0 million workers with long tenure permanently lost their job during the three-year period between 1999 and 2001 due to plant move or closing, a position that was shifted or abolished, or insufficient work (BLS, 2002b). Because the 2002 supplement covers the recent recession, fewer workers (two out of three) were reemployed as of the survey date. The earnings losses as of 2002 were larger as well, compared with displaced workers in the 2000 survey.

Box 4.2

Trade and Aggregate Employment

Overall, growth in U.S. employment has remained strong over the past four decades as the degree of openness of the U.S. economy expanded. For example, Figure 4.9 plots the employment-to-population ratio—the share of the U.S. population who are employed—along with total trade activity's share of GDP. Again, while the business cycle swings are evident, the longer-run pattern is one of successively higher and higher employment rates with each business cycle peak. The rising employment rate over this period reflects, in large part, the increased labor force participation of women discussed in Chapter Two. Yet, the growing importance of trade in the U.S. economy did not hinder the absorption of these new workers into the labor force (Burtless et al., 1998). Moreover, in the business cycle expansion of the 1990s, while trade represented close to one-quarter of the economy, the unemployment rate reached remarkable lows.

It is the case that the share of employment in the manufacturing sector has been steadily declining, from 43 percent of full-time equivalent employment in the private sector as of 1960 to 23 percent by 2001.[25] But the shift of employment from the goods-producing to the services-producing sectors is part of a long-run trend associated with shifting consumption patterns and productivity gains that predates the growth of trade in the U.S. economy in the postwar era (Kletzer, 2002). Burtless et al. (1998) estimate that trade played at most a small role in the overall decline in manufacturing employment between 1960 and 1994. Instead of the actual decline of 15 percentage points over that period, if the entire trade deficit after 1975 had been eliminated, the decline in the share of manufacturing in overall employment would have been 14 percentage points.

As another example, consider the case of the evidence regarding the effects of NAFTA on U.S. employment. Prior to the passage of NAFTA, extraordinary claims were made of a "giant sucking sound" that repre-

---

[25]Based on data from the Bureau of Economic Analysis, National Income Product Accounts, for 1960 and 2001 (see http://www.bea.doc.gov/bea/dn1.htm).

Box 4.2—continued

sented the movement of jobs and capital south across the Rio Grande. Rigorous studies at the time indicated the benefits would be small but positive for the United States and large and positive for Mexico (Burfisher, Robinson, and Thierfelder, 2001). It has been challenging to isolate the effects of NAFTA, given other economic and policy changes that coincided with the greater openness of trade between the United States and Mexico. However, research indicates that imports from Mexico potentially displaced about 37,000 U.S. jobs annually, primarily in manufacturing (as compared with employment growth during the 1990s of about 200,000 jobs per month). When accounting for increased exports, the consensus among studies is that NAFTA has no overall effect on aggregate employment (Burfisher, Robinson, and Thierfelder, 2001).

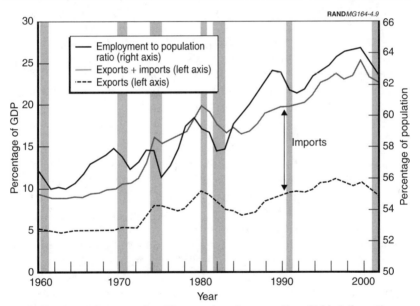

SOURCES: BEA U.S. International Transactions Accounts Data, Table 1 (http://www.bea.gov/bea/international/bp_web); BEA NIPA Tables, Table 1.1 (http://www.bea.gov/bea/dn/nipaweb/SelectTable.asp); BLS Labor Force Statistics from the CPS, Series ID LNS12300000 (http://data.bls.gov/cgi-bin/surveymost?ln); and NBER Business Cycle Expansions and Contractions (http://www.nber.org/cycles/).

NOTE: Gray shading marks business cycle recessions (from peak to trough).

Figure 4.9—U.S. Trade and Employment-to-Population Ratio, 1960–2002

workers (Helwig, 2001).[26] Among long-tenured workers displaced during that period, nearly four in five were reemployed as of February 2000 (Helwig, 2001). The typical, or median, worker displaced in the late 1990s experienced a little more than five weeks of unemployment before finding a new job. Earlier in the 1990s, when the labor market was weaker, the typical unemployment spell was about three weeks longer. Less than one in two displaced workers who were reemployed relied on unemployment insurance benefits, while one in five exhausted their benefits by the time they found a new job. About half of all reemployed workers switched to a different industry but most stayed in the same occupation.

While the typical or median reemployed displaced worker during 1997 or 1998 reported no loss in earnings between their old and new job, workers who remained employed over the same period experienced an average increase of 10 percent in earnings. In recessionary periods, the short-term earnings loss among those reemployed is closer to 15 percent (Helwig, 2001). Studies of the longer-term consequences of job displacement suggest permanent earnings losses in the range of 5 to 15 percent (Kletzer, 1998). In the case of workers displaced from import-competing manufacturing jobs, earnings losses are considerably larger for those reemployed in the trade or services sector compared with those who are reemployed in manufacturing (Kletzer, 2000).

Because the phenomenon of trade-related displacement in the IT sector and IT-enabled services sector is a relatively recent phenomenon, researchers have not focused on the specific consequences of job loss for these workers. Other studies of job displacement suggest that, in general, more-educated workers are reemployed more rapidly than their less-educated counterparts and their relative earnings losses tend to be smaller, presumably because their skills are more transferable from one job to the next (Kletzer, 1998). This suggest that, while painful, trade-related job loss associated with higher-skilled services sector employment (e.g., IT-related jobs) may not be as costly in terms of unemployment and permanent

---

[26]Kletzer's (1998) survey article reports displacement rates closer to 10 percent when displaced workers of any tenure are counted relative to the pool of all workers.

wage loss as earlier waves of blue-collar, trade-related, job displacement were.

To the extent that global economic integration has distributional consequences in the form of job losses for some U.S. workers, economists have long noted that the aggregate gains to the country can be used, through the tax and transfer system, to provide assistance to those workers. This approach places the spotlight on domestic policy, rather than on trade policy, through programs such as Trade Adjustment Assistance (TAA), established in 1962 and reauthorized in 2002. The program provides for up to 104 additional weeks of income support (called Trade Readjustment Allowances) once unemployment insurance benefits are exhausted for workers whose job loss is associated with increased import competition (including those affected by NAFTA, as well as "secondary" workers of an upstream supplier or downstream producer).[27] Other benefits include up to 104 weeks of training, job search allowances, relocation allowances, and tax credits for assistance with health insurance coverage. An Alternative TAA Program, provided for with the 2002 TAA reauthorization but not yet implemented, allows qualified workers age 50 and above who are reemployed full-time to receive for up to two years, in lieu of other benefits, half the difference between their previous wage and their new wage, up to a maximum of $10,000. This represents a form of insurance against earnings losses associated with trade-related displacement. The 2002 reauthorization also established a TAA program for farmers.

Although nearly 228,000 workers were certified under the TAA program in fiscal year 1999, far fewer received readjustment allowances (37,000) or training (32,000), primarily because they were reemployed before they were eligible to claim benefits (U.S. GAO, 2000). In the latter part of the 1990s, the largest numbers of trade-affected displaced workers in these programs were in the apparel and textile industries. Limited data indicate that the program meets with some success in reemployment rates and the extent of wage replacement.

---

[27]As part of the Trade Adjustment Assistance Reform Act of 2002, the basic income support period of 52 weeks was extended by 26 weeks for those involved in training, and another 26 weeks for those requiring remedial education. For a summary of the 2002 Act, see http://www.doleta.gov/tradeact/2002act_summary.cfm.

Global Competition Has Had Modest Effects on the Wage Structure to Date

Just as technology has been linked to the growing wage gap between more- and less-skilled workers, economists have pointed to globalization as another driver of falling real wages for low-skill workers and, concomitantly, rising wage disparities. Thus, some have argued that increased trade with low-wage countries not only is responsible for the loss of jobs in the United States, but also for putting downward pressure on U.S. wages. The pressure is believed to be particularly heavy on less-skilled U.S. workers, who must now compete with their counterparts in other countries who are paid considerably lower wages. The trends in wages by education level reported in Figure 3.8 confirm that real wages have been declining since the 1970s for workers with a high school education or less, while they have been rising for more-educated workers.

The argument that trade has depressed average wages is not supported by the evidence. For one thing, jobs in export-oriented sectors are associated with higher wages on average; in the goods sector, for example, export-related jobs pay 13 to 16 percent more than those not related to export.[28] More to the point, Burtless et al. (1998) show that the stagnation in wage growth since 1973 is attributable to the slower productivity growth after that year, not to changes in patterns of trade.

It has been more challenging to determine the effect of trade on relative wages between workers of different education or skill levels, or overall wage inequality. Indeed, economists have been intensively studying and debating the relationship between globalization and the U.S. wage structure for at least a decade, using a number of approaches (see Box 4.3).[29] While some differences can be found across studies, most analysts find a relatively modest effect (see, for example, reviews by Freeman, 1995; Richardson, 1995). Perhaps 10 to 20 percent of the relative wage decline of the wages of low-skilled

---

[28]See the Office of the U.S. Trade Representative data available at http://www.ustr.gov/outreach/statemap.shtml.

[29]For a discussion of the strengths and weaknesses of the various approaches see Burtless (1995), Freeman (1995), Collins (1998), Krugman (2000), and Leamer (2000).

Box 4.3

Methods for Assessing the Contribution of Trade to the Changing Wage Structure

The expectation that the wage structure is linked to trade comes from a classical theorem in trade economics stating that trade between two countries will result in the equalization of factor prices, such as the wages of less- and more-skilled workers (Bhagwati and Dehejia, 1994; Helpman, 1999).[30] *The challenge in testing this theory is to make inferences about the U.S. wage structure in a situation that we do not observe: the absence of the growth of trade in the last several decades.*

In the absence of observing this situation, one set of studies proceeds by examining labor quantities associated with domestic production and trade. The effect on relative wages by education level is determined by comparing the actual level of low-skill employment in import-competing industries with what employment would have been if all imports were produced in the United States. The same comparison is made regarding U.S. exports. These comparisons are based on the following market relations: By purchasing imports from low-wage countries, the United States reduces the effective demand for low-skilled domestic workers, thereby placing downward pressure on low-skill wages. U.S. exports of higher-skilled products to low-income countries raise the effective demand for higher-skilled workers and consequently their wages. By assessing the implicit shifts in the balance between supply and demand for workers by skill level as a result of trade, the implied effect on relative wages can be assessed. Studies by Murphy and Welch (1991); Katz and Murphy (1992); Borjas, Freeman, and Katz (1992, 1996, 1997); Sachs and Shatz (1994); Wood (1994, 1995); and Krugman (1995, 2000) among others adopt this "factor content" approach.

---

[30]This theorem derives from the Heckscher-Ohlin-Samuelson two-factor, two-good model of trade. Trade theorists have considered more-complex variations on this model and identified the strong assumptions that must hold for the factor price equalization theorem to extend to an n-factor, n-good world. These strong assumptions have cast doubt on the ability of this model to explain real-world wage patterns, and certainly limit the applicability of full factor price equalization (Bhagwati and Dehejia, 1994).

> **Box 4.3—continued**
>
> *Another set of studies, in contrast, has proceeded by considering the effects of trade on the prices of goods produced by low-skilled workers and then making inferences about the demand for low-skilled labor and hence the effect on their wages. According to the trade model, prices should fall in the import-competing industries (and ultimately all industries employing low-skilled labor), thereby lowering the relative wages of lower-skilled U.S. workers. The lower cost of labor should lead industries in both the traded and nontraded sectors to increase their employment of lower-skilled workers. In these studies, then, analysts determine whether price changes in import-competing industries and labor utilization by industry are consistent with the model's predictions. This approach has been employed in studies by Lawrence and Slaughter (1993), Sachs and Shatz (1994, 1998), and Leamer (1998, 2000), among others.*

workers can be attributed to trade (Krugman, 1995; Freeman, 1995; Collins, 1998).[31] As noted in Chapter Three, the changes in the wage structure have been attributed to the confluence of several factors rather than to a single cause. In sorting out the relative importance of various factors, studies that consider multiple explanations generally give less weight to trade than to the role of technology or other supply-side factors (e.g., slower growth in the number of educated workers, immigration) or the combined effect of various institutional factors (e.g., the minimum wage, unionization) (see the related discussion in Chapter Three and the references cited therein).

Several explanations support the general finding that trade effects on the wages of low-skilled U.S. workers have been relatively modest to date (Freeman, 1995). One is that most U.S. trade is with other industrialized countries (see the discussion above), where wage levels are comparable, or with faster-growing newly industrializing countries where wages and other production costs are rising along with skill levels. Depending on which countries are counted as having low

---

[31]Among the studies that find effects above this consensus view are those by Wood (1994, 1995) (who attributes all the rise in inequality to trade) and Leamer (1993, 1994, 1998). In contrast, Bhagwati (1999) has argued that increased trade between high-wage and low-wage countries will not reduce wages in the former but may actually have a favorable effect.

wages, trade with such countries as a share of GDP ranges in the low to mid-single digits (Burtless et al., 1998; Krugman, 2000). A second explanation is that in the 1980s and beyond, less than 15 percent of U.S. employment was in the manufacturing sector (the sector most affected by trade with low-income countries). Most low-skilled workers are employed in such nontradable services as retail trade and other personal services. In the future, if trade in services that involve more highly skilled jobs continues to grow, trade will affect a larger share of the workforce, so the effect on the wage structure could become larger over time. However, to the extent that more-skilled U.S. workers now face greater competition from workers overseas, it may serve to dampen the rate of growth of wages among more educated workers, thereby lowering wage disparities.

While trade may be associated with a modest increase in wage dispersion among groups of workers defined by education level, a potential benefit from the increased competition induced by greater economic openness is a reduction in wage discrimination. Economists have long argued that discrimination is difficult to maintain in an increasingly competitive environment because discrimination is costly in terms of resource utilization. Provided markets are competitive, employers who do not discriminate would be able to drive those who do out of the market. In a recent study, Black and Brainerd (2002) show that the increased product market competition associated with growing trade in the 1980s and 1990s was also associated with a narrowing of the male-female wage gap, an effect strongest in those industries that were most highly concentrated (i.e., in those sectors where the effect of import competition would be the strongest). The evidence is weaker but still suggests that greater competition from trade also increased the relative employment of women and women in management positions and reduced the wage gap between white and nonwhite men. This potential benefit would be expected to continue as the share of trade in the economy expands even further.

Global Competition May be Tied to Changing Employment Relationships

In addition to concerns about adverse wage and employment consequences of globalization, the increased competition from abroad has raised concerns that globalization has weakened the traditional employer-employee relationship, with long-term implicit contracts giving way to less stable relationships. As a result of competition from abroad, there is a reduced expectation that U.S. workers will be employed with a given employer or in a given industry for much or all of their working life. Rather, it is argued that workers face a greater likelihood of being displaced as firms downsize or relocate plants overseas to take advantage of lower wages. This may be manifested in greater job instability (i.e., job turnover for voluntary or involuntary reasons) or in increased job insecurity (i.e., involuntary job loss). Recent research, however, largely fails to find any strong patterns of rising instability or insecurity in the U.S. labor market, particularly in the 1990s as the economy became even more open to trade (see Neumark, 2000, and the studies included in the same edited volume). On the other hand, survey data on workers' perceptions of job insecurity have been rising through the mid-1990s (Aaronson and Sullivan, 1998).

Other studies have looked for a more direct link between changing employment contracts and global competition. They have begun with the proposition that, once workers are hired, their wages are determined through policies internal to the firm, such as administrative rules and customs only weakly tied to external market conditions. Bertrand (1999) focuses on whether employers, in the face of increased import competition, still shield workers' wages from competitive pressures. Based on data from 1976 to 1992, the analysis indicates that industries that face greater import competition show a greater responsiveness of wages to current labor market conditions (e.g., the unemployment rate). These results suggest that competitive pressures stemming from foreign trade can weaken employers' use of implicit contracts that shield workers' wages from the vagaries of the external labor market. If so, the labor market would operate more like a spot market with wages determined by current employment conditions.

ECONOMIC GLOBALIZATION AND THE FUTURE OF WORK

The second half of the twentieth century, particularly the last several decades, can be considered the start of a new era of globalization. For the world as a whole and the United States in particular, the movement has been toward greater economic integration in terms of trade, capital flows, and the flow of labor and ideas. To some extent, the future implications of globalization for the U.S. labor market depend on the path taken by the United States and other countries with respect to further trade and capital market liberalization, a process that could lose some of its recent momentum as trade negotiators confront some of the more contentious issues, such as agricultural subsidies, labor standards, the environment, and intellectual property rights. At the same time, the technological forces that have spurred greater economic integration in the last several decades will further reduce the costs associated with global integration on a wider scale. Thus, a high degree of openness with the rest of the world can be expected to be a defining characteristic of the U.S. labor market in the coming decades, with both the opportunities and challenges such economic globalization presents.

The evidence to date of the consequences of globalization for the U.S. economy indicates that there have been both aggregate effects and distributional consequences. For the economy and for the labor market as a whole, trade has generally produced favorable outcomes: continued employment growth because of expanded markets, high rates of innovation and productivity gains as a result of more competitive markets, and rising standards of living. At the same time, trade has distributional consequences as labor, capital, and other inputs are reallocated toward their most productive uses. For U.S. workers, that means job declines in some sectors of the economy, counterbalanced by job creation in others. This is similar to the effect of technology discussed in the prior chapter: gains to the economy as a whole from innovation and technological progress but distributional consequences as new technologies displace workers or alter the skill content of jobs.

Given the links between the era of globalization discussed in this chapter and the technological advances discussed in the prior chapter, it is not surprising that many of the implications for U.S. labor markets in the future are interrelated. Again, we will turn to these issues in Chapter Five but offer a preview here.

- *The reach of global competition.* As the U.S. economy became more open to world markets in the past half-century, the focus has been on the ability of U.S. manufacturers to compete in a global economy. Likewise, globalization was expected to have the greatest effect on lower-skilled U.S. workers, given the abundance of lower-skilled workers in low-wage countries overseas. The expansion of trade to cover more sectors of the economy, such as various IT-enabled services, will extend the reach of global competition to new sectors of the economy, as well as to the higher-skilled workers they employ.

- *Skill requirements for the workforce.* In Chapter Three, we focused on the implications of technological advances in terms of the demand for skilled labor, particularly those sectors that involve high technology. In a similar vein, the U.S. comparative advantage in world trade is based on sustaining a highly-skilled labor force. Many of the industries with strong competitive positions, such as the IT sector and tradable services—are precisely those that require a highly skilled workforce.

- *The dynamics of work.* Issues of job displacement and job instability suggest that workers facing rapid technological advances and open global markets will need to upgrade their marketable skills throughout their working life. Workers displaced by foreign imports may need to seek reemployment in another sector of the economy that requires a different set of skills. Workers exposed to new technologies may experience a change in their job content that requires learning new skills for working with the technology or for navigating within a restructured workplace. Such training may be provided on the job or through formal learning opportunities available through the public and private sectors.

- *The nature of firms and work.* Just as new technologies have led to changes in the way firms are organized and work is conducted across a broad array of economic sectors, global competition is reinforcing those trends. The vertical disintegration of firms and the associated increased specialization within firms is manifested on a global scale in the vertical disintegration of production and specialization of countries in stages of the production process. The same technologies that support telecommuting for U.S. workers extend on a global scale to international teams coordinating efforts across vast geographic distances. Higher-skilled U.S. workers can market their talents in a worldwide labor market as freelance talent or within multinational organizations.

These implications and others are explored in the next chapter, as are the challenges they present for the public and private sectors in responding to the future of work in the twenty-first century.

Chapter Five

IMPLICATIONS FOR WORK IN THE TWENTY-FIRST CENTURY

In the preceding chapters, we have examined three forces that will influence the world of work in the twenty-first century. The *demographic* trends point to a workforce that will not grow as rapidly as in the past but will continue to evolve in terms of its composition by gender, age, race and ethnicity, language, and family responsibilities. The labor force may grow more rapidly if some population groups increase their participation in the labor market, and skill will be the defining characteristic of future workers. At the same time, ongoing *technological progress* in information technologies, biotechnology, and nanotechnology will continue to reshape production processes, the task content of jobs, how firms are organized, where work is conducted, and the delivery of work-related education and training. Such technologies will demand—and reward—a highly skilled workforce, but one that may be increasingly less tied to particular locations for job performance. Finally, advances in IT and other factors have contributed to the increased economic *globalization* of the U.S. economy. U.S. firms and workers increasingly compete in a worldwide marketplace that generates aggregate benefits for the U.S. population but also spawns both winners and losers as a result of a more open economy.

As we noted in the first chapter, the three forces we have examined do not move independently of one another but can be expected to have important interactive effects. For example, we discussed in Chapter Four the role of the IT revolution in promoting greater economic integration among world economies as communication and data transmission costs have fallen and as long-distance interactions have become more manageable. In turn, for the U.S. economy and other countries, the increased openness to world markets generates greater competitive pressures to stay on the cutting edge of techno-logical innovations through R&D and investments in the productive capacity of the workforce. Together, the forces of technology and globalization are altering the nature of work, the organization of firms, and where work is conducted.

Technological advances can alter the composition of the U.S. work-force by enhancing the health and longevity of the population or by providing incentives for individuals to remain in the labor force or leave as job skill requirements change. In turn, the skills of the workforce can shape the future course of technological progress through high-end knowledge in the sciences and engineering or through the ability to adapt to changing technologies in the work-place. Also, the aging population drives demand for pharmaceutical products and high-tech medical devices, thereby spurring and directing growth in the development and manufacturing of the underlying technologies. Interactions also occur between the demo-graphic composition of the workforce and economic globalization. To the extent that labor becomes more mobile in an economically integrated world, the workforce in any given country is a function, in part, of the size and composition of the immigrant population. Immigrants, in turn, can foster further economic integration through their strong international networks or through return migration that transmits knowledge across international boundaries.

Given these interactions, we seek to anticipate the implications of these interrelated and interacting forces for the future of work. These issues are relevant from the perspective of current and future work-ers who wish to anticipate the trends to come and how these workers might respond in terms of investments in their human capital and other decisions throughout their working lives. Other issues pertain to choices that employers make about how to organize their work-places, invest in their employees, and structure employee compen-sation. Policymakers at the federal, state, and local levels also make decisions that shape the laws and regulations governing the work-place and make other policies that may provide incentives or disin-centives for behavior on the part of workers or employers. Other interested parties include public- and private-sector education and training institutions that help shape the quality of the future work-force.

The affected areas may be summarized as follows:

- *The organization of production.* Technological advances and globalization are pushing firms toward vertical disintegration and specialization, decentralized decisionmaking, and attaching a premium to acquiring and sustaining knowledge as a means of achieving competitive advantage. In some sectors, these trends could result in the disintegration of firms to the individual level in the form of numerous IT-enabled, networked, self-employed individuals—or "e-lancers."

- *The nature of employer-employee relationships and work location.* The forces driving the reorganization of production will also increase the fraction of work performed in such nonstandard arrangements as self-employment, contract work, and temporary help. As advances in IT continue to weaken the bonds between work and place, a greater proportion of the labor force will be working at home or in other locations removed from their employer's headquarters.

- *Safety, security, and privacy.* Technological advances may provide both solutions (e.g., through ergonomics) and challenges (e.g., via nanoscale materials that may be inhaled) to workplace safety. Workplace security, in the face of terrorist or other security threats to workers in the United States or overseas, raises issues regarding the balance between public-sector investments in workplace security and those of the private sector. Privacy concerns will become more prominent as a result of various technological advances that facilitate employee monitoring and access to sensitive information.

- *The nature of work and job skill requirements.* Future technological developments will increase the demand for highly skilled workers while demographic and other factors will drive demand for traditionally lower-skilled jobs in various services. The labor market will require employees adaptable throughout the course of their careers to changing technology and product demand. In this context, consideration must be given to how the U.S. education and training system can evolve to better meet the needs of the twenty-first century workforce. Technology-mediated learning may help meet training challenges and support lifelong learning.

- *The size and composition of the workforce.* Slower labor force growth ahead will increase the pressure to ensure that all segments of the population participate in the labor force. Accommodations of various types could aid the participation of older people, women with children, and those with disabilities. Technological advances may aid the labor force participation of people with disabilities by alleviating the disabilities themselves or their impact on the ability to work.

- *Compensation in the form of wages and benefits.* The mechanisms driving greater wage disparities in the recent past, namely technological change and globalization among others, can be expected to exert the same pressures in the near term. In the absence of a strong increase in the supply of skilled workers in response to the higher returns to education, wage dispersion will likely remain at current levels or continue to widen. Meanwhile, a variety of factors may weaken the tie between employment and access to fringe benefits. Employers that do offer benefits may move toward more-personalized structures, tailored to meet the circumstances of each employee.

We have raised most of these points previously in the study. This chapter integrates them and highlights several important implications and challenges. With that objective in mind, we will be more speculative than definitive while we identify some of the wide-ranging implications of these three forces for the future of work.

NEW PARADIGMS FOR THE ORGANIZATION OF PRODUCTION

The forces of technology and globalization have implications for the nature of business organizations in the future. The chief thrust of organizational evolution will be decentralization, perhaps to the point at which some firms will disappear altogether, replaced by networks of individuals.

Structure of Firms

Three shifts are evident in the form that business organizations are expected to take in the future. One is the movement from vertically integrated business organizations to less–vertically integrated, specialized firms. Another is the shift within firms away from command-and-control leadership styles to decentralized management and employee empowerment across all levels of the organization. The third is the paradigm of knowledge-based organizations, where intellectual capital becomes an important asset for generating competitive advantage in U.S. and worldwide markets.

As discussed in Chapters Three and Four, technology and globalization are fundamentally altering the organization of firms, from a model calling for ownership of as much of the production pipeline as possible to one of vertically disintegrated specialization. Such specialization allows firms, which may remain as large as ever, to exploit their comparative advantage in the provision of particular goods and services and to outsource functions that are peripheral to the core business. While outsourcing has been common for such functions as security and cleaning, increasingly firms are contracting such activities as industrial design, manufacturing processes, business processing tasks, human resources, IT, and other business activities that used to be considered central. While these functions may have once been located in the same city, state, or country, outsourcing is now available on a global scale. Other manifestations of the disintegration of the vertically integrated corporate structure are large companies that have divided into semiautonomous or autonomous units that interact almost as if they were separate companies. Global teams assembled for specific projects that subsequently dissolve provide another example of more decentralized business activity.

Vertical disintegration is fostered by new communication and information technologies that reduce the costs of coordination across entities that would be otherwise bureaucratically integrated in one organization. These technologies allow coordination across geographically dispersed entities connected through electronic networks. Work products, data, and information can be transmitted rapidly and inexpensively, eliminating the need for hierarchical coordination structures. As the Internet and other information technologies reduce the costs of acquiring and exchanging information, more decentralized, market-based coordination within and between organizations can take the place of centralized bureaucracies. Within this business form, firms are more efficient and flexible in their ability to respond to local or global market conditions and to technological change, shedding or adding functions (and labor) through supply chains as conditions warrant.

Other technologies are expected to support this trend as well. For example, vertical disintegration and outsourcing may be facilitated by the shift toward rapid prototyping, the ability to combine computer-assisted design with rapid fabrication methods in manufacturing (Antón, Silberglitt, and Schneider, 2001). Rapid prototyping allows companies to develop multiple inexpensive prototypes that can be tested before committing capital infrastructure to production of the items. A more agile manufacturing capability would allow companies to outsource the production of goods designed and tested in-house.

The same forces behind the transition to a more decentralized organizational form also support the shift to decentralized decisionmaking processes within organizations. Chapter Three noted the movement toward providing frontline employees with greater authority and decisionmaking through various participatory, high-performance workplace systems; we also indicated the productivity advantages to firms that adopt such practices. Striking the right balance between empowerment and control will be an important management element in the future workplace (Malone, 1997b). Instead of serving a command and control function, corporations may exist to provide the rules, standards, and culture that define the environment within which more autonomous employees operate (Malone and Laubacher, 1998).

We have discussed the continuing shift to a services-based economy, combined with the global competitive pressures and growing importance of technology in both the manufacturing and services sectors. As a result of these trends, an increased emphasis is being placed on knowledge as the key source of comparative advantage for businesses and their employees in the twenty-first century economy (Earl and Scott, 1999; Zack, 2003). While the concepts of knowledge workers, knowledge organizations, and knowledge management have taken on a variety of meanings, at the core, knowledge embodies another economic input that combines with capital, labor, or natural resources to produce goods and services. In this context, knowledge is more than just technology but also embodies understanding of markets, customers, suppliers, business processes, best practices, and other invisible assets of the organization.

Classic examples of knowledge-based industries include software, financial services, and consulting (although not all firms in these industries are necessarily organized as knowledge-based institutions). This paradigm, however, embraces potentially all industries to the extent that there is knowledge in what firms in the industry do, how they do it, and why that adds value to the output of goods or services (Zack, 2003). The increased emphasis placed on knowledge work is manifested in the creation of chief knowledge officers in many corporations to help manage intellectual capital and create an environment supportive of knowledge development. These positions are often distinct from the human resource and IT functions (Earl and Scott, 1999; Herschel and Nemati, 2000).

The E-Lancing Model

Following the vertical disintegration and decentralization of the firm to one extreme, some analysts posit the eventual disappearance of large corporations, even to the point where the basic unit of the economy is no longer the corporation but the individual (Malone and Laubacher, 1998). Just as the hierarchical corporation defined the organization of industry in the twentieth century, some argue that the new form of business organization for the twenty-first century will be based on electronically connected networks of free-lancers, or "e-lancers." Comparisons are made to the Hollywood model of production, in which each project brings together a new team of individuals and small specialized firms—actors, directors, screenwriters, producers, and so on—to provide the range of required skills and expertise. This is in contrast to the previous model of the big studios that controlled the entire production process during the 1920s to the 1940s. In this new business model, individuals may compete in a global market for project opportunities and may work on multiple projects at any given time. Project teams continually dissolve as old projects are completed and form as new projects begin. Project involvement may last for as little as a day or two and may involve collaborators distributed over the globe.

Variants of this form of work organization are operating in some sectors of the economy today. However, the present system of employment laws and regulations, the provision of employee benefits, and the tax treatment of benefits are generally predicated on the traditional employer-employee model. Issues associated with a more decentralized e-lance model of production include access to such traditional employee benefits provided by employers as health, life, and disability insurance, and pensions. Furthermore, tax treatment of such benefits in traditional employment relationships differs from that for independent contractors or the self-employed (Malone, 1997a). The vision of a labor market defined by companies of one or a few individuals also raises concerns over the nature of social interactions in such transient, virtual organizations. These organizational forms also place the risk of ensuring sufficient demand for the individual's talents on the individual worker, who now must market his or her services and manage time allocation across projects. Responsibility for ongoing skills investment also rests with the individual. The distribution of earned income may also be more dispersed under this more decentralized model, which no longer imposes a corporate internal wage structure and which more closely ties rewards to the open-market value of an individual's talents.

In response to some of these concerns, visionaries in this field anticipate the growth of worker associations in which membership and benefits would be independent of a particular employment relationship (Malone, 1997a; Laubacher and Malone, 1997; Malone and Laubacher, 2002). These associations would be the principal mechanism for linking e-lancers to a "home base" and for providing access to the types of benefits provided by traditional employers. Again, taking a cue from Hollywood, the Screen Actors Guild (SAG) provides a model of such a confederation of individuals in which a share of members' base pay goes toward providing health benefits, pensions, and professional development programs. Such associations could also provide insurance against poor outcomes (e.g., spells of unemployment), as well as opportunities for training, mentoring, social interaction, and professional identity. They could also provide clearinghouses for matching workers to projects by using the Internet. In addition to SAG, organizations exist now to provide all or some of these benefits for other professional groups. Such organizations include the National Association for the Self-Employed; the Freelancers Union, established by Working Today; and labor unions in the construction trades (Laubacher and Malone, 1997). Other existing professional or community groups (e.g., school or employer alumni associations) may take on these functions in the future, or new organizations may be established, defined by occupational groups or geographic areas, to take on this role.

The future evolution of organizational forms in the next 10 to 15 years is not expected to rapidly converge on any one particular model. Instead, organizations are expected to adapt in response to the nature of innovation, markets, networks, and information costs (Langlois and Robertson, 1995). Thus, we can expect large corporations to continue to exist, albeit with greater specialization of function than in the past, while the prevalence of decentralized networks of small organizations grows. Within these new paradigms of specialized firms, decentralized decisionmaking, and knowledge-based organizations, employers in the coming decades will require a workforce with well-developed analytical skills and communication and collaboration skills. While these approaches do not necessarily affect the orientation and task content of jobs for all employees in a firm, a growing segment of the workforce can be expected to require these skills.

SHIFTS IN EMPLOYMENT RELATIONSHIPS AND WHERE WORK IS PERFORMED

Concurrent with the changes in the organization of production and the internal organization of firms, the demographic, technology, and globalization forces are also operating to change the nature of employer-employee relationships and the locations where work is performed. We can expect an increase in the fraction of workers in such nonstandard work arrangements as self-employment, contract work, temporary help, and lease agreements. Technological advances and the changing makeup of the labor force also suggest growth in such nontraditional workplace arrangements as home-based work and telecommuting. These changes are likely to lead to adjustments in the delivery of employee benefits, in social insurance programs, and in workplace laws and regulations, all of which evolved in the context of twentieth-century work arrangements.

Shifts to Nonstandard Work Arrangements

Changes in the organization of firms suggest a new paradigm for the nature of the employment relationship as well (Malone and Laubacher, 2002). At one extreme are jobs that essentially offer lifetime employment with a long-term employer-employee relationship governed by the internal labor market and procedures of the firm. At the other extreme are the e-lance jobs described above: freelance work that takes place over weeks and months, often in collaborative teams. These employment relationships are governed by the market and mediated by institutional rules. One variant of the form consists of "expert spot markets" in which the duration of work might be a few hours or minutes.[1] Between these two extremes fall jobs that are more permanent than freelance work yet do not promise lifetime employment. Such jobs imply a more tenuous, "at-will" employment relationship that will last as long as conditions are favorable from the perspective of both the employer and the employee. While long-term employment has been more common, less-permanent employment arrangements have taken root and are likely to become more prevalent in the face of rapid technological change and competitive market pressures (Cappelli, 2003; see also Jacoby, 2003, for a contrasting view).

As discussed in Chapter Three, almost one in ten workers is currently in an alternative or flexible work arrangement. These workers are primarily independent contractors but also include on-call workers, temporary-help agency workers, and workers employed by contract firms. When self-employed individuals and those working part-time are included, about one in four workers is currently in a "nonstandard work arrangement" (Wenger, 2003). Taking an even broader view, surprisingly few workers today are employed in what might be thought of as a "traditional" job. One estimate for California revealed that, in 1999, just one in three workers held only one dayshift on-site job that was permanent, full-time, year-round, and paid by the employer as a regular employee (Institute for Health Policy Studies, 1999). While the economywide use of such work

---

[1]An example is Guru.com (soon to be Emoonlighter.com), which matches experts in IT, creative design, office administration, and business consulting with organizations seeking top professional advice.

arrangements does not seem to have changed much (aside from cyclical fluctuations) in the past two decades, many analysts anticipate growth in the number of workers in nonstandard work arrangements (Neumark and Reed, 2002). This trend may be driven by technology and changes in the organization of work that could lead to greater numbers of e-lancers, as discussed above. It could also result from increases in labor force participation among subgroups of the population, such as the disabled or older workers, who have a preference for more flexible work arrangements (see the discussion below).

For many workers, nonstandard work arrangements are a matter of choice: They offer entrepreneurial opportunities and greater autonomy (for independent contractors and the self-employed), or they meet the needs of workers who want more flexibility in their work schedules (for temporary-help and on-call workers). For other workers, such jobs are a point of entry into the labor market, a source of income while obtaining additional schooling, or jobs of last resort; for yet others, they provide a useful bridge to retirement. The fraction of workers in nonstandard arrangements who prefer full-time wage and salary employment is highest among temporary-help agency workers and those on call (Wenger, 2003). The preference is lowest for the self-employed and self-employed independent contractors. This demarcation also divides the relative pay for nonstandard work: The self-employed and independent contractors receive higher wages on average than those in standard work arrangements, while the reverse is true for part-time workers, temporary-help workers, and on-call workers.

To the extent that the ranks of workers in nonstandard work arrangements grow in the future, one issue will be access to traditional workplace benefits. Part-time employees, whether in nonstandard or standard employment relationships, typically do not qualify for such benefits as health insurance and pensions. Even full-time workers in nonstandard arrangements, however, are less likely to receive these two benefits than are full-time wage and salary workers (Wenger, 2003). Similarly, workers in nonstandard work arrangements are less likely to receive company-sponsored training to update their skills. Responsibility for the initiative and burden of continuing adult learning is therefore shifting onto individual workers. More generally, shifts in employment relationships have implications for workers' access to the full range of tangible and intangible benefits that come with traditional full-time employment relationships: economic security through employment continuity and subsidized employee welfare benefits, professional development through training and other opportunities, career progression through internal labor markets, and social connections to workplace colleagues and a sense of professional identity (Laubacher and Malone, 1997). It may be worthwhile to implement policies promoting health and pension coverage among workers in nonstandard arrangements, whether through the tax code or access through business or professional associations. The latter may be modeled on the worker associations as discussed above (Laubacher and Malone, 1997). As noted, such associations may also perform some functions traditionally provided by employers, such as training and professional development, job matching, and social connections.

Growth in Distance Work

As technology permits a delinking of work and place, new workplace arrangements may evolve to meet the needs of employers and various segments of the labor force in traditional work arrangements. Many wage and salary jobs—particularly those involving goods production and face-to-face service provision—will continue to be tied to a designated work site where productivity is highest and workers can be appropriately monitored. However, off-site work, whether at home or at a third site, is potentially relevant for a growing segment of the labor force, such as many of the IT occupations slated to grow rapidly (e.g., computer software engineers and desktop publishers; see Hecker, 2001). Part-time or full-time telecommuting can allow employers to accommodate the needs of workers who care for children at home or for a sick family member. Older workers and the disabled may also benefit from nontraditional workplace arrangements.

Despite the growth in nontraditional workplace arrangements, few data exist on implications of mixed home-office work and telecommuting, and their implications are not entirely clear. There are indications that home-based work or telecommuting may be disruptive to family relationships and be socially isolating (NSF, 2002). Some evidence suggests that telecommuting and face-to-face interactions are complements rather than substitutes so that workers who telecommute have increased working hours at home without a corresponding decrease in the time spent in the office (Autor, 2001).

Some evidence also suggests that there is a strong unmet demand for telecommuting among today's workforce. In a survey conducted in January 2000, 41 percent of workers reported that they could perform their job while telecommuting from another location with access to a phone, fax, and Internet connection. Yet only 16 percent of workers were offered this option, and just 9 percent reported they actually telecommuted one day or more a week (Heldrich Center for Workforce Development, 2000). In terms of benefits, telecommuters in the same survey reported being more productive and having higher job satisfaction, although this may have been because those who chose telecommuting were predisposed to such reactions. If such benefits accrue to others as well, there is potential for a growing pool of workers to be productively engaged in arrangements not based on the traditional workplace.

With the "death of distance" afforded by telework and other forms of virtual work, some have suggested that geographic place will become even less relevant in the future world of work. In one view, technologies that allow individuals to locate anywhere and connect to virtual workplaces might make cities obsolete.[2] Another perspective suggests that the economy of the early twenty-first century will not be centered in the old megacities or even such older suburbs as Long Island and the San Fernando Valley. Instead, it will emanate from the new high-tech centers, or "nerdistans," represented by Silicon Valley, and Routes 128 and 495 near Boston (Kotkin, 2000; Kotkin and Siegel, 2000). In the United States, high-tech enclaves are emerging on the fringes of major metropolitan areas or in such smaller urban areas as Albuquerque, New Mexico; Austin, Texas; and Raleigh, North Carolina. Just as technology supports the vertical disintegration of large corporate forms, the same forces foster the vertical disintegration of geographic space into smaller horizontal cities with specialized agglomeration. These regions are supported by networks of firms that gain advantage in terms of an educated labor pool, R&D, and

---

[2]This extreme view considers only workplace requirements. There may be very good cultural or social reasons that keep cities relevant. For example, museums, sports arenas, and concert halls need a certain critical mass of potential visitors to remain viable.

other intellectual and business exchanges. The primary drivers are the infrastructure and amenities that support the exchange of information and knowledge, rather than the need to exploit such geographic features as rivers and ports. The Internet and other information technologies have also expanded opportunities for more-rural areas, which offer other quality-of-life amenities for those who can take advantage of virtual work (Kotkin and Siegel, 2000).

With more workers employed at virtual work sites, one potential policy issue concerns the location of teleworkers in jurisdictions having employment regulations or employment-related social insurance programs differing from those in their employer's jurisdiction. Workers based at home in a different state from their employer are one example; those located in another country from their employer provide another. The recent case of a Florida resident who, prior to becoming unemployed, worked from her home for a company in New York state illustrates the challenges that lie ahead (Baker, 2003). The New York State Court of Appeals ruled that the former employee was not eligible for New York unemployment benefits because she was unavailable for work in New York state. The state of Florida ruled that the individual was not eligible for benefits in that state either.

The New York–Florida case is unlikely to be the last. Such issues can be expected to arise in regard to a range of employment-related regulations and benefits. For example, California is one of the first states to establish paid family and medical leave support by employer contributions to the state disability insurance program. Will employees of California-based firms working from home in another state be eligible for benefits under the California program? Will employers be required to contribute premiums for unemployment insurance, disability insurance, or workers' compensation in every state where their employees are based, even if it is just one employee in a given state? To the extent that work and workers migrate virtually across state boundaries more easily in the decades ahead, information technologies may minimize the transaction costs associated with employers interacting with multiple jurisdictions and programs. If future case law holds that the relevant laws and benefits are those that apply where an individual physically works, mobile workers may choose where to live based on the attractiveness of a state or locality's employment-related policies. Thus, instead of fashioning a business climate appealing solely to traditional businesses, state and local policymakers may also compete for free-lancers, independent contractors, the self-employed, and other virtual workers to fashion their jurisdictions as desirable places to locate.

Other Changes in Employer-Employee Relationships

Changes in business organization, management structures, and employment relationships have other implications for the relationship between employers and their employees in more-traditional employment relationships (Blair and Kochan, 2000). On the one hand, shifts in organizational form and the use of nonstandard work arrangements weaken the bonds between employers and their employees. On the other hand, many employers increasingly recognize the human capital and knowledge base of their employees as a critical asset. Within this context, the use of high-performance workplace practices that give greater decisionmaking authority to frontline employees is blurring the traditional distinction between "labor" and "management." Likewise, when workers become owners through employee stock ownership plans or shared governance arrangements (whereby they collectively have an equity stake in their firm and are represented on the board), the dynamics of labor-management relations can change. Workers become more vested in the financial success of their employer and gain additional decisionmaking power. At the same time, these changing roles require workers to develop more substantive knowledge of the business and to engage in collective decisionmaking. It is expected that these dynamics will continue to evolve along with changes in organizational form and the organization of work within firms.

Changes in the nature of the employment relationship also have implications for unionization rates in the U.S. labor market. The long-run trend, driven by the decline in traditionally unionized industries and other factors, has been toward falling rates of union representation among the U.S. workforce. As of 2002, just 13 percent of wage and salary workers were union members, compared with the peak in the 1950s of 35 percent (BLS, 2003c). Union representation may be further eroded by growth in the labor force among demographic groups and in occupations and industries that have not historically been unionized.

At the same time, unions are responding to the competitive pressures of the global marketplace with strategies to increase membership (Freeman, 2002). For example, many unions view the Internet and other communications technologies as key resources for addressing the needs of an increasingly diverse workforce. Increased economic integration of the world's economies have led unions to use the Internet to create a "new internationalism" linking workers and their shared issues around the globe.

OTHER WORKPLACE DIMENSIONS: SAFETY, SECURITY, AND PRIVACY

In addition to the implications of demographics, technology, and globalization for workplace arrangements, other aspects of the workplace will likely be affected by these forces. In this section, we focus on three in particular: safety, security, and privacy.

Workplace safety has been a traditional area of concern for business and government. While such concerns may have focused in the past on high-risk industries in the goods-producing sector, such as extractive industries or factory production using dangerous machinery, workplace safety and security issues now resonate with virtually all employers and the entire workforce. In the coming decades, the aging of the workforce may raise new safety concerns in the workplace in traditional or emerging industries. For example, workers age 65 and older have been shown to experience higher rates of permanent disabilities and workplace fatalities than their younger counterparts do in the same industries and occupations (Mitchell, 1988). At the same time, new technologies may provide solutions for improving worker safety, from the use of ergonomic equipment by office workers to safety improvements in traditional manufacturing plants. Emerging technologies may also present their own health and safety concerns as workers are exposed to potentially hazardous chemical or biological materials. For example, critics of the pace of development of products derived from nanotechnology contend that health risks might be associated with inhaling or ingesting nanoscale materials (Feder, 2003).

Beyond traditional concerns about occupational health and safety, since the terrorist attacks on September 11, 2001, U.S. employers and workers from offices to factories to physical plants see themselves as potential targets. However, recent data suggest that employers have only modestly increased security spending since the attacks (Whiting and Cavanagh, 2003). Of the more than 300 businesses surveyed nationwide, the typical (or median) company increased security spending by about 4 percent. At one extreme, about 7 percent of companies increased their spending by 50 percent or more. Spending increases were highest in critical infrastructure industries, such as transportation, energy and utilities, financial services, IT, health care, and media and telecommunications. Companies in such northeast U.S. cities as Boston and New York also reported spending more. Fewer than one in four companies reported creating a specialized security position or chief security officer.

At the same time, insurance costs have been increasing, and companies report paying more for risk management services as well. It is not clear what the balance should be between public-sector investments in workplace security and private-sector security investments—especially when companies are reluctant to devote funds that do not add to the bottom line. In addition, self-protection on the part of firms in one industry may lead terrorists to substitute other, more vulnerable targets, a potential unintended consequence or negative externality. In this context, Lakdawalla and Zanjani (2002) argue that more-efficient protection may result from government subsidies promoting more-complete insurance against terrorism, complemented by public-sector security efforts.

Concerns about workplace safety and security must be considered in the context of an increasingly open economy. In terms of traditional safety concerns, efforts to promote greater workplace safety through regulation may have implications for the competitiveness of U.S. industry to the extent that such practices are costly and not followed by our competitors. In terms of emerging workplace security issues, a more mobile and geographically dispersed workforce creates security concerns for U.S. businesses operating at home, but even more so for those operating abroad. Recent terrorist attacks overseas have targeted places where U.S. citizens based in other countries work, live, and congregate, as well as other interests identified with the United States (e.g., embassies and military facilities). Residents in other countries employed by U.S. multinationals may also become targets of such attacks.

While IT is spurring the trend toward a more productive and competitive workforce, potential downsides also exist from the electronic means used to communicate and conduct work on the job. One area of concern is workplace privacy. There is evidence of increased use of technology to monitor employees and their activities on the job (Schulman, 2001). Some of this oversight is desirable to improve worker performance, to prevent shirking and other forms of unproductive behavior, and to allow employers to monitor workers who are off-site. Privacy advocates are concerned that workers may not be aware of such monitoring and the consequences involved. Other privacy concerns revolve around the use of personal data, such as medical, financial, and criminal records, for employment screening and evaluation. With future advances in biotechnology, the potential for misuse of results from genetic screening will become another area of concern. This is already an issue of debate in the United Kingdom. Under proposals put forth by the British government, every child born in the country could be genetically screened and the results could be stored to plan their future health care (Firn, 2003).

THE CHANGING NATURE OF WORK AND THE SKILL REQUIREMENTS OF JOBS

The twenty-first century labor market is expected to demand a more skilled workforce whose members are adaptable throughout their career course to changing technology, product demand, and global competition, along with a lesser-skilled services-oriented workforce. As the reach of the technologies described in Chapter Three grows, an increasing fraction of the workforce will develop or produce high-technology products and services, or interface with these new technologies as part of the tasks they perform. A key challenge for the public and private sectors will be developing an education and training system that responds to the needs of the twenty-first century labor market.

A Continued Emphasis on Highly Skilled Employment

As Chapters Two, Three, and Four have indicated, the skills of the workforce will increasingly be the defining characteristic that determines the extent to which an economy can develop and exploit new technologies and compete in the global marketplace. A highly skilled workforce will be needed to realize and take advantage of change in IT, biotechnology, and nanotechnology. The shift in organizational forms and the nature of employment relationships also favor strong cognitive and entrepreneurial skills. For example, as noted in Chapter Three, knowledge workers require high-level cognitive skills for managing, interpreting, validating, transforming, communicating, and acting on information. Valued skills include such nonroutine analytic skills as abstract reasoning, problem-solving, communication, and collaboration. Workers with these skills can perform tasks that require higher-skill human action not easily codified into computer software.

In addition, independent contractors, freelancers, and others in alternative work arrangements will require strong entrepreneurial skills to market their products and services, as well as the capacity to manage their time and workload in a nonhierarchical environment. These workers and others who increasingly interact in a global marketplace and participate in global work teams will also require the skills needed to collaborate and interact in diverse cultural and linguistic settings (Marquardt and Horvath, 2001). Individuals who can exploit diversity to generate new knowledge about customers, suppliers, products, and services will be more likely to succeed in a competitive global environment. Advances in technology in the form of real-time translators or other devices may facilitate these interactions to some extent, but the human factor is likely to remain paramount.

While technological change places a priority on maintaining a highly skilled workforce, the forces of global integration exert the same pressure. The U.S. standard of living in open world trade is predicated on maintaining a highly productive, educated workforce. Such a workforce characterizes high-tech sectors of the economy—for example, aerospace, computers and office machinery, communications equipment, and pharmaceuticals—in which the United States maintains a large share of the world's production. A growing emphasis on knowledge workers and knowledge-based organizations can further define a source of competitive advantage for U.S. workers and employers. As noted in Chapter Two, however, the United States does not rank very high among developed countries in schoolchildren's achievement or in adult skills, despite educational attainment levels unmatched by other developed countries. Moreover, many newly industrializing countries and rapidly growing developing countries are heavily investing in the education of their populations. Just as Indian computer scientists and software engineers now compete for jobs once held by U.S.-based workers, other countries with more highly skilled workforces are poised to compete in the world labor market as well.

One expectation is that the rise in the college wage premium will induce more young people to complete a postbaccalaureate degree. Indeed, some evidence of a supply response exists. The percentage of high school graduates who went on to college grew from 52 percent in 1970 to 67 percent in 1997. However, perhaps in response to enticing immediate job opportunities in the booming economy, that percentage subsequently dipped to 63 percent in 2000. Technology in the future may improve the flow of information about future labor market prospects to youth, who often misperceive the returns for staying in school and acquiring more education or training (Blank, 1998).

Demand for highly skilled labor in the recent past in some sectors has been met, in part, by highly skilled temporary foreign workers (so-called specialty occupation workers, H-1B visa category). In fiscal year 2001, 331,000 H-1B visas were approved, of which 58 percent were for computer-related jobs. As a result of the widespread retrenchments in the IT industry, only 198,000 H-1B visas were approved the next year (INS, 2003a). In the face of potential shortages of skilled workers, U.S. immigration policy can be expected to continue to play an important role in meeting the need for a skilled workforce. At the same time, the globalization of production may mean that, rather than bringing foreign workers to the United States, U.S. employers will bring the jobs to foreign workers. This may not be an option for a large portion of very skilled jobs because of the importance of location for some aspects of employment, but it may become more common, judging from the recent outsourcing of white-collar work overseas.

It is also important to recognize that there will continue to be considerable demand for jobs traditionally requiring lower skill levels in such service sectors as retail trade, eating establishments, health care, child care, and other personal services. Much of this demand is driven by demographic factors. These include an aging population that consumes more health care and other personal services and the increased labor force participation of women, which leads to substitution of market-purchased personal services for their home-produced equivalents. Because these services are not tradable on the international market, the low-skilled workers that produce them are not directly affected by competition from less-expensive workers overseas.

BLS has projected that, of the 15 occupations with the largest absolute increases in employment through 2010, 10 will be lower-skill service-related occupations, such as food service workers; customer service representatives; retail salespersons; and nursing aides, orderlies, and attendants (Hecker, 2001). Among the occupations projected to grow the fastest between 2000 and 2010, personal and home care aides, medical assistants, social and human service assistants, and home health aides rank in the top 15. None of these jobs typically requires postsecondary education, although training often is an important component of job preparation. In addition, more of these jobs in the future are likely to incorporate new technologies but typically with intuitive interfaces accessible to individuals who are not technologically sophisticated (Anderson et al., 2000). For example, as technology becomes more pervasive in health care delivery, home health care workers and other support personnel may employ information "appliances" to manage health data, monitor vital signs, and direct treatment regimes.

Adapting to a Dynamic Career

Although little evidence had been found as of the late 1990s that a marked increase in job instability or job insecurity had occurred, there are signs that worker tenure—the length of time spent on the job—may be falling among some groups of workers, particularly men (Kruse and Blasi, 1998; Neumark, 2000). This may be an early indicator that the labor market may be shifting toward less job stability. As discussed above, a variety of forces appear to be shifting the workforce away from more permanent or lifetime jobs toward less permanent, even nonstandard, employment relationships. Even within more standard employment relationships, less stability may result from job displacements caused by technological change or competition from trade. For example, technological change can lead to worker displacement as technology substitutes for human labor or technological advances shift production from old to new industries. The growing reach of globalization beyond the manufacturing sector and into the services sector suggests that a greater fraction of the workforce may face the prospects of job displacement caused by trade. Chapter Four noted the movement of IT and other IT-enabled service-sector jobs to overseas locations in lower-wage countries. Current estimates place the magnitude of the imports associated with these jobs at less than one-twentieth of 1 percent of GDP. Nonetheless, there may be a tipping point at which enough U.S. firms have adopted the practice that it becomes necessary for others to follow suit in order to remain competitive (Gongloff, 2003; Greenhouse, 2003).

Shifts in demand across occupations and industries will be less costly for individuals who can retrain to meet new skill requirements when old capabilities become obsolete. Thus, it will not only be initial education and skills acquisition prior to labor market entry but also training and retraining as part of lifelong learning that will influence the skills of the U.S. labor force. Greater turnover within traditional employment relationships and shifts to nonstandard employment relationships also spotlight the importance of fringe benefits that are portable across jobs, or even independent of jobs (in the case of freelancers, for example).

The prospects of continued or even accelerating job displacement as a result of technological change and trade also invite consideration of current and future policies to help workers adjust to these shocks. Chapter Four discussed the current role of trade adjustment assistance programs that essentially provide additional weeks of traditional unemployment benefits as well as job training for those who lost their jobs because of import competition. To the extent that future labor markets evolve to place a greater emphasis on small business forms, such as freelance work and self-employment, these adjustment programs may be tailored to promote nonstandard employment opportunities among displaced workers. This emphasis is already present in the traditional unemployment insurance program. For example, some states provide self-employment assistance programs to allow eligible unemployed workers to start their own business rather than searching for another wage or salary job (Karoly and Zissimopoulos, forthcoming).[3] The U.S. Department of Labor and the Small Business Administration have joined in a demonstration called Project GATE (Growing America Through Enterprise), which promotes self-employment through microenterprise, in this case in urban and poor rural areas.

An Education and Training System for the Twenty-First Century

Meeting the needs of the future workforce in terms of skill and the capacity for lifelong learning will require an education and training system that is up to the challenge. The present U.S. education and training system largely evolved to meet the needs of the early twentieth century workforce, and the basic parameters have changed little since that time.[4] The system that evolved was predicated on the model of first obtaining education and knowledge until young adulthood, followed by entry into the labor force and a career lasting 40 years or more (Greenspan, 2001). Additional training required for a given occupation might be acquired early in the individual's working life, with the expectation that such training would remain relevant for his or her entire career. Increasingly, this system is less relevant for the twenty-first century workforce. Given the pace of technological change and the evolution of the business world, skills obtained early may become obsolete. The new model for workforce education and training is predicated on the need for continuous learning

---

[3]A monthly allowance, equivalent to the unemployment insurance benefit, is paid to eligible individuals while they work full-time establishing their small business. Individuals are also provided technical assistance and business training opportunities.

[4]As the economy shifted in the early part of the twentieth century from one based on agriculture to one based on manufacturing, the system of public secondary education developed, in part, in response to the demand for even more literate workers with the analytical skills required for the growing number of factory and office jobs (Goldin and Katz, 1998, 1999a). High schools expanded and the percentage of youth that attended high schools rose. The system of higher education also responded with expanded opportunities in public and private institutions for contributing to scientific knowledge and the professions (Goldin and Katz, 1999b). One dimension of the system has been changing in recent years. The U.S. system of community colleges has been expanding its focus to include not only traditional students who enter after high school completion but also returning adults who seek opportunities for skill upgrading and retraining through degree and nondegree programs (Leigh and Gill, 1997).

throughout the working life, a process of lifelong learning involving training and retraining that continues well past initial entry into the labor market.

Providing an education and training system for the twenty-first century workforce represents a challenge for both the private and public sectors. The first challenge is to improve educational outcomes at the primary and secondary levels of education. As discussed in Chapter Two, many children and youth fail to meet achievement standards and expectations for proficiency even in basic math and reading skills. Dropout rates remain high for some demographic groups, such as Hispanics. Failure to graduate from high school or to graduate with sufficient skills in math, reading, and the sciences required for the higher-skilled jobs of the future potentially limits the lifelong job market prospects of less well-prepared labor market entrants. Educational reform at the primary and secondary levels remains at the top of the nation's policy agenda, as evidenced by such federal initiatives as the Leave No Child Behind Act of 2001. A focus on improving educational outcomes in mathematics and the sciences is particularly crucial given the future pace of technological change and extent of global competition (National Commission on Mathematics and Science Teaching for the 21st Century, 2000). As discussed in Chapter Two, the use of technology-mediated learning to improve educational outcomes offers tremendous promise, but such methods must be implemented appropriately to have their full effect.

The second challenge is developing opportunities for lifelong learning through formal and informal training opportunities. While employers can be expected to support some opportunities for acquiring job-specific training, they are less likely to invest in the general skills of their workers because these skills are more readily transferable to another employer (Becker, 1975). Yet, employers make substantial investments in training their workforces, whether through on-the-job training, by formal training programs at corporate universities, or through partnerships established with such external training institutions as community colleges. One recent employer survey indicated, for example, that 80 percent of employers provide some type of formal training, although employers vary in the nature and depth of training they provide (Lynch and Black, 1995). However, training rates rose with education levels, indicating less-skilled workers do not have the same access to employer-provided training as higher-skilled workers (Ahlstrand, Bassi, and McMurrer, 2003).

In the twenty-first century labor market, opportunities for continued education and training may become an important fringe benefit used by employers to attract and retain a highly skilled workforce (Ahlstrand, Bassi, and McMurrer, 2003). For example, United Parcel Service (UPS) currently has a program called "Earn and Learn"™ designed to "recruit and retain qualified student employees by providing them with cash reimbursements and student loans for college."[5] The program, initiated in 1999 and now available in 51 locations, provides reimbursement for tuition and fees: up to $3,000 per year and $15,000 lifetime for part-time employees and up to $4,000 per year and $20,000 lifetime for part-time management employees. Loans are forgiven as individuals continue their employment with UPS. Such opportunities may become more prevalent as employers compete for well-qualified workers. On the other hand, to the extent that employment relationships evolve toward nontraditional forms, the burden of continuous skills upgrading will fall on the individual. As noted earlier, worker associations may help provide high-quality training opportunities and other forms of professional development for their members.

The need for lifelong learning in a future labor market identified by rapid technological changes and shifting demand spurred by international trade is one area in which technology itself may provide a solution. As noted in Chapter Three, the Internet and other communications technologies offer great potential for improving worker skills through technology-mediated learning. For instance, companies may create online training courses for new workers or update the training of workers previously hired and provide access to training and reference materials whenever needed. Government trade assistance programs may take advantage of distance learning to help workers retool for reemployment. Such efforts would benefit from the ADL Initiative, designed to reduce the costs of making e-learning materials available (see Chapter Three).

---

[5]For details on this program, see http://www.pressroom.ups.com/mediakits/human resources/earnandlearn/0,1374,,00.html.

Technology-mediated learning offers the advantage of individualized learning programs that can be accessed "any time, any place," an important feature for workers who want to advance their skills but face challenges in balancing their work and family obligations. The flexibility to schedule distance-learning sessions to accommodate other work-life demands may allow more individuals to take advantage of such opportunities. In addition, as e-learning materials become more common in routine work processes (e.g., the use of wearable devices with procedural information to supplement prior training and reduce errors), continuous training and lifelong learning may become a reality.

Training and skill-upgrading through technology-mediated learning may turn out to be less expensive and more effective than using traditional approaches. If so, it may increase the percentage of the labor force that can take advantage of learning opportunities through private sources (e.g., employers, work associations, postsecondary institutions) or public sources (e.g., publicly provided job-training programs). While there is some evidence of the effectiveness of distance learning at the postsecondary level, the effectiveness and cost advantages for job training are relatively unproven (Autor, 2001; NSF, 2002). Thus, it remains to be seen whether this promising approach will be viable for maintaining and upgrading the skills of the workforce.

In any event, workers appear to be open to distance-learning opportunities. According to a survey conducted in January 2000, 61 percent of workers expressed interest in receiving education and training through distance learning, yet just 26 percent had participated in such opportunities (Heldrich Center for Workforce Development, 2000). Rates of past participation in distance learning rise with education and income levels and the extent of IT use on the employee's current job, yet the overall interest in distance learning is equal across income levels.

More-educated workers are more likely to have participated in traditional training programs. Thus, it is important to determine whether the lower-skilled workers can take advantage of e-learning and other technology-driven learning opportunities when such training would be beneficial. This is the population that faced declining real wages in the recent past and for whom skill upgrading is often a challenge.

For example, public training and job-search programs aimed at disadvantaged workers often fail to produce much in the way of earnings increases, although recent welfare-to-work programs for low-income mothers and intensive job-skills development for youth are exceptions (Blank, 1998; Karoly, 2001; Grogger, Karoly, and Klerman, 2002). Jobs held by lower-skilled workers often do not allow the workers to be absent for training, which further limits their ability to upgrade their skills. At the same time, case study evidence suggests that employers of low-skill workers have yet to take advantage of e-learning opportunities. This seems particularly well suited for lower-skilled employees, given the need for more flexibility about when training takes place and the possibility for making training an integral part of job performance (Ahlstrand, Bassi, and McMurrer, 2003). This points to the broader issue of access to technology-driven education and training opportunities among the least advantaged populations.

A third challenge, particularly in the high-technology field, is to meet the growing need for scientists and engineers who can advance the new technologies in the laboratories, develop the applications, and then bring them to market. The United States, for example, is generally regarded as a leader in R&D for nanotechnologies, yet, with major investments by such countries as Japan, it will be a challenge to retain that lead (NNI, 2003). Continued leadership in the field requires sufficient scientific personnel, often with the multidisciplinary training required to contribute to emerging cross-cutting fields, such as biotechnology and nanotechnology, to make the basic scientific discoveries and translate them into commercial applications. Retaining global leadership also requires entrepreneurs in the business field who are capable of bringing new applications to the global marketplace. At each step of the process of scientific discovery, applications development, and market development, the United States faces vigorous competition from other countries with highly trained scientific personnel backed by public and private resources invested in R&D and market development.

SUPPLYING THE WORKFORCE NEEDS OF THE FUTURE

Demographic trends, technological change, and globalization all have implications for the future composition of the U.S. workforce.

From the demographic perspective, the aging of the baby boom and the relative size of later cohorts imply slow growth in the labor force in the near future and even slower growth thereafter. At the same time, claims on such entitlement programs as Medicare and Social Security are projected to rise dramatically. Another demographic reality is that the U.S. workforce has become and will continue to become more diverse in its racial and ethnic composition. Increasingly, however, minority group representation has become blended, creating an even more complex racial and ethnic mosaic. Within this context, a key challenge for the future is ensuring that the pool of potentially available labor is fully utilized. Employer policies and public policies may encourage (or discourage) greater labor force participation among such key demographic groups as older workers, the disabled, and women.

Slower Labor Force Growth and Possible Labor Shortages

As discussed in Chapter Two, current demographic forecasts estimate no change in the growth rate of the labor force in the coming decade and even a likely slowdown after that. Such projections depend critically on assumptions regarding underlying population growth rates (immigration being one important factor) and rates of labor force participation among demographic subgroups.

If labor force growth proceeds at the projected rate, it will be difficult for the U.S. economy to maintain its recent rates of growth in aggregate output. The U.S. economy of the 1990s managed high rates of growth with a labor force that grew about as fast as what is projected for the coming decade. As discussed in Chapter Three, strong growth in productivity helped propel the economy forward. At the same time, the labor market of the 1990s boom was extremely tight, which suggests that any future periods of rapid growth will also face tight labor markets and skill shortages in some areas (Lofgren, Nyce, and Schieber, 2003).

How will employers likely respond to potential worker shortages in the future? From the perspective of supply and demand, the first possibility is that wages will increase in the face of worker shortages. The effectiveness of higher wages will depend on how much more labor is supplied in response to increased wages and the extent to which wage increases cause employers to alter production processes or substitute other inputs. Alternatively, employers may seek to recruit workers more aggressively, perhaps from nontraditional labor pools, or they may lower their hiring standards. For skilled workers, such recruitment may also take place within foreign labor pools, with H-1B visas used to import qualified workers from overseas. Alternatively, employers may migrate more-skilled jobs with high vacancy rates overseas to where the workers are, rather than bring the workers to the jobs.

As for less-skilled workers, wages did rise during the tight labor market of the 1990s, and employers were apparently more willing to hire a range of disadvantaged workers, including minorities, welfare recipients, and those with fewer educational credentials or less experience (Holzer, Raphael, and Stoll, 2003). At the same time, employers used more-sophisticated screens, such as tests and background checks, to identify suitable candidates. Although some of these trends reversed as the economy weakened in 2000 and 2001, the hiring prospects of less-skilled workers may improve with the next economic expansion and expectations of slower labor force growth. The expected growth of Internet use for recruitment and screening may or may not be favorable for lower-skilled workers. They may benefit to the extent that information costs for job seekers and employers are reduced, providing for more-rapid and better job matches. Lower-skilled workers will only benefit, however, if they have access to and take advantage of these new technologies for job search and recruitment.

Employing All Available Skills in the Future Workforce

Labor force growth rates can exceed current projections to the extent that labor force participation can rise for groups not fully employed. Thus, an important issue is whether there is scope for tapping underutilized labor force capacity. Based on the labor force participation trends discussed in Chapter Two, opportunities to retain greater numbers of older workers who might otherwise retire early have arisen and some evidence exists that older workers are already choosing to stay in the workforce longer. Greater attention to work–family life balance issues may increase the labor force participation of women, particularly those with children. Other demographic groups that may be targets for greater inclusion are individuals with work-limiting disabilities, low-income women with children, former military personnel, and immigrants.

Recruiting a workforce from diverse population groups presents both opportunities and challenges. To the extent that pools of skilled and semiskilled workers remain untapped, there may be ways to increase the size of the available workforce and resolve short-term or chronic skill shortages. Yet barriers to increasing access to job opportunities for population groups with traditionally low rates of labor market participation may be encountered. For example, women with children may face child care barriers; people with disabilities may be hindered by their physiological condition or its interaction with workplace conditions; older prospective workers may experience issues related to care for an ailing spouse; and so on. More generally, current participation rates reflect a balance among desire for income, health, family responsibilities, nonlabor income, and other factors. For participation to rise, some elements need to shift, for example, by a higher wage offer, an accommodation of a health condition, an accommodation of family responsibilities, a removal of pension incentives to retire young, and so on.

From the perspective of employers, strategies to make working more attractive than remaining out of the labor force are not cost-free. In tight labor markets, employers may offer higher wages, with obvious cost implications. They may also offer more-attractive work conditions (such as flexible scheduling or telecommuting) or more-generous fringe benefits (such as time off for family emergencies, on-site child care, or assistance with elder care). Such improved working conditions and benefits also imply potentially nontrivial costs. In their negotiations over compensation, prospective workers and firms may trade off cash wages, working conditions, and benefits.[6] The key challenge will be to identify the compensation mix that attracts the most new workers for any given total cost increase. Dollar for dollar, some subpopulations may be far more responsive to better working conditions or more-generous benefits than to higher wages. Some

---

[6]Economists generally find that the costs of various employer-provided benefits are shifted to employees in the form of lower wages (see, for example, Gruber, 1994). All else being equal, to the extent that employees seek more work-related benefits, employers would be expected to reduce wages to leave total compensation unchanged.

employers may even want to customize their offers to the preferences and family circumstances of individual applicants. Such institutional features as internal wage structures and the minimum wage or other government labor market regulations may preclude such adjustments.

The rising labor force participation rate of women has been a key source of labor force growth in recent decades. Whether that trend continues will depend to a great extent on working parents' ability to balance work and family. As a woman enters the labor force, not all of her homemaker responsibilities will be transferred to others. These dual work and homemaker responsibilities can strain a woman's limits on time and effort. Women (and their spouses or partners who share in homemaking responsibilities) are therefore likely to increasingly favor family-friendly workplace policies and benefits. These may include child care at work, health and wellness programs, (more-generous) parental leave, family emergency leave, vacation time, unpaid leave, and so on (Honig and Dushi, 2003).

The cost and quality of child care, in particular, appear to be important factors in determining mothers' labor force participation (see the review provided by Blau, 2001). While not widespread, employer-provided or -sponsored child care is becoming available. Overall, 4 percent of firms offer some form of support for private child care, such as on-site child care or subsidized off-site child care (BLS, 1998). Medium-size and large firms are somewhat more likely to offer child care (7 percent), and it is disproportionately offered to professional and technical employees (15 percent). In addition, a number of states are moving toward implementing universal pre-kindergarten programs for children as young as age 3 or 4. Further efforts on the part of the private or public sectors to affect the availability of child care could promote modestly greater work participation among women with young children.

Working adults may also face greater demands from their parents or parents-in-law. The proportion of elderly requiring help with daily activities increased from 35 percent in 1984 to nearly 43 percent 10 years later (Tracey, 2000). To provide this help, middle-aged and older workers may increasingly prefer work arrangements with flexible scheduling and perhaps assistance with arranging elder care (Honig and Dushi, 2003). Individuals who need to care for both children and parents—the so-called sandwich generation—will be particularly squeezed. This type of dual responsibility appears to be becoming more common (Raphael and Schlesinger, 1994).

New technologies may offer solutions for helping workers address the balance between their jobs and caregiving responsibilities at home. Motivated by the expected sharp increase in the number of individuals suffering from Alzheimer's disease, technologists are developing applications using radio-frequency tags to monitor the movements of memory-impaired elderly persons living at home (Dishman, 2003). Other potential IT applications include improving access to health information and medical records, monitoring vital signs remotely, and monitoring patient adherence to treatment regimes (e.g., medications and other therapies). Such assistive technologies would potentially reduce the time and other costs facing adult family caregivers and lower the stress associated with balancing work and family needs.

Another group with relatively low labor force participation is older men and women. For a variety of reasons, it appears that older workers may already be shifting toward longer work careers. Employer behavior and government policies may further stimulate or slow that trend. For example, older workers are more likely to be in poor health, and employers may be able to retain them by accommodating their special needs. Hurd and McGarry (1999) found that workplace flexibility and employers' accommodation of older workers increased the length of older workers' anticipated work-life. Older workers may require more flexibility in hours or responsibilities than their younger counterparts do. More than half of workers age 59 and older in the 2000 Health and Retirement Study preferred to gradually reduce hours worked, with equal pay per hour (Panis et al., 2002). At the same time, 63 percent stated that their employer would not let older workers move to a less demanding job with lower pay if they wanted to. Signs that employers may be gradually adopting policies that will appeal to older workers and increase their retention have emerged. For example, phased retirement programs that allow a gradual reduction in hours are becoming more common, although fewer than one in five firms offered them as of 1999 (Lofgren, Nyce, and Schieber, 2003).

Technology may have an effect on the timing of labor force withdrawal for older workers. Workers who receive substantial on-the-job training are more likely to work longer to recoup the investment in job skills. Thus, access to new technologies and the training to take advantage of them may further determine the length of career and the path to retirement. Moreover, the aforementioned delinking of work and place brought about by new technologies may benefit older workers. By combining work at home and in the office, the physical needs of older workers may be better accommodated. Home-based work may also allow older workers in some occupations to work from home and care for an ill spouse while continuing to work.

Government policies may also have implications for the ability to increase participation in the labor market at advanced ages. For example, government policies limit employers' ability to adjust benefits for older workers to account for changes in preferences for health insurance, pension benefits, and other employee benefits as workers age. Employers are also constrained—through downward rigidity of wages or lumpiness of health insurance benefits—in their ability to adjust total compensation in line with changes in productivity or hours worked at older ages. A more gradual transition to retirement could be facilitated by greater flexibility for older workers and their employers to renegotiate such terms of employment as wage levels, health insurance coverage, pension accumulation, and perhaps weekly hours and the nature of workers' responsibilities. For example, as part of a process of phased retirement, it may be beneficial for older workers to receive pension benefits early while shifting to part-time work, or not to accumulate additional pension rights (Panis et al., 2002; Purcell, 2000).

Employers and workers who would like to agree on such phased retirement currently face legal obstacles. Under current IRS rules, it is generally illegal to pay pension benefits to an active employee who has not yet reached the plan's normal retirement age. It is therefore illegal for employees between the early and normal retirement ages to partially retire (shift to part-time work and collect partial pension benefits). Some employers are calling on Congress to amend the tax code to allow them greater flexibility in designing phased retirement programs for their employees (Purcell, 2000). In 2000, legislation with that purpose failed to become law.

As discussed in Chapter Three, medical breakthroughs now and in the future may improve the functioning of those with such disabilities as blindness, deafness, and paralysis. To the extent that these advances become a reality, it will shift the emphasis away from workplace accommodations for those with disabilities to obtaining access to the latest medical advances in order to treat progressive or permanent disabilities. Such treatments will likely be expensive, at least initially, but the increase in economic productivity that results may outweigh the costs of remediation.

Even without such advances, technologies can improve the functioning of individuals with disabilities so they can participate in meaningful work or continue a career once they become ill. Some of these technologies may be employed in the workplace along with other accommodations, but disabled workers, especially those less able to travel, may also be able to take advantage of telecommuting. Indeed, there is some evidence indicating that telecommuting is on the rise among workers with disabilities, with expectations that 10 to 20 percent of disabled workers will be telecommuting within 10 years (Tahmincioglu, 2003). Likewise, new medical treatments for chronic illnesses and life-threatening diseases may improve the quality of life for individuals with these afflictions, thereby increasing the length of their participation in the labor market.

An important component of increasing the labor force participation of less-represented groups is matching workers to jobs. Here again, technology may play a role in reducing information barriers associated with job search. In particular, the Internet is growing in importance as a tool for matching employers with potential employees (Autor, 2001; Freeman, 2002). Workers now post resumes on Internet job boards and search online job banks for openings; employers advertise job openings on their own websites or in job banks and search online resumes for viable candidates; and employers and job candidates make contact through various communication technologies (e.g., online job applications or e-mail exchanges). In some cases, intermediaries for these services are for-profit firms (e.g., Monster.com) while others are offered by the public sector, such as the U.S. Department of Labor's America's Job Bank (www.ajb.org). Unemployed job seekers already use the Internet at about the same rate as they use traditional help-wanted ads (about 15 percent), and

7 percent of employed workers regularly search on the Internet for new job opportunities (Autor, 2001).

While the Internet offers tremendous potential for facilitating and speeding employer-employee matches and improving their quality, it remains a challenge to ensure that access to this technology is widely available across the diverse population of potential employees. Indeed, in the area of technology, a concern recurs perennially regarding the "digital divide" that precludes some individuals and population subgroups from fully exploiting the transition to the information age (Bikson and Panis, 1999; U.S. DOC, 2002).

CHANGING THE REWARDS TO WORK

As discussed in Chapters Three and Four, past and future trends in technology and globalization have important implications for the U.S. wage structure, including the growth in average wages, changes in the wage distribution, and the nature of compensation arrangements. While overall wage growth will likely occur, given expected increases in productivity, little evidence suggests that the trend toward greater wage dispersion will be reversed. In addition, a variety of factors may weaken the tie between employment and access to various fringe benefits. At the same time, employers that offer benefits may move toward more personalized benefit structures, tailored to meet the circumstances of a given employee.

Average Wages and the Wage Distribution

Chapter Three highlighted the potential for continued technological progress to sustain the higher rates of productivity growth attained in the second half of the 1990s. Such continued productivity gains would support growth in real wages (or total compensation to the extent that compensation patterns shift from wages to benefits). Future trends in technology, globalization, and demographics are also likely to affect the distribution of wages just as they have in the past several decades. As discussed in Chapters Three and Four, the persistent rise in wage disparities—particularly in the 1980s as measured by the wage differential by education level—is attributable to a number of factors, including technological change that favors more-skilled workers, and, to a lesser extent, increased economic globalization of the U.S. economy. While debate continues about the relative contributions of these and other factors in the past, the mechanisms driving wider wage disparities are expected to exert the same pressures in the near term (Johnson, 1997). In the absence of a strong increase in the supply of skilled workers in response to the higher returns to education, wage dispersion—particularly as measured by the gap between more- and less-educated workers—will likely remain at current levels or even continue to widen. At the same time, the relative stability of wage inequality over much of the 1990s' economic expansion and the attenuation of the growth in the college wage premium during the same period may indicate that wage disparities have reached a plateau and may not increase further as they did during the 1980s (Card and DiNardo, 2002a, 2002b).

More-significant shifts in the organization of production and the nature of employment relationships, such as those discussed above, also have implications for the distribution of labor market rewards. An increase in the proportion of the workforce in nontraditional relationships would be expected to produce a more dispersed distribution of earnings. Among the self-employed, there is more dispersion in earnings compared with wage and salary workers, with more of the self-employed reporting earnings below zero as well as very high earnings (Hamilton, 2000). The same might be true of the distribution of earned income among e-lancers and other independent workers. For these workers, rewards are more closely tied to how an individual's talents are valued on the open market, and while many will succeed, others will fail. In some cases, the outcomes for independent workers may exhibit the "winner take all" feature associated with markets for sports professionals and entertainers (Frank and Cook, 1995; Autor, 2001). Just as there are global star athletes and artists, professionals in medicine, law, architecture, financial services, consulting, and corporate management may increasingly be dominated by a few "stars" with worldwide reputations and large rewards.

An issue for future labor market policy is the potential impact of changes in the wage structure on labor market behavior. For example, reduced labor market opportunities for low-skill workers has been linked to their earlier withdrawal from the labor force (Juhn, 1992). Participation rates among lower-skilled younger workers may also decline in the face of reduced labor market opportunities. Wage opportunities also affect participation decisions among lower-skill women, such as those making the transition from welfare to work. To the extent that the increased openness of the U.S. economy places downward pressure on the wages of lower-skill workers, the supply of workers may fall, further exacerbating the slow overall growth of the labor force.

Employer-Provided Benefits and Other Forms of Compensation

Beyond wages and salaries, employer-provided benefits—particularly health insurance and pension benefits—are the other important dimension of the compensation system. As of 2001, 54 percent of U.S. workers were covered by health insurance on the current job under their own employer.[7] For some, this is a fully subsidized benefit; others contribute some or all of the premium cost. Even for those who pay the full premium, the cost of group health insurance coverage is typically considerably less than the cost of individual coverage purchased in the private market. In the same year, 55 percent of the U.S. labor force worked for an employer that offered a pension plan, although just 43 percent were included in their employer's plan.[8] Over time, employers have shifted away from providing DB pension plans to DC plans, a shift that transfers retirement security risk from employers to employees.[9] Other important employer-provided benefits include retiree health benefits; life and disability insurance; sick, vacation, and holiday pay; and subsidized child care and transportation costs.

Within this setting, the demographic, technology, and globalization forces reviewed in the previous chapters have important implications for employer-provided benefits as a whole and for specific

---

[7]Based on data from the March 2002 CPS, available at http://ferret.bls.census.gov/macro/032002/noncash/toc.htm.

[8]Based on the March 2002 CPS; see previous footnote.

[9]In DB plans, lifelong guaranteed benefits are based on the worker's wage history, tenure, and age. In DC plans, a lump-sum benefit is based on employer and employee contributions and accumulated interest on plan balances. Uncertainty about accumulated interest generates investment risk. Uncertainty about the potential to outlive one's DC plan balance involves longevity risk.

components of the benefits package. In terms of the demographic shifts, the changing composition of the workforce may have implications for who has access to employer-provided benefits and the effect of benefit structures on worker recruitment and retention. Older workers, for example, may prefer a package of benefits different from one preferred by younger workers, particularly if they already have access to pension or retiree health benefits through a prior job. Immigrant workers who intend to return to their home country may prefer more portable forms of deferred compensation, such as DC pension plans. In addition, future policy changes with respect to such social insurance programs as Social Security and Medicare may have implications for the structure of benefit plans offered by employers. For example, future Social Security reforms may reduce the incentive for workers to retire early, an incentive that may be reinforced or counterbalanced by shifts in employer pension plan features. Ultimately, the provision of employee benefits may shift toward more personalized benefit structures, with more workers able to select benefits that fit their circumstances with corresponding adjustments in cash compensation. Information technologies and outsourcing may support this trend by reducing the costs associated with managing a more complex system of employee benefits.

Benefit coverage in the aggregate or for particular subgroups will be affected by the use of alternative or flexible work arrangements, such as contract, leased, or part-time employment, which are less likely to provide benefits than traditional jobs are. Growth in freelancing and self-employment may further erode the tie between employment and access to health insurance, pensions, and other benefits. As a result of global competition, employers may face a growing pressure to reduce overall compensation costs to maintain more competitive cost structures. This may lead to reductions in the generosity of benefits or loss of benefit coverage altogether. On the other hand, in some sectors in which competition for high-quality employees is strong, fringe benefits may be an important component of the total compensation package offered to attract and retain top talent.

In response to a more dynamic economy, employer-provided benefits could be made more portable so that job transitions do not necessarily entail lost access to benefits. For example, COBRA (Consolidated Omnibus Budget Reconciliation Act of 1985) allows workers to purchase health insurance at the employer-group rate for 18 to 36 months following certain qualifying events that lead to health insurance loss. Future progress with respect to retirement income security may depend on greater portability of pension benefits. The worker association model discussed earlier in the context of e-lancers provides one approach for providing access to group-rate benefits that is independent of the nature of the employment relationship and job transitions.

As noted in Chapter Three, new forms of compensation—performance-based pay, profit sharing, stock options—have become more common in recent years for employees who did not previously work under such arrangements. To the extent that these approaches favorably affect recruitment, motivation, and retention, they may become more prevalent. However, some of the enthusiasm for these new compensation arrangements has been tempered by the recent economic downturn and the dot-com bust, exposing workers to the downside risk of such variable compensation systems. Recently, Microsoft—a company that has created more than 1,000 millionaires since its founding in 1975—announced it would no longer grant stock options to employees but instead shift to awarding stock directly (Markoff and Leonhardt, 2003). This move was reportedly in response to concerns from new employees that, in a slower economy, they would not benefit from an incentive-based pay system that relied on stock options.[10] At the same time, stock options remain an important component of the compensation package in many high-tech start-up companies that rely on a workforce willing to innovate and take risks.

CONCLUSIONS

The demographic, technology, and globalization forces that have been the focus of this book have wide-ranging implications for the future of the U.S. labor market. While the future course for the workplace and workforce is not known with certainty, we can gain some sense of the direction in which trends will run and of the challenges the private and public sectors will face. To a large extent, the

---

[10]Companies are also under pressure to treat stock options granted to employees as an expense.

U.S. labor market in the next 10 to 15 years will be shaped by the decisions of millions of economic actors, from workers to firms, from the least to the most skilled, and from small businesses to large multinational corporations. Market forces in the U.S. economy and increasingly in the world economy will determine who works, what jobs they will hold, the type of work arrangements they will face, and the compensation they receive.

Given the multitude of actors, any prediction more specific than that cannot be made with great confidence. However, some trends appear more likely than not. Among the more important of those is that employer-employee relationships and work arrangements will be redefined, as corporations increasingly specialize and worker-entrepreneurs become more numerous. Worker skills will determine the competitiveness of the U.S. labor force. A college education will still be a critical qualification, but the most successful workers will be those who can retrain in midlife in response to technological change and shifting demand. As the growth in the labor force subsides, employers will compete to attract currently underrepresented groups, such as women, older people, and persons with disabilities. Accommodations will undoubtedly be made to their desires for more flexible work arrangements. The latter will be facilitated by advances in IT, as will the need for retraining.

Many of the institutional features of the U.S. labor market evolved in the context of an earlier era—such features as the laws and regulations that govern employment, hours, wages, fringe benefits, occupational health and safety, and so on. In some cases, these policies need to be reexamined in light of the evolution of the labor market in the coming decades. Are there distortions or unintended consequences associated with current policies that preclude desirable market adjustments? Are policies put in place to address market failures in the past less relevant, given parameters that exist today and their likely future evolution? Are there new market failures that policy can address? Are there distributional consequences that could make a case for government intervention? These questions merit a more detailed examination in the context of the future of the workforce, workplace, and compensation in the twenty-first century.

BIBLIOGRAPHY

Aaronson, Daniel, and Daniel G. Sullivan, "The Decline of Job Security in the 1990s: Displacement, Anxiety, and Their Effect on Wage Growth," *Federal Reserve Bank of Chicago Economic Perspectives*, Vol. 22, No. 1, 1998, pp. 17–43.

Abernathy, Frederick H., John T. Dunlop, Janice H. Hammond, and David Weil, "Globalization in the Apparel and Textile Industries: What Is New and What Is Not," in Martin Kenney and Richard Florida, eds., *Locating Global Advantage: Industry Dynamics in a Globalizing Economy*, Palo Alto, Calif.: Stanford University Press, forthcoming.

Abraham, Katherine G., and Susan K. Taylor, "Firms' Use of Outside Contractors: Theory and Evidence," *Journal of Labor Economics*, Vol. 14, No. 3, July 1996, pp. 394–424.

Acemoglu, Daron, "Technical Change, Inequality, and the Labor Market," *Journal of Economic Literature*, Vol. 40, No. 1, March 2002, pp. 7–72.

Ahlstrand, Amanda L., Laurie J. Bassi, and Daniel P. McMurrer, *Workplace Education for Low-Wage Workers*, Kalamazoo, Mich.: W. E. Upjohn Institute for Employment Research, 2003.

Akass, Clive, "Terahertz Chips: Too Hot to Handle?" *vnunet.com: U.K. Technology News, Reviews and Downloads*, July 3, 2002 (available at http://www.vnunet.com/features/1129818).

Allen, Steven G., "Technology and the Wage Structure," *Journal of Labor Economics*, Vol. 19, No. 2, 2001, pp. 440–483.

American Anthropological Association, *American Anthropological Association Response to OMB Directive 15: Race and Ethnic Standards for Federal Statistics and Administrative Reporting*, 1997, available at http://www.aaanet.org/gvt/ombdraft.htm.

American Society for Training and Development (ASTD), "1998 Learning Technology Research Report," 1998, available at http://www.astd.org/virtual_community/research/1998_learning_techn ologies.html

Andersen, Torben M., and Tryggvi Thor Herbertsson, "Measuring Globalization," Working Paper No. W03:03, Reykjavik, Iceland: Institute of Economic Studies, University of Iceland, July 2003.

Anderson, Patricia M., and Phillip B. Levine, "Child Care and Mothers' Employment Decisions," in Rebecca M. Blank and David Card, eds., *Finding Jobs: Work and Welfare Reform*, New York: Russell Sage Foundation, 2000.

Anderson, Robert H., Philip S. Antón, Steven C. Bankes, Tora Kay Bikson, Jonathan Caulkins, Peter Denning, James A. Dewar, Richard O. Hundley, and C. Richard Neu, *The Global Course of the Information Revolution: Technological Trends, Proceedings of an International Conference*, Santa Monica, Calif.: RAND Corporation, CF-157-NIC, 2000.

Antón, Philip S., Richard Silberglitt, and James Schneider, *The Global Technology Revolution: Bio/Nano/Materials Trends and Their Synergies with Information Technology by 2015*, Santa Monica, Calif.: RAND Corporation, MR-1307-NIC, 2001.

Appelbaum, Eileen, "The Transformation of Work and Employment Relations in the U.S.," paper presented at the conference on "Workforce/Workplace Mismatch? Work, Family, Health, and Well-Being," Washington, D.C., May 2003, available at http://www.popcenter.umd.edu/conferences/nichd.

Arquilla, John, and David Ronfeldt, eds., *Networks and Netwars: The Future of Terror, Crime, and Militancy*, Santa Monica, Calif.: RAND Corporation, MR-1382-OSD, 2001.

Autor, David H., "Wiring the Labor Market," *Journal of Economic Perspectives*, Vol. 15, No. 1, Winter 2001, pp. 25–40.

Autor, David H., Frank Levy, and Richard Murnane, "Upstairs, Downstairs: Computer-Skill Complementarity and Computer-Labor Substitution on Two Floors of a Large Bank," Working Paper No. 7890, Cambridge, Mass.: National Bureau of Economic Research, September 2000.

_____, "The Skill Content of Recent Technological Change: An Empirical Exploration," MIT Department of Economics Working Paper No. 01-22, September 2002.

Autor, David H., Lawrence F. Katz, and Alan B. Krueger, "Computing Inequality: Have Computers Changed the Labor Market?" Working Paper No. 5956, Cambridge, Mass.: National Bureau of Economic Research, March 1997.

_____, "Computing Inequality: Have Computers Changed the Labor Market?" *Quarterly Journal of Economics*, Vol. 113, November 1998, pp. 1169–1213.

Baily, Martin Neil, "The New Economy: Post-Mortem or Second Wind?" *Journal of Economic Perspectives*, Vol. 16, No. 2, Spring 2002, pp. 3–22.

Baily, Martin Neil, and Hans Gersbach, "Efficiency in Manufacturing and the Need for Global Competition," *Brookings Papers on Economic Activity, Microeconomics*, 1995, pp. 307–347.

Baily, Martin Neil, and Robert Z. Lawrence, "Do We Have a New E-Conomy?" Working Paper No. 8243, Cambridge, Mass.: National Bureau of Economic Research, April 2001.

Baker, Al, "Telecommuter Loses Case for Benefits," *New York Times*, July 3, 2003, p. A19.

Bakos, Yannis, "The Emerging Landscape for Retail E-Commerce," *Journal of Economic Perspectives*, Vol. 15, No. 1, Winter 2001, pp. 69–80.

Baldwin, Robert E., "Openness and Growth: What's the Empirical Relationship?" Working Paper No. 9578, Cambridge, Mass.: National Bureau of Economic Research, March 2003.

Bartel, Ann P., "Formal Employee Training Programs and Their Impact on Labor Productivity: Evidence from a Human Resources Survey," Working Paper No. 3026, Cambridge, Mass.: National Bureau of Economic Research, 1989.

Bartel, Ann P., and Nachum Sicherman, "Technological Change and the Retirement Decisions of Older Workers," *Journal of Labor Economics*, Vol. 11, No. 1, 1993, pp. 162–183.

Bean, Frank. D., and Marta Tienda, *The Hispanic Population of the United States*, New York: Russell Sage Foundation, 1987.

Becker, Gary S., *Human Capital*, 2nd edition, Chicago: University of Chicago Press, 1975.

Bell, Daniel, and Stephen R. Graubard, eds., *Toward the Year 2000: Work in Progress*, printed in the summer issue of *Daedalus*, 1967.

Bell, Daniel, and Stephen R. Graubard, "Preface to the MIT Edition," in Daniel Bell and Stephen R. Graubard, eds., *Toward the Year 2000: Work in Progress*, reprinted from the 1967 summer issue of *Daedalus*, Cambridge, Mass.: MIT Press, 1997.

Berman, Eli, John Bound, and Zvi Grilliches, "Changes in the Demand for Skilled Labor Within U.S. Manufacturing: Evidence from the Annual Survey of Manufactures," *Quarterly Journal of Economics*, Vol. 109, May 1994, pp. 367–397.

Bertrand, Marianne, "From the Invisible Handshake to the Invisible Hand? How Import Competition Changes the Employment Relationship," Working Paper No. 6900, Cambridge, Mass.: National Bureau of Economic Research, January 1999.

Bhagwati, Jagdish, "Play It Again, Sam: A New Look at Trade and Wages," in *Trade, Growth and Development: Essays in Honor of Professor T.N. Srinivasan*, Vol. 242 of Contributions to Economic Analysis, New York: Elsevier Science, North-Holland, 1999.

_____, "Borders Beyond Control," *Foreign Affairs*, Vol. 82, No. 1, January–February 2003, pp. 98–104.

Bhagwati, Jagdish, and Vivek H. Dehejia, "Freer Trade and Wages of the Unskilled: Is Marx Striking Again?" in Jagdish Bhagwati and

Marvin H. Kosters, eds., *Trade and Wages: Leveling Wages Down?* Washington, D.C.: American Enterprise Institute, 1994, pp. 36-75.

Bikson, Tora K., and Constantijn W. A. Panis, *Citizens, Computers, and Connectivity: A Review of Trends*, Santa Monica, Calif.: RAND Corporation, MR-1109-MF, 1999.

Black, Sandra E., and Elizabeth Brainerd, "Importing Equality? The Impact of Globalization on Gender Discrimination," Working Paper No. 9110, Cambridge, Mass.: National Bureau of Economic Research, August 2002.

Blair, Margaret M., and Thomas A. Kochan, "Introduction," in Margaret M. Blair and Thomas A. Kochan, eds., *The New Relationship: Human Capital in the American Corporation*, Washington, D.C.: Brookings Institution Press, 2000, pp. 1–27.

Blank, Rebecca M., "Enhancing Opportunities, Skills and Security of American Workers," paper prepared for the Aspen Institute Domestic Strategy Group, 1998, available at http://www.aspen institute.org/Programt2.asp?bid=868.

Blank, Rebecca, David Card, and Philip Robins, "Financial Incentives for Increasing Work and Income Among Low-Income Families," in Rebecca Blank and David Card, eds., *Finding Jobs: Work and Welfare Reform*, New York: Russell Sage Foundation, 2000.

Blau, David M., *The Child Care Problem: An Economic Analysis*, New York: Russell Sage Foundation, 2001.

Blundell, Richard, and Thomas Macurdy, "Labor Supply: A Review of Alternative Approaches," in Orley Ashenfelter and David Card, eds., *Handbook of Labor Economics*, Volume 3A, Amsterdam, The Netherlands: North-Holland, 1999.

Board of Trustees of the Federal Old-Age and Survivors Insurance and Disability Insurance (OASDI) Trust Funds, *The 2003 Annual Report*, Washington, D.C.: Social Security Administration, 2003.

Boards of Trustees of the Hospital Insurance and Supplementary Medical Insurance Trust Funds, *The 2003 Annual Report*, Washington, D.C.: Center for Medicare and Medicaid Services, 2003, available at http://cms.hhs.gov/publications/trusteesreport/2003/tr.pdf.

Bond, Phillip J., "Nanotechnology: Evolution and Revolution," keynote address delivered to the NanoBusiness Alliance, New York, May 13, 2003.

Bordo, Michael D., Barry Eichengreen, and Douglas A. Irwin, "Is Globalization Today Really Different Than Globalization a Hundred Years Ago?" Working Paper No. 7195, Cambridge, Mass.: National Bureau of Economic Research, June 1999.

Borjas, George J., Richard B. Freeman, and Lawrence F. Katz, "On the Labor Market Effects of Immigration and Trade," in George J. Borjas and Richard B. Freeman, eds., *Immigration and the Work Force: Economic Consequences for the United States and Source Areas*, Chicago: University of Chicago Press, 1992, pp. 213–244.

_____, "Searching for the Effect of Immigration on the Labor Market," *American Economic Review*, Vol. 86, No. 2, 1996, pp. 246–251.

_____, "How Much Do Immigration and Trade Affect Labor Market Outcomes?" *Brookings Papers on Economic Activity*, Vol. 1997, No. 1, 1997, pp. 1–67.

Bound, John, and George Johnson, "Changes in the Structure of Wages During the 1980s: An Evaluation of Alternative Explanations," *American Economic Review*, Vol. 82, No. 3, June 1992, pp. 371–392.

Bresnahan, Timothy F., Erik Brynjolfsson, and Lorin M. Hitt, "Information Technology and Recent Changes in Work Organization Increase the Demand for Skilled Labor," in Margaret M. Blair and Thomas A. Kochan, eds., *The New Relationship: Human Capital in the American Corporation*, Washington, D.C.: Brookings Institution Press, 2000, pp. 145–184.

_____, "Information Technology, Workplace Organization, and the Demand for Skilled Labor: Firm-Level Evidence," *Quarterly Journal of Economics*, Vol. 117, No. 1, February 2002, pp. 339–376.

Brynjolfsson, Erik, and Lorin M. Hitt, "Beyond Computation: Information Technology, Organizational Transformation and Business

Performance," *Journal of Economic Perspectives*, Vol. 14, No. 4, Fall 2000, pp. 23–48.

Bureau of Citizenship and Immigration Services, *2002 Yearbook of Immigration Statistics*, forthcoming. Select tables and sections are prepublished at http://www.bcis.gov/graphics/shared/aboutus/statistics/ybpage.htm.

Bureau of Economic Analysis (U.S. Department of Commerce), "Annual Personal Saving as Percentage of Disposable Personal Income," tabulations based on National Income and Product Accounts, 2003, available at http://www.bea.gov/bea/dn/saverate.xls.

Bureau of Labor Statistics (BLS), "Chapter 13: Employment Projections," *BLS Handbook of Methods*, Washington, D.C., 1997.

_____, "Employer-Sponsored Child Care Benefits," *Issues in Labor Statistics*, Washington, D.C., August 1998.

_____, *Report on the American Workforce, 1999*, Washington, D.C.: BLS, 1999, available at http://www.bls.gov/opub/rtaw/pdf/rtaw1999.pdf.

_____, "Contingent and Alternative Employment Arrangements, February 2001," news release, Washington, D.C., May 24, 2001.

_____, "Work at Home in 2001," news release, Washington, D.C., March 1, 2002a.

_____"Worker Displacement, 1999–2001," news release, Washington, D.C., August 21, 2002b.

_____, *Series Report*, Washington, D.C., 2003a, available at http://data.bls.gov/cgi-bin/srgate.

_____, *Consumer Expenditures in 2001*, Washington, D.C., 2003b, available at http://www.bls.gov/cex/csxann01.pdf.

_____, "Union Members in 2002," news bulletin, USDL 03-88, Washington, D.C., February 25, 2003c.

Burfisher, Mary E., Sherman Robinson, and Karen Thierfelder, "The Impact of NAFTA on the United States," *Journal of Economic Perspectives*, Vol. 15, No. 1, Winter 2001, pp. 125–144.

Burkhauser, Richard V., J. S. Butler, Yang-Woo Kim, and Robert R. Weathers, "The Importance of Accommodation on the Timing of Male Disability Insurance Application: Results from the Survey of Disability and Work and the Health and Retirement Study," *Journal of Human Resources*, Vol. 34, No. 3, 1999, pp. 589–611.

Burnham, James B., "Why Ireland Boomed," *The Independent Review*, Vol. 7, No. 4, Spring 2003, pp. 537–556.

Burtless, Gary, "International Trade and the Rise in Earnings Inequality," *Journal of Economic Literature*, Vol. 33, No. 2, June 1995, pp. 800–816.

_____, "Technology, Organization, and the Demand for Skilled Labor: Comment," in Margaret M. Blair and Thomas A. Kochan, eds., *The New Relationship: Human Capital in the American Corporation*, Washington, D.C.: Brookings Institution Press, 2000, pp. 185–190.

Burtless, Gary, Robert Z. Lawrence, Robert E. Litan, and Robert J. Shapiro, *Globaphobia: Confronting Fears About Open Trade*, Washington, D.C.: Brookings Institution Press, 1998.

Butler, Jim, "Robotics and Microelectronics: Mobile Robots as Gateways into Wireless Sensor Networks," *Technology@Intel Magazine*, May 2003, available at http://www.intel.com/update/contents/it05031.htm#overview.

Cappelli, Peter, "Career Jobs Are Dead," in Olivia S. Mitchell, David S. Blitzstein, Michael Gordon, and Judith F. Mazo, eds., *Benefits for the Workplace of the Future,* Philadelphia: University of Pennsylvania Press, 2003, pp. 203–225.

Card, David, and John E. DiNardo, "Skill Biased Technological Change and Rising Wage Inequality: Some Problems and Puzzles," Working Paper No. 8769, Cambridge, Mass.: National Bureau of Economic Research, February 2002a.

_____, "Technology and U.S. Wage Inequality: A Brief Look," *Federal Reserve Bank of Atlanta Economic Review*, Vol. 87, No. 3, 2002b, pp. 45–62.

Carmichael, Mary, "Help from Far Away," *Newsweek*, May 12, 2003, p. E16.

Central Intelligence Agency (CIA), *The World Factbook 2002*, 2003, available at http://www.cia.gov/cia/publications/factbook.

Chomo, Grace V., "Free Trade Agreements Between Developing and Industrialized Countries: Comparing the U.S.-Jordan FTA with Mexico's Experience Under NAFTA," Office of Economics Working Paper No. 2002-01-B, Washington, D.C.: U.S. International Trade Commission, January 2002.

Collins, Susan M., "Economic Integration and the American Worker," in Susan M. Collins, ed., *Imports, Exports and the American Worker*, Washington, D.C.: Brookings Institution Press, 1998, pp. 3–45.

Commission on Technology and Adult Learning, *A Vision of E-Learning for America's Workforce*, 2001, available at http://www.uncwil.edu/dpscs/pdfs/A_Vision_of_ELearning_for_America_Workforce.pdf.

Congressional Budget Office (CBO), *The Role of Computer Technology in the Growth of Productivity*, Washington, D.C., 2002.

Council of Economic Advisors (CEA), *Economic Report of the President*, Washington, D.C.: U.S. Government Printing Office, 2003.

Council of Europe, *Recent Demographic Developments in Europe 2000*, Strasbourg, Luxembourg: Council of Europe Press, 2000, available at http://www.scb.se/eng/omscb/eu/TFR-en.xls.

Council of the European Union, "Recommendation 92/241/EEC of 31 March 1992 on Childcare," 1992, http://europa.eu.int/scadplus/leg/en/cha/c10916.htm (accessed August 29, 2003).

Daly, Mary, "A Fine Balance: Women's Labor Market Participation in International Comparison," in Fritz W. Scharpf and Vivian A.

Schmidt, eds., *Welfare and Work in the Open Economy,* Vol. II, New York: Oxford University Press, 2000.

Day, Jennifer Cheeseman, and Kurt J. Bauman, "Have We Reached the Top? Educational Attainment Projections of the U.S. Population," Working Paper Series, No. 43, Washington, D.C.: U.S. Bureau of the Census, 2000.

Destler, I. M., "Trade Policy at a Crossroads," in Henry J. Aaron and Robert D. Reischauer, eds., *Setting National Priorities: The 2000 Election and Beyond,* Washington, D.C.: Brookings Institution Press, 1999, pp. 73–93.

DiNardo, John E., and Jorn-Steffen Pischke, "The Returns to Computer Use Revisited: Have Pencils Changed the Wage Structure Too?" *Quarterly Journal of Economics,* Vol. 112, February 1997, pp. 291–303.

DiNardo, John E., Nicole Fortin, and Thomas Lemieux, "Labor Market Institutions and the Distribution of Wages, 1973–1992: A Semi-Parametric Approach," *Econometrica,* Vol. 64, September 1996, pp. 1001–1044.

Dishman, Eric, "Exploring Technology's Caring Side," *New York Times,* July 20, 2003.

Earl, Michael J., and Ian A. Scott, "What Is a Chief Knowledge Officer?" *Sloan Management Review,* Vol. 40, No. 2, Winter 1999, pp. 29–38.

Economides, Nicholas, and David Encaoua, *International Journal of Industrial Organization on the Economics of Networks,* Vol. 14, No. 6, 1996, pp. 673–886.

Emery, Gail Repsher, "Distance Learning Revs Up Integrators," *Washington Technology,* Vol. 15, No. 19, January 8, 2001. http://www.washingtontechnology.com/news/15_19/workplace/15079-1.html (accessed August 29, 2003).

Engardio, Pete, "Perilous Currents in the Offshore Shift," *Business-Week* (online version), February 3, 2003, available at http://www.businessweek.com/print/magazine/content/03_05/b3818051.htm?mz.

Engardio, Pete, Aaron Bernstein, and Manjeet Kripalani, "The New Global Job Shift," *BusinessWeek*, February 3, 2003, p. 50.

Feder, Barnaby J., "Nanotechnology Group to Address Safety Concerns," *New York Times*, July 7, 2003, p. C6.

Feenstra, Robert C., "Integration of Trade and Disintegration of Production in the Global Economy," *Journal of Economic Perspectives*, Vol. 12, No. 4, Autumn 1998, pp. 31–50.

Feldstein, Martin, "Aspects of Global Economic Integration: Outlook for the Future," Working Paper No. 7899, Cambridge, Mass.: National Bureau of Economic Research, September 2000.

Firn, David, "Britain Looks at Expanding Genetic Testing," *Financial Times*, June 25, 2003, p. 1.

Fortin, Nicole M., and Thomas Lemieux, "Institutional Changes and Rising Wage Inequality: Is There a Linkage?" *Journal of Economic Perspectives*, Vol. 11, No. 2, 1997, pp. 75–96.

Frank, Robert H., and Philip J. Cook, *The Winner-Take-All Society*, New York: The Free Press, 1995.

Frankel, Jeffrey A., "Globalization of the Economy," in Joseph S. Nye, Jr., and John D. Donahue, eds., *Governance in a Globalizing World*, Washington, D.C.: Brookings Institution Press, 2000.

Freeman, Richard B., "Are Your Wages Set in Beijing?" *Journal of Economic Perspectives*, Vol. 9, No. 3, Summer 1995, pp. 57–80.

Freeman, Richard B., "Labor Market Institutions and Earnings Inequality," *New England Economic Review*, May/June 1996, pp. 157–168.

_____, "The Labor Market in the New Information Economy," Working Paper No. 9254, Cambridge, Mass.: National Bureau of Economic Research, October 2002.

Friedberg, Leora, "The Impact of Technological Change on Older Workers: Evidence from Data on Computer Use," Working Paper No. 8297, Cambridge, Mass.: National Bureau of Economic Research, May 2001.

Fullerton, Howard, "Labor Force Participation: 75 Years of Change, 1950–98 and 1998–2025," *Monthly Labor Review*, December 1999, pp. 3–12.

Fullerton, Howard, and Mitra Toossi, "Labor Force Projections to 2010: Steady Growth and Changing Composition," *Monthly Labor Review*, November 2001, pp. 21–38.

Garr, Doug, "The Human Body Shop," *Technology Review*, April 2001, pp. 73–79.

Gelbach, Jonah B., "Public Schooling for Young Children and Maternal Labor Supply," *American Economic Review*, Vol. 92, No. 1, March 2002, pp. 307–322.

Gill, Brian P., P. Michael Timpane, Karen E. Ross, and Dominic J. Brewer, *Rhetoric Versus Reality: What We Know and What We Need to Know About Vouchers and Charter Schools*, Santa Monica, Calif.: RAND Corporation, MR-1118-EDU, 2001.

Goho, Alexandra M., "10 Emerging Technologies That Will Change the World: Injectible Tissue Engineering," *Technology Review*, February 2003, p. 38.

Goldin, Claudia, *Understanding the Gender Gap: An Economic History of American Women*, New York: Oxford University Press, 1990.

Goldin, Claudia, and Lawrence F. Katz, "The Origins of Technology-Skill Complementarity," *Quarterly Journal of Economics*, Vol. 113, No. 3, 1998, pp. 693–732.

_____, "Human Capital and Social Capital: The Rise of Secondary Schooling in America, 1910 to 1940," *Journal of Interdisciplinary History*, Vol. 29, Spring 1999a, pp. 683–723.

_____, "The Shaping of Higher Education: The Formative Years in the United States, 1890 to 1940," *Journal of Economic Perspectives*, Vol. 13, Winter 1999b, pp. 37–62.

Gongloff, Mark, "U.S. Jobs Jumping Ship," *CNN/Money*, March 13, 2003, available at http://money.cnn.com/2003/03/13/news/economy/jobs_offshore/.

Goodman, Peter S., "China Calling with Cell-Phone Standard," *Washington Post*, July 25, 2003a, p. E1.

Goodman, Peter S., "White-Collar Work a Booming U.S. Export," *Washington Post*, April 2, 2003b, p. E1.

Gordon, Robert J., "Does the 'New Economy' Measure Up to the Great Inventions of the Past?" *Journal of Economic Perspectives*, Vol. 14, No. 4, Fall 2000, pp. 49–74.

Gordon, Robert J., "Hi-Tech Innovation and Productivity Growth: Does Supply Create Its Own Demand?" working paper, Northwestern University, December 2002.

Gottschalk, Peter, "Inequality, Income Growth, and Mobility: The Basic Facts," *Journal of Economic Perspectives*, Vol. 11, No. 2, 1997, pp. 21–40.

Greenhouse, Steven, "I.B.M. Explores Shift of Some Jobs Overseas," *New York Times*, July 22, 2003, p. C1.

Greenspan, Alan, "The Growing Need for Skills in the 21st Century," remarks before the U.S. Department of Labor 21st Century Workforce Summit, Washington, D.C., June 20, 2001, available at http://www.federalreserve.gov/boarddocs/speeches/2001/20010620/default.htm.

Grissmer, David, Ann Flanagan, Jennifer Kawata, and Stephanie Williamson, *Improving Student Achievement: What State NAEP Test Scores Tell Us*, Santa Monica, Calif.: RAND Corporation, MR-924-EDU, 2000.

Grogger, Jeffrey, "The Effects of Time Limits, the EITC, and Other Policy Changes on Welfare Use, Work, and Income Among Female-Headed Families," *Review of Economics and Statistics*, Vol. 85, No. 2, 2003, pp. 394–408.

Grogger, Jeffrey, Lynn A. Karoly, and Jacob Alex Klerman, *Consequences of Welfare Reform: A Research Synthesis*, Santa Monica, Calif.: RAND Corporation, DRU-2676-DHHS, July 2002.

Grossman, Gene M., and Elhanan Helpman, "Outsourcing in a Global Economy," Working Paper No. 8728, Cambridge, Mass.: National Bureau of Economic Research, January 2002.

Gruber, Jonathan, "The Incidence of Mandated Maternity Benefits," *American Economic Review*, Vol. 84, No. 3, June 1994, pp. 622–641.

Hamilton, Barton H., "Does Entrepreneurship Pay? An Empirical Analysis of the Returns of Self-Employment," *Journal of Political Economy*, Vol. 108, No. 3, June 2000, pp. 604–631.

Hanushek, Eric A., "The Long Run Importance of School Quality," Working Paper No. 9071, Cambridge, Mass.: National Bureau of Economic Research, July 2002.

Hanushek, Eric A., and Dennis D. Kimko, "Schooling, Labor-Force Quality, and the Growth of Nations," *American Economic Review*, Vol. 90, No. 5, December 2000, pp. 1184–1208.

Hatton, Timothy H., and Jeffrey G. Williamson, "What Fundamentals Drive World Migration?" Working Paper No. 9159, Cambridge, Mass.: National Bureau of Economic Research, September 2002.

Hecht, Jeff, "Wavelength Division Multiplexing," *Technology Review*, March/April 1999, available at http//www.technologyreview.com/articles/print_version/hecht0399.asp.

Hecker, Daniel E., "Occupational Employment Projections to 2010," *Monthly Labor Review*, Vol. 124, No. 11, November 2001, pp. 57–84.

Heldrich Center for Workforce Development at Rutgers, *Nothing but Net: American Workers and the Information Economy*, February 2000, available at http://wdr.doleta.gov/conference/2001_papers_1.cfm.

Helpman, Elhanan, "The Structure of Foreign Trade," *Journal of Economic Perspectives*, Vol. 13, No. 2, 1999, pp. 121–144.

Helwig, Ryan T., "Worker Displacement in a Strong Labor Market," *Monthly Labor Review*, Vol. 124, No. 6, June 2001, pp. 13–28.

Herschel, Richard T., and Hamid R. Nemati, "Chief Knowledge Officer: Critical Success Factors for Knowledge Management," BRINT

Institute, 2000, available at http://www.brint.com/members/online/20090319/cko/cko_1.html.

Hibbard, Justin, "The Learning Revolution," *Information Week,* March 9, 1998, available at http://www.informationweek.com/672/72iurev.htm.

Hicks, Diana, Tony Breitzman, Dominic Olivastro, and Kimberly Hamilton, "The Changing Composition of Innovative Activity in the U.S.: A Portrait Based on Patent Analysis," *Research Policy,* Vol. 30, 2001, pp. 681–703.

Hillner, Jennifer, "Venture Capitals," *Wired,* No. 8.07, July 2000.

Hipple, Steven, and Karen Kosanovich, "Computer and Internet Use at Work in 2001," *Monthly Labor Review,* February 2003, pp. 26–35.

Hoffman, Bruce, *Inside Terrorism,* New York: Columbia University Press, 1998.

Holmes, Stanley, "The New Cold War at Boeing," *BusinessWeek,* February 3, 2003.

Holzer, Harry J., Steven Raphael, and Michael A. Stoll, "Employers in the Boom: How Did the Hiring of Unskilled Workers Change During the 1990s?" Discussion Paper No. 1267-03, Madison, Wisc.: Institute for Research on Poverty, June 2003.

Honig, Marjorie, and Irena Dushi, "How Demographic Change Will Drive Benefit Design," in Olivia Mitchell, David Blitzstein, Michael Gordon, and Judith Mazo, eds., *Benefits for the Workplace of the Future,* Philadelphia: University of Pennsylvania Press, 2003.

Huang, Gregory T., "10 Emerging Technologies That Will Change the World: Molecular Imaging," *Technology Review,* February 2003, p. 42.

Hufbauer, Gary, "World Economic Integration: The Long View," *Economic Insights,* Vol. 30, 1991, pp. 26–27.

Hummels, David, Jun Ishii, and Kei-Mu Yi, "The Nature and Growth of Vertical Specialization in World Trade," *Journal of International Economics,* Vol. 54, No. 1, June 2001, pp. 75–96.

Hummels, David, Dana Rapoport, and Kei-Mu Yi, "Vertical Specialization and the Changing Nature of World Trade," *Federal Reserve Bank of New York Economic Policy Review*, June 1998, pp. 79–99.

Hundley, Richard O., Robert H. Anderson, Tora K. Bikson, and C. Richard Neu, *The Global Course of the Information Revolution: Recurring Themes and Regional Variations*, Santa Monica, Calif.: RAND Corporation, MR-1680-NIC, 2003.

Hurd, Michael D., and Michael J. Boskin, "The Effect of Social Security on Retirement in the Early 70's," *Quarterly Journal of Economics*, Vol. 99, No. 4, 1984, pp. 767–790.

Hurd, Michael D., and Kathleen McGarry, "Prospective Retirement: Effects of Job Characteristics, Pensions, and Health Insurance," unpublished manuscript, RAND Corporation, 1999.

IBM, "IBM's 'Millipede' Project Demonstrates Trillion-Bit Data Storage Density," *IBM Research News*, June 11, 2002a, available at http://www.research.ibm.com/resources/news/20020611_millipe de.shtml.

_____, "IBM Scientists Build World's Smallest Operating Computer Circuits," *IBM Research News*, October 24, 2002b, available at http://www.research.ibm.com/resources/news/20021024_cascad e.shtml.

_____, "IBM Announces World's Smallest Working Silicon Transistor," *IBM Research News*, December 9, 2002c, available at http://www.research.ibm.com/resources/news/20021209_transistor.sht ml.

_____, "Scientists Announce First 3-D Assembly of Magnetic and Semiconducting Nanoparticles," *IBM Research News*, June 25, 2003, available at http://www.research.ibm.com/resources/news/20030625_assembly.shtml.

Ichniowski, Casey, Thomas A. Kochan, David Levine, Craig Olson, and George Strauss, "What Works at Work: Overview and Assessment," *Industrial Relations*, Vol. 35, No. 3, July 1996, pp. 299–333.

Immigration and Naturalization Service (INS), *2000 Statistical Yearbook of the Immigration and Naturalization Service*, Washington, D.C.: U.S. Government Printing Office, 2002.

_____, *2001 Statistical Yearbook of the Immigration and Naturalization Service*, Washington, D.C.: U.S. Government Printing Office, 2003a.

_____, Office of Policy and Planning, *Estimates of the Unauthorized Immigrant Population Residing in the United States: 1990 to 2000*, 2003b, available at http://www.bcis.gov/graphics/shared/about us/statistics/Ill_Report_1211.pdf.

Information Technology Association of America (ITAA), *2003 Workforce Survey*, May 23, 2003, available at http://www.itaa.org/workforce/studies/03execsumm.pdf.

Institute for Health Policy Studies, "The California Work and Health Survey, 1999: Who Succeeds and Who Fails in the New World of Work," San Francisco: Institute for Health Policy Studies, September 6, 1999, available at http://www.medicine.ucsf.edu/programs/cwhs/1999/dayone/toc.html.

Intel Labs, "New Transistors for 2005 and Beyond," 2001, available at ftp://download.intel.com/research/silicon/TeraHertz.short.pdf.

International Monetary Fund (IMF), "Globalization: Threat or Opportunity?" issue brief, January 2000, available at http://www.imf.org/external/np/exr/ib/2000/041200.htm.

_____, "The Information Technology Revolution," *World Economic Outlook: Trade and Finance*, September 2001, pp. 105–144, available at http://www.imf.org/external/pubs/ft/weo/2001/02/index.htm.

_____, "Trade and Financial Integration," *World Economic Outlook: The Information Technology Revolution*, October 2002, pp. 108–146, available at http://www.imf.org/external/pubs/ft/weo/2002/02/index.htm.

International Telecommunication Union, "Key Global Telecom Indicators for the World Telecommunication Service Sector," 2001, available at http://www.itu.int/ITU-D/ict/statistics/at-glance/Key telecom99.html.

International Telework Association and Council (ITAC), "Telework Facts and Figures," available at http://www.workingfromany where.org/resources/abouttelwork.htm, accessed July 7, 2003.

Iwata, Edward, "Intel Chip Breakthrough Validates Moore's Law," *USA Today*, November 26, 2001, available at http://www.usatoday. com/tech/techreviews/2001/11/26/intel-breakthrough.htm.

Jacoby, Sanford M., "Are Career Jobs Headed for Extinction?" in Olivia S. Mitchell, David S. Blitzstein, Michael Gordon, and Judith F. Mazo, eds., *Benefits for the Workplace of the Future*, Philadelphia: University of Pennsylvania Press, 2003, pp. 178–202.

Johnson, George, "Changes in Earnings Inequality: The Role of Demand Shifts," *Journal of Economic Perspectives*, Vol. 11, No. 2, 1997, pp. 41–54.

Johnston, William B., and Arnold E. Packer, *Workforce 2000: Work and Workers for the 21st Century*, Indianapolis, Ind.: Hudson Institute, 1987.

Jorgenson, Dale W., Mun S. Ho, and Kevin J. Stiroh, "Projecting Productivity Growth: Lessons from the U.S. Growth Resurgence" *Federal Reserve Bank of Atlanta Economic Review*, Vol. 87, No. 3, 2002, pp. 1–13.

Judy, Richard W., and Carol D'Amico, *Workforce 2020: Work and Workers in the 21st Century*, Indianapolis, Ind.: Hudson Institute, 1997.

Juhn, Chinhui, "Decline of Male Labor Market Participation: The Role of Declining Market Opportunities," *Quarterly Journal of Economics*, Vol. 107, No. 1, 1992, pp. 79–122.

Kapteyn, Arie, and Constantijn Panis, "The Size and Composition of Wealth Holdings in the United States, Italy, and the Netherlands," Santa Monica, Calif.: RAND Corporation, DRU-2767-DOL, March 2002.

Karoly, Lynn A., "Investing in the Future: Reducing Poverty Through Human Capital Investments," in Sheldon H. Danziger and Robert H. Haveman, eds., *Understanding Poverty*, New York and Cambridge, Mass.: Russell Sage Foundation and Harvard University Press, 2001, pp. 314–356.

Karoly, Lynn A., and Julie Zissimopoulos, *Self-Employment and the 50+ Population*, Washington, D.C.: AARP, forthcoming.

Katz, Lawrence F., and David Autor, "Changes in the Wage Structure and Earnings Inequality," in Orley Ashenfelter and David Card, eds., *Handbook of Labor Economics*, Volume III, Amsterdam, The Netherlands: Elsevier, 2000.

Katz, Lawrence F., and Kevin M. Murphy, "Changes in Relative Wages, 1963–1987: Supply and Demand Factors," *Quarterly Journal of Economics*, Vol. 197, February 1992, pp. 35–78.

Kletzer, Lori G., "Job Displacement," *Journal of Economic Perspectives*, Vol. 12, No. 1, Winter 1998, pp. 115–136.

_____, "Trade and Job Loss in U.S. Manufacturing, 1979–94," in Robert C. Feenstra, ed., *The Impact of International Trade on Wages*, Chicago: University of Chicago Press, 2000.

_____, *Imports, Exports, and Jobs*, Kalamazoo, Mich.: W. E. Upjohn Institute for Employment Research, 2002.

Kotkin, Joel, *The New Geography of Work: How the Digital Revolution Is Reshaping the American Landscape*, New York: Random House, 2000.

Kotkin, Joel, and Fred Siegel, *Digital Geography: The Remaking of City and Countryside in the New Economy*, Indianapolis, Ind.: The Hudson Institute, 2000.

Krueger, Alan B., "How Computers Have Changed the Wage Structure: Evidence from Microdata, 1984–1989," *Quarterly Journal of Economics*, Vol. 108, No. 1, 1993, pp. 33–60.

Krugman, Paul, "Growing World Trade: Causes and Consequences," *Brookings Papers on Economic Activity*, Vol. 1995, No. 1, 1995, pp. 327–362.

_____, "Technology, Trade and Factor Prices," *Journal of International Economics*, Vol. 50, 2000, pp. 51–71.

Kruse, Douglas, and Joseph Blasi, "The New Employee-Employer Relationship," paper prepared for the Aspen Institute Domestic Strategy Group, 1998, available at http://www.aspeninstitute.org/Programt2.asp?bid=870.

Kuenzi, Jeffrey, and Clara A. Reschovsky, *Home-Based Workers in the United States: 1997*, P70-78, Washington, D.C.: U.S. Bureau of the Census, 2001.

Lakdawalla, Darius, Dana Goldman, Jayanta Bhattacharya, Michael Hurd, Geoffrey Joyce, and Constantijn Panis, "Forecasting the Nursing Home Population," *Medical Care*, Vol. 41, No. 1, January 2003, pp. 8–20.

Lakdawalla, Darius, and George Zanjani, "Insurance, Self-Protection, and the Economics of Terrorism," Working Paper No. 9215, Cambridge, Mass.: National Bureau of Economic Research, September 2002.

Landefeld, J. Steven, and Ralph Kozlow, "Globalization and Multinational Companies: What Are the Questions, and How Well Are We Doing in Answering Them?" U.S. Bureau of Economic Analysis Working Paper, June 12, 2003.

Langlois, Richard N., and Paul L. Robertson, *Firms, Markets and Economic Change*, New York: Routledge, 1995.

Laubacher, Robert J., and Thomas W. Malone, "Flexible Work Arrangements and 21st Century Worker Guilds," Initiative on Inventing the Organizations of the 21st Century Working Paper No. 4, Cambridge, Mass.: Massachusetts Institute of Technology, October 1997.

Lawrence, Robert Z., and Matthew J. Slaughter, "International Trade and American Wages in the 1980s: Giant Sucking Sound or Small Hiccup?" *Brookings Papers on Economic Activity: Microeconomics*, No. 2, 1993, pp. 161–226.

Leamer, Edward E., "U.S. Wages and the Mexican-U.S. Free Trade Agreement," in P. Garber, ed., *The Mexico-U.S. Free Trade Agreement*, Cambridge, Mass.: MIT Press, 1993, pp. 57–128.

_____, "Trade, Wages and Revolving Door Ideas," Working Paper No. 4716, Cambridge, Mass.: National Bureau of Economic Research, 1994.

_____, "In Search of Stolper-Samuelson Linkages Between International Trade and Lower Wages," in Susan M. Collins, ed., *Imports, Exports and the American Worker*, Washington, D.C.: Brookings Institution Press, 1998, pp. 141–214.

_____, "What Is the Use of Factor Contents?" *Journal of International Economics*, Vol. 50, 2000, pp. 17–49.

Lee, Sharon M., "Using the New Racial Categories in the 2000 Census," the Annie E. Casey Foundation and the Population Reference Bureau, 2001, available at http://www.aecf.org/kidscount/racial 2000.pdf.

Leigh, Duane E., and Andrew M. Gill, "Labor Market Returns to Community Colleges: Evidence for Returning Adults," *Journal of Human Resources*, Vol. 32, No. 2, Spring 1997, pp. 334–353.

Leibowitz, Arleen, and Jacob A. Klerman, "Explaining Changes in Married Mothers' Employment Over Time," *Demography*, Vol. 32, No. 3, 1995, pp. 365–378.

Lemonick, Michael D., and Alice Park, "The Truth About SARS," *Time*, May 5, 2003, pp. 48–57.

Leonhardt, David, "Globalization Hits a Political Speed Bump," *New York Times*, June 1, 2003.

Lillard, Lee A., and Hong Tan, *Training: Who Gets It and What Are Its Effects on Employment and Earnings?* Santa Monica, Calif.: RAND Corporation, R-3331, 1986.

Litan, Robert E., and Alice M. Rivlin, "The Economy and the Internet: What Lies Ahead?" in Robert E. Litan and Alice M. Rivlin, eds., *The Economic Payoff from the Internet Revolution*, Washington, D.C.: Brookings Institution Press, 2001, pp. 1–28.

Lofgren, Eric P., Steven A. Nyce, and Sylvester J. Schieber, "Designing Total Reward Programs for Tight Labor Markets," in Olivia S. Mitchell, David S. Blitzstein, Michael Gordon, and Judith F. Mazo, eds., *Benefits for the Workplace of the Future,* Philadelphia: University of Pennsylvania Press, 2003, pp. 151–177.

Lucking-Reiley, David, and Daniel F. Spulber, "Business-to-Business Electronic Commerce," *Journal of Economic Perspectives,* Vol. 15, No. 1, Winter 2001, pp. 55–68.

Lynch, Lisa M., and Sandra E. Black, "Beyond the Incidence of Training: Evidence from a National Employer Survey," Working Paper No. 5231, Cambridge, Mass.: National Bureau of Economic Research, August 1995.

Mahon, Rianne, "Child Care: Toward What Kind of 'Social Europe'?" *Social Politics: International Studies in Gender, State & Society,* Vol. 9, 2002, pp. 343–379.

Malone, Thomas W., "American Worker at a Crossroads Project," testimony for the U.S. House of Representatives, Committee on Education and the Workforce, Subcommittee on Oversight and Investigations, October 29, 1997a, available at http://edworkforce.house.gov/hearings/105th/oi/awp102997/malone.htm.

_____, "Is Empowerment Just a Fad? Control, Decisionmaking, and IT," *Sloan Management Review,* Vol. 38, No. 2, Winter 1997b, pp. 23–35.

Malone, Thomas W., and Robert J. Laubacher, "The Dawn of the E-Lance Economy," *Harvard Business Review,* September–October 1998, pp. 145–152.

_____, "Retreat of the Firm and the Rise of Guilds: The Employment Relationship in an Age of Virtual Business," Initiative on Inventing the Organizations of the 21st Century Working Paper No. 33, Cambridge, Mass.: Massachusetts Institute of Technology, July 2002.

Manton, Kenneth G., "Forecasting the Nursing Home Population" (comment), *Medical Care,* Vol. 41, No. 1, 2003, pp. 21–24.

Manton, Kenneth, Larry Corder, and Eric Stallard, "Chronic Disability Trends in the Elderly United States Populations, 1982–1994," *Proceedings of the National Academy of Sciences*, Vol. 94, 1997, pp. 2593–2598.

Markoff, John, and David Leonhardt, "Microsoft Will Award Stock, Not Options, to Employees," *New York Times*, July 9, 2003, p. A1.

Marquardt, Michael J., and Lisa Horvath, *Global Teams: How Top Multinationals Span Boundaries and Cultures with High-Speed Teamwork*, Palo Alto, Calif.: Davies-Black Publishing, 2001.

Mason, Karen Oppenheim, and Karen Kuhlthau, "The Perceived Impact of Child Care Costs on Women's Labor Supply and Fertility," *Demography*, Vol. 29, No. 4, November 1992, pp. 523–543.

Mataloni, Raymond J., Jr., "U.S. Multinational Companies: Operations in 2000," *Survey of Current Business*, December 2002, pp. 111–122.

McCarthy, John C., "3.3 Million U.S. Services Jobs to Go Offshore," brief, Forrester TechStrategy, November 11, 2002.

Mewhirter, Erin, and Michael Fullerton, "The Trade Act of 2002: What Does It All Mean?" *Export America*, International Trade Administration, U.S. Department of Commerce, November 2002, pp. 20–21, available at http://www.ita.doc.gov/exportamerica/TechnicalAdvice/ta_tradeAct2002.pdf.

Meyer, Bruce D., and Dan T. Rosenbaum, "Making Single Mothers Work: Recent Tax and Welfare Policy and Its Effects," Working Paper No. 749, Cambridge, Mass.: National Bureau of Economic Research, 2000.

Mincer, Jacob, "Human Capital, Technology, and the Wage Structure: What Do Time Series Show?" Working Paper No. 3581, Cambridge, Mass.: National Bureau of Economic Research, January 1991.

Mishel, Lawrence, Jared Berstein, and Heather Boushey, *The State of Working America 2002/2003*, Ithaca, N.Y.: Cornell University Press, 2003.

Mitchell, Olivia S., "The Relation of Age to Workplace Injuries," *Monthly Labor Review*, July 1988, pp. 8–13.

Moe, Michael, and Henry Blodgett, *The Knowledge Web*, Merrill Lynch & Co., Global Securities Research & Economics Group, Global Fundamental Equity Research Department 2000.

Moncarz, Roger, and Azure Reaser, "The 2000–10 Job Outlook in Brief," *Occupational Outlook Quarterly*, Spring 2002.

Morello, Diane, "U.S. Offshore Outsourcing Leads to Structural Changes and Big Impact," Gartner, Inc., July 23, 2003, available at http://www.gartner.com.

Moulton, Brent, "Bias in the Consumer Price Index: What Is the Evidence?" *Journal of Economic Perspectives*, Vol. 10, No. 4, Fall 1996, pp. 159–177.

Murphy, Kevin F., and Finis Welch, "The Role of International Trade in Wage Differentials," in Marvin H. Kosters, ed., *Workers and Their Wages: Changing Patterns in the United States*, Washington, D.C.: American Enterprise Institute, 1991, pp. 39–76.

Murphy, Kevin F., and Finis Welch, "The Structure of Wages," *Quarterly Journal of Economics*, Vol. 107, February 1992, pp. 285–326.

"Nanotech Executive Summary," *Technology Review*, October 12, 2001, available at http//www.technologyreview.com/articles/print_version/wo_nanotech101.asp.

National Academy of Sciences (NAS), *Beyond Discovery: Designer Seeds*, Washington, D.C.: Office on Public Understanding of Science, National Academy of Sciences, October 1998.

_____, *Transgenic Plants and World Agriculture*, Washington, D.C.: National Academy of Sciences Press, July 2000.

_____, *Animal Biotechnology: Science-Based Concerns*, Washington, D.C.: National Academy of Sciences Press, 2002.

National Center for Education Statistics, *Comparative Indicators of Education in the United States and Other G-8 Countries: 2002*, Washington, D.C.: U.S. Department of Education, Institute of Education Sciences, NCES 2003-026, 2003.

National Center for Health Statistics (NCHS) (Centers for Disease Control and Prevention), *Vital Statistics of the United States, 1995, Preprint of Vol. II, Mortality, Part A Sec 6 Life Tables*, Hyattsville, Md., 1998.

_____, *Vital Statistics of the United States, 1999, Volume I, Natality*, Hyattsville, Md.: NCHS, 2001, available at http://www.cdc.gov/nchs/datawh/statab/unpubd/natality/natab99.htm.

_____, *Births: Final Data for 2001*, National Vital Statistics Reports, Vol. 51, No. 2, 2002a, available at http://www.cdc.gov/nchs/data/nvsr/nvsr51/nvsr51_02.pdf.

_____, *United States Life Tables, 2000*, National Vital Statistics Reports, Vol. 51, No. 3, 2002b, available at http://www.cdc.gov/nchs/data/nvsr/nvsr51/nvsr51_03.pdf.

_____, "Births, Marriages, Divorces, and Deaths: Provisional Data for November 2001," *National Vital Statistics Reports*, Vol. 50, No. 13, September 11, 2002c, available at http://www.cdc.gov/nchs/data/nvsr/nvsr50/nvsr50_13.pdf.

National Commission on Mathematics and Science Teaching for the 21st Century, *Before It's Too Late: A Report to the Nation*, Washington, D.C.: U.S. Department of Education, September 2000.

National Institutes of Health (NIH), *Investments, Progress, and Plans: Selected Examples from FY 1999–2003*, Bethesda, Md.: Office of the Director, NIH, June 2001.

National Intelligence Council (NIC), *Global Trends 2015: A Dialogue About the Future with Nongovernmental Experts*, Washington, D.C., December 2000.

National Nanotechnology Initiative (NNI), *Nanotechnology: Opportunity and Challenge for Industry*, University of California at Los Angeles, September 10, 2001.

_____, *Nanotechnology Workshop: From the Laboratory to New Commercial Frontiers, Final Report*, Center for Nanoscale Science and Technology, Rice University, February 28, 2003.

National Science Foundation (NSF), *Science and Engineering Indicators, 1998*, Washington, D.C., 1998.

_____, *Societal Implications of Nanoscience and Nanotechnology*, Washington, D.C., March 2001.

_____, *Science and Engineering Indicators, 2002*, Washington, D.C., 2002.

National Telecommunications and Information Administration (NTIA), *A Nation Online: How Americans Are Expanding Their Use of the Internet*, Washington, D.C., U.S. Department of Commerce, February 2002.

Neal, Margaret B., Leslie B. Hammer, Krista J. Brockwood, Suzanne Caubet, Cari L. Colton, Terry Hammond, Emily Huang, Jo Isgrigg, and Angela Rickard, *A Work-Family Sourcebook for Employers: Supporting Employees with Child and Elder Care Needs*, Portland, Oreg.: Portland State University, 2001.

Neumark, David, "Changes in Job Stability and Job Security: A Collective Effort to Untangle, Reconcile, and Interpret the Evidence," in David Neumark, ed., *On the Job: Is Long-Term Employment a Thing of the Past?* New York: Russell Sage Foundation, 2000, pp. 1–27.

Neumark, David, and Deborah Reed, "Employment Relationships in the New Economy," Working Paper No. 8910, Cambridge, Mass.: National Bureau of Economic Research, April 2002.

Nordhaus, William D., "Productivity Growth and the New Economy," *Brookings Papers on Economic Activity*, No. 2, 2002a, pp. 211–244.

_____, "The Progress of Computing," working draft, March 2002b, available at http://www.econ.yale.edu/~nordhaus/homepage/recent_stuff.html.

Obstfeld, Maurice, "The Global Capital Market: Benefactor or Menace?" *Journal of Economic Perspectives*, Vol. 12, No. 4, Fall 1998, pp. 9–30.

Oeppen, Jim, and James W. Vaupel, "Broken Limits to Life Expectancy," *Science*, No. 292, 2002, pp. 1029–1030.

Oliner, Stephen D., and Daniel E. Sichel, "The Resurgence of Growth in the Late 1990s: Is Information Technology the Story?" *Journal of Economic Perspectives*, Vol. 14, No. 4, Fall 2000, pp. 3–22.

_____, "Information Technology and Productivity: Where Are We Now and Where Are We Going?" *Federal Reserve Bank of Atlanta Economic Review*, Vol. 87, No. 3, 2002, pp. 15–44.

Olshansky, Jay S., Bruce A. Carnes, and Aline Désesquelles, "Prospects for Human Longevity," *Science*, No. 291, 2001, pp. 1491–1492.

Organisation for Economic Co-operation and Development (OECD), *Education at a Glance*, Paris: OECD, 2001.

_____, *Literacy in the Information Age: Final Report of the International Adult Literacy Survey*, Paris, 2003a.

_____, *Literacy Skills for the World of Tomorrow: Further Results from PISA 2000*, Paris, 2003b.

_____, *Trends in International Migration: Continuous Reporting System on Migration*, Annual Report, Paris, 2003c.

O'Rourke, Kevin H., and Jeffrey G. Williamson, *Globalization and History: The Evolution of a Nineteenth-Century Atlantic Economy*, Cambridge, Mass.: MIT Press, 2000.

Panis, Constantijn, Michael Hurd, David Loughran, Julie Zissimopoulos, Steven Haider, and Patricia St. Clair, "The Effects of Changing Social Security Administration's Early Entitlement Age and the Normal Retirement Age," Santa Monica, Calif.: RAND Corporation, DRU-2903-SSA, June 2002.

Paugh, Jon, and John C. Lafrance, *The U.S. Biotechnology Industry*, Washington, D.C.: U.S. Department of Commerce, Office of Technology Policy, July 1997.

Postrel, Virginia, "Economic Scene: Vertical Integration Worked Well in Its Day," *New York Times*, June 19, 2003, p. C2.

Purcell, Patrick J., "Older Workers: Employment and Retirement Trends," *Monthly Labor Review*, October 2000, pp. 19–30.

Rai, Saritha, "India Is Regaining Contracts with U.S.," *New York Times*, December 25, 2002.

Raphael, Dennis, and Benjamin Schlesinger, "Women in the Sandwich Generation: Do Adult Children Living at Home Help?" *Journal of Women and Aging*, Vol. 6, 1994, pp. 21–45.

Rebick, Marcus, "The Japanese Approach to Finding Jobs for Older Workers," in Olivia S. Mitchell, ed., *As the Workforce Ages: Costs, Benefits and Policy Challenges*, Ithaca, N.Y.: ILR Press, 1993, pp. 103–124.

Redl, Franz X., Kyung S. Cho, Christopher B. Murray, and Stephen O'Brien, "Three-Dimensional Binary Superlattices of Magnetic Nanocrystals and Semiconductor Quantum Dots," *Nature*, Vol. 423, June 26, 2003, pp. 968–971.

Reich, Robert B., *The Future of Success*, New York: Alfred A. Knopf, 2001.

Richardson, J. David, "Income Inequality and Trade: How to Think, What to Conclude," *Journal of Economic Perspectives*, Vol. 9, No. 3, Summer 1995, pp. 33–55.

Rotman, David, "Molecular Memory," *Technology Review*, May 2001, available at http//www.technologyreview.com/articles/print_version/patents50501.asp.

Roush, Wade, "10 Emerging Technologies That Will Change the World: Wireless Sensor Networks," *Technology Review*, February 2003, p. 37.

Sachs, Jeffrey D., and Howard J. Shatz, "Trade and Jobs in U.S. Manufacturing," *Brookings Papers on Economic Activity*, Vol. 1, 1994, pp. 1–84.

_____, "International Trade and Wage Inequality in the United States: Some New Results," in Susan M. Collins, ed., *Imports, Exports and the American Worker*, Washington, D.C.: Brookings Institution Press, 1998, pp. 215–254.

Salmi, Minna, "Analysing the Finnish Homecare Allowance System: Challenges to Research and Problems of Interpretation," in Laura

Kalliomaa-Puha, ed., *Perspectives of Equality—Work, Women and Family in the Nordic Countries and EU*, Copenhagen, Denmark: Nordic Council of Ministers, 2000.

Saxenian, AnnaLee, *Silicon Valley's New Immigrant Entrepreneurs*, San Francisco: Public Policy Institute of California, 1999.

_____, *Local and Global Networks of Immigrant Professionals in Silicon Valley*, San Francisco: Public Policy Institute of California, 2002.

Scarpetta, Stefano, Andrea Bassanini, Dirk Pilat, and Paul Schreyer, "Economic Growth in the OECD Area: Recent Trends at the Aggregate and Sectoral Level," Working Paper No. 248, OECD Economics Department, 2000, available at http://www.oecd.org/dataoecd/15/6/1885257.pdf.

Scheve, Kenneth, and Matthew J. Slaughter, "Economic Insecurity and the Globalization of Production," Working Paper No. 9339, Cambridge, Mass.: National Bureau of Economic Research, November 2002.

Schmidt, Charlie, "Beyond the Bar Code," *Technology Review*, March 2001, available at http//www.technologyreview.com/articles/print_version/schmidt0301.asp.

Schoeni, Robert, Kevin McCarthy, and Georges Vernez, *The Mixed Economic Progress of Immigrants*, Santa Monica, Calif.: RAND Corporation, MR-763-IF/FF, 1996.

Schroeder, Michael, "Thaw with Pakistan Likely to Draw Jobs to India: Outsourcing, Finance Firms Greet News with Optimism as Wage Savings Beckon," *New York Times*, May 8, 2003a.

_____, "States Fight Exodus of Jobs: Lawmakers, Unions Seek to Block Outsourcing," *Wall Street Journal*, June 3, 2003b.

Schulman, Andrew, "The Extent of Systematic Monitoring of Employee Email and Internet Use," The Privacy Project, July 9, 2001, available at http://www.privacyfoundation.org/workplace/technology/extentpf.html.

Scigliano, Eric, "10 Emerging Technologies That Will Change the World: Nano Solar Cells," *Technology Review*, February 2003, p. 39.

Sharma, Amol, "India Winning Higher-Status Jobs from U.S.," *Christian Science Monitor*, June 18, 2003.

Smith, James P., "Introduction," in James P. Smith and Barry Edmonston, eds., *The Immigration Debate: Studies on the Economic, Demographic, and Fiscal Effects of Immigration*, Washington, D.C.: National Academy Press, 1998.

_____, "Race and Ethnicity in the Labor Market: Trends Over the Short and Long Term," in Neil J. Smelser, William Julius Wilson, and Faith Mitchell, eds., *America Becoming: Racial Trends and Their Consequences*, Vol. II, Washington, D.C.: NAS, 2001, pp. 52–97.

_____, "Assimilation Across Latino Generations," *American Economic Review*, Vol. 93, No. 2, May 2003, pp. 315–319.

Solow, Robert, "We'd Better Watch Out," *New York Times Book Review*, July 12, 1987, p. 36.

Spillman, Brenda C., and Liliana E. Pezzin, "Potential and Active Family Caregivers: Changing Networks and the 'Sandwich Generation,'" *Milbank Quarterly*, Vol. 78, 2000, pp. 347–374.

Stone, Brad, "Seeing Is Believing: Hope for the Blind," *Newsweek*, May 19, 2003, pp. 63–64.

Su, Betty W., "The U.S. Economy to 2010," *Monthly Labor Review*, Vol. 124, No. 11, November 2001, pp. 3–20.

Tahmincioglu, Eve, "By Telecommuting, the Disabled Get a Key to the Office, and a Job," *New York Times*, July 20, 2003.

Taylor, Alan M., "Globalization, Trade, and Development: Some Lessons from History," Working Paper No. 9326, Cambridge, Mass.: National Bureau of Economic Research, November 2002.

Thornburg, David, *The New Basics: Education and the Future of Work in the Telematic Age*, Alexandria, Va.: Association for Supervision and Curriculum Development, 2002.

Toossi, Mitra, "A Century of Change: The U.S. Labor Force, 1950–2050," *Monthly Labor Review*, May 2002, pp. 15–28.

Topel, Robert H., "Factor Proportions and Relative Wages: The Supply-Side Determinants of Wage Inequality," *Journal of Economic Perspectives*, Vol. 11, No. 2, 1997, pp. 55–74.

Tracey, Elizabeth, "Costs of Care for Elderly Growing," *Reuters Health Information*, November 14, 2000.

Triplett, Jack E., "The Solow Productivity Paradox: What Do Computers Do to Productivity?" *Canadian Journal of Economics*, Vol. 32, No. 2, 1999, pp. 309–334.

Triplett, Jack E., and Barry P. Bosworth, "'Baumol's Disease' Has Been Cured: IT and Multifactor Productivity in U.S. Services Industries," Brookings Institution Working Paper, July 2002.

Trupin, Laura, Douglas S. Sebesta, Edward Yelin, and Mitchelle P. LaPlante, "Trends in Labor Force Participation Among Persons with Disabilities, 1983–1994," *Disability Statistics Report*, Vol. 10, Washington, D.C.: U.S. Department of Education, National Institute on Disability and Rehabilitation Research, 1997.

Tynan, Trudy, "Dictionary's 11th Edition Adds 10,000 Words, Casting a Wide Web," *Philadelphia Inquirer*, July 3, 2003, p. A14.

United Nations (UN), Department of Economic and Social Affairs, Population Division, "World Population Ageing: 1950–2050," ST/ESA/SER.A/207, New York, 2001, available at http://www.un.org/esa/population/publications/worldageing19502050.

_____, *International Migration, 2002*, New York, October 2002, available at http://www.un.org/esa/population/publications/ittmig2002/Migration2002.pdf.

UN Commission on Trade and Development (UNCTAD), Division on Investment, Technology and Enterprise Development, *World Investment Report 2002: Transnational Corporations and Export Competitiveness*, September 17, 2002, available at http://r0.unctad.org/wir/.

UN Development Programme, *Human Development Report 2001: Making New Technologies Work for Human Development*, New York: Oxford University Press, 2001.

U.S. Bureau of the Census, *Historical Statistics of the United States: Colonial Times to 1970*, Bicentennial Edition, Part 1, Washington, D.C., 1975.

_____, *School Enrollment—Social and Economic Characteristics of Students: October 1980*, Current Population Reports, P20-362, Washington, D.C. 1981, available at http://www.census.gov/ population/www/socdemo/school/p20-362.html.

_____, *Quarterly Population Estimates, 1980–1990*, Washington, D.C., 2001a, available at http://eire.census.gov/popest/archives/ national/nat_80s_detail.php.

_____, *Resident Population Estimates for the 1990s*, Washington, D.C., 2001b, available at http://eire.census.gov/popest/archives/ national/nat_90s_detail/nat_90s_1.php.

_____, *School Enrollment—Social and Economic Characteristics of Students: October 2000*, PPL-148, Washington, D.C., 2001c, available at http://www.census.gov/population/www/socdemo/ school/ppl-148.html.

_____, *International Data Base Population Pyramids*, Washington, D.C., 2002a, available at http://www.census.gov/ipc/www/ idbpyr.html.

_____, *National Population Projections*, Washington, D.C., 2002b, available at http://www.census.gov/population/www/projec tions/natsum-T3.html.

_____, *Statistical Abstract of the U.S.*, Washington, D.C., 2002c.

_____, *Disability Data from March Current Population Survey*, Washington, D.C., 2003a, available at http://www.census.gov/ hhes/www/disable/disabcps.html.

_____, *The Foreign-Born Population in the United States: March 2002*, P20-539, Washington, D.C.: U.S. Bureau of the Census, 2003b.

U.S. Department of Agriculture (USDA), "Benefits of NAFTA," *FAS-online*, Foreign Agricultural Service, July 2001 available at http://www.fas.usda.gov/itp/policy/nafta/nafta_backgrounder.htm.

U.S. Department of Commerce (U.S. DOC), *Digital Economy 2000*, Washington, D.C., June 2000.

_____, *U.S. Jobs from Exports*, Washington, D.C., February 2001.

_____, *Visions 2020*, Washington, D.C., September 2002.

_____, *Education and Training for the Information Technology Workforce*, Washington, D.C., April 2003.

U.S. Department of Education, National Center for Education Statistics, *Distance Education at Degree-Granting Postsecondary Institutions: 2000–2001*, 2003, available at http://nces.ed.gov/pubs2003/2003017.pdf.

U.S. Department of Health and Human Services (DHHS), Administration for Children and Families, Office of Planning, Research and Evaluation, *Temporary Assistance for Needy Families (TANF Program): Third Annual Report to Congress*, Washington, D.C., August 2000.

U.S. Department of Homeland Security (DHS), Office of Immigration Statistics, Office of Management, *2002 Yearbook of Immigration Statistics*, Washington, D.C.: U.S. Government Printing Office, forthcoming, select tables as used in the text are prepublished and available at http://www.bcis.gov/graphics/shared/aboutus/statistics/ybpage.htm.

U.S. Department of Labor (DOL), Employee Benefits Security Administration, Office of Policy and Research, "Abstract of 1998 Form 5500 Annual Reports," *Private Pension Plan Bulletin*, No. 11, Winter 2001–2002, 2002, available at http://www.dol.gov/ebsa/PDF/1998pensionplanbulletin.pdf.

_____, *A Chartbook of International Comparisons: United States, Europe, Asia*, Washington, D.C., April 2003.

U.S. Department of State, Bureau of Consular Affairs, *2002 Report of the Visas Office*, forthcoming.

U.S. General Accounting Office, *Trade Adjustment Assistance: Trends, Outcomes, and Management Issues in Dislocated Worker Programs*, Washington, D.C., GAO-01-59, October 2000.

U.S. House of Representatives, Committee on Ways and Means, *2000 Green Book: Background Material and Data on Programs Within the Jurisdiction of the Committee on Ways and Means*, Washington, D.C.: U.S. Government Printing Office, October 2000.

U.S. Patent and Trademark Office, *Patent Counts by Class by Year, January 1977–December 31, 2001*, April 2002a, available at http://www.uspto.gov/web/offices/ac/ido/oeip/taf/cbcby.pdf.

_____, *U.S. Patent Activity, Calendar Years 1790–2001*, April 2002b, available at http://www.uspto.gov/web/offices/ac/ido/oeip/taf/h_counts.htm.

Waldman, Amy, "More 'Can I Help You?' Jobs Migrate from U.S. to India," *New York Times*, May 11, 2003.

Walker, James R., "The Effect of Public Policies on Recent Swedish Fertility Behavior," *Journal of Population Economics*, Vol. 8, 1995, pp. 223–251.

Wallman, Katherine, S. Evinger, and S. Schecter, "Measuring Our Nation's Diversity: Developing a Common Language for Data on Race/Ethnicity," *American Journal of Public Health*, Vol. 90, No. 11, 2000, pp. 1704–1708.

Warschauer, Mark, "Demystifying the Digital Divide," *Scientific American*, August 2003, pp. 42–47.

Wenger, Jeffrey, "Share of Workers in 'Nonstandard' Jobs Declines," Economic Policy Institute Briefing Paper, Washington, D.C.: Economic Policy Institute, April 2003.

The Wharton School, University of Pennsylvania, "The Rush to Send Back-Office Business Overseas," Knowledge@Wharton Special Section, October 2002a, available at http://knowledge.wharton.upenn.edu/100902_ss.html.

_____, "What Works, What Doesn't: Lessons from Two Companies That Outsource Back-Office Tasks," Knowledge@Wharton Brief, December 18, 2002b, available at http://knowledge.wharton. upenn.edu/articles.cfm?catid=13&articleid=693.

_____, "An Aging, Fatter Population Drives Demand for New Medical Devices," *Managing Technology*, March 26, 2003, available at http://knowledge.wharton.upenn.edu/articles.cfm?articleid=740& catid=14.

Whiting, Meredith Armstrong, and Thomas E. Cavanagh, *Corporate Security Management: Organization and Spending Since 9/11*, New York: The Conference Board, July 2003.

Williamson, Jeffrey G., "Globalization, Labor Markets and Policy Backlash in the Past," *Journal of Economic Perspectives*, Vol. 12, No. 4, 1998, pp. 51–72.

Wood, Adrian, *North-South Trade, Employment and Inequality: Changing Fortunes in a Skill-Driven World*, Oxford, United Kingdom: Clarendon Press, 1994..

Wood, Adrian, "How Trade Hurt Unskilled Workers," *Journal of Economic Perspectives*, Vol. 9, No. 3, Summer 1995, pp. 57–80.

Woodall, Pam, "Untangling E-Conomics," *The Economist*, September 21, 2000.

World Bank, "What Is Globalization," briefing paper, April 2000, available at http://www1.worldbank.org/economicpolicy/globali zation/ag01.html.

_____, *Globalization, Growth and Poverty: Building and Inclusive World Economy*, New York: Oxford University Press and the World Bank, 2002a.

_____, *World Development Indicators, 2002*, New York, 2002b.

_____, "Lessons from a Celtic Tiger: Irish Prime Minister Delivers Address at World Bank," DevNews Media Center, New York: The World Bank Group, May 17, 2003a, available at http://web.world bank.org/WBSITE/EXTERNAL/NEWS/0,,pagePK:34382~piPK:3443 9,00.html.

_____, *World Development Indicators, 2003*, New York, 2003b.

World Trade Organization, *International Trade Statistics, 2002*, 2002, available at http://www.wto.org/english/res_e/statis_e/its2002_e/its2002_e.pdf.

_____, *Annual Report 2003*, Geneva, Switzerland, 2003.

Wortman, Marc, "Medicine Gets Personal," *Technology Review*, January/February 2001.

Zack, Michael H., "Rethinking the Knowledge-Based Organization," *MIT Sloan Management Review*, Vol. 44, No. 4, Summer 2003, pp. 67–71.